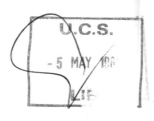

Responses to Population Growth in India

edited by
Marcus F. Franda

The Praeger Special Studies program—
utilizing the most modern and efficient book
production techniques and a selective
worldwide distribution network—makes
available to the academic, government, and
business communities significant, timely
research in U.S. and international economic, social, and political development.

Responses to Population Growth in India

Changes in Social, Political, and Economic Behavior

PRAEGER SPECIAL STUDIES IN INTERNATIONAL ECONOMICS AND DEVELOPMENT

Praeger Publishers   New York   Washington   London

Library of Congress Cataloging in Publication Data
Main entry under title:

Responses to population growth in India.

    (Praeger special studies in international economics
and development)
    Includes bibliographical references and index.
    1. India—Population—Addresses, essays, lectures.
2. India—Economic conditions—1947-   Addresses,
essays, lectures. 3. India—Social conditions—
Addresses, essays, lectures. I. Franda, Marcus F.
HB3639.R47   301.32'9'54   75-8405
ISBN 0-275-00940-8

PRAEGER PUBLISHERS
111 Fourth Avenue, New York, N.Y. 10003, U.S.A.

Published in the United States of America in 1975
by Praeger Publishers, Inc.

Published for The Asia Society

Printed in the United States of America

To Krishan Bhatia

ACKNOWLEDGMENTS

The conference that resulted in this volume was organized by the India Council of the Asia Society, under the direction of Abraham Weisblat. Other members of the council that played key roles in determining the nature of the subject matter and format of the conference were Kempton Dunn, Lawrence A. Veit, Lionel Landry, Konrad Bekker, Thomas Graham, and Phillips Talbot, president of the Asia Society. The indispensable coordinator of the conference, at all stages, was Kempton Dunn.

Funds for staging the conference were provided by the Ford Foundation and the Johnson Foundation. The logistics at Wingspread —the conference center of the Johnson Foundation in Racine, Wisconsin—were most skillfully handled by Rita Goodman, Leslie Paffrath, and their staff. Vonnie Franda played an especially important role as rapporteur at the conference and in readying manuscripts both for the conference and the press. Typing assistance was most ably and speedily provided by Rose Shablak, Thelma Mayer, and B. D. Diwan. The tapes from the conference were accurately converted to typed manuscript by Emily Faber.

The editor wishes to thank everyone who attended the conference, whether as chairman, panelist, or observer, both for the lively and stimulating discourse that they created and for their permission to use papers and transcripts in this volume. Space limitations have resulted in the need for considerable pruning and editing, most of which has been done by the participants themselves. Without the willing understanding and cooperation of those authors and panelists who have had to condense severely their original contributions, this volume would not have been possible.

Acknowledgment must also be given to the American Universities Field Staff, which has allowed portions of my <u>Fieldstaff Reports</u>, summarizing the conference, to be used in my introductory essay in this volume.

Finally, special mention should be made of the role of Krishan Bhatia, whose eloquent statements at Wingspread reflected his deep knowledge of India, his unique ability to express thoughtful criticism in a most constructive manner, and his faith in Indian democracy and the people of India. Krishan was a very special person to many of us. His untimely death on December 9, 1974, shortly after he had returned from Wingspread to Washington, leaves a void in Indian journalism and public affairs.

CONTENTS

Chapter	Page

LIST OF TABLES AND FIGURE

1

INTRODUCTION AND SUMMARY OF THE CONFERENCE

Marcus F. Franda

This volume includes the papers, as well as the discussion and comments, presented at a conference sponsored by the Asia Society, November 13-16, 1974.

The theme of the conference was "Societal Responses to Population Change in India," which thus encouraged the participants to direct their attention to some of the more neglected aspects of population-related studies in one of the most populous nations in the world. The conference was prompted by the observation that, while the question of population growth in India has received considerable attention and funding since the mid-1950s, most studies of India's population have been primarily demographic or biological, and most of the international discourse on India's population has resulted either in finger-pointing or hand-wringing exercises. The purpose of the conference organizers in bringing together scholars, journalists, and public affairs figures from India, the United States, Canada, and England was to learn more about the adjustments to greater population densities already occurring in India in a manner that might stimulate further thought and work in this field and contribute to international understanding of one of the major phenomena of our time.

As Phillips Talbot pointed out in his introductory remarks to the conference, we know that there are two people in most towns and villages of India for every one who was there in the 1930s and 1940s. If we had asked these people three decades ago what adjustments they would need to make if the population of their communities should double over the next 30 years, they would not have been able to answer. Yet the doubled numbers do live there now, and we know that the residents have made numerous and varied cultural and social responses to this doubling, in a whole range of living patterns. It is these adaptations that were the subjects of concern at the conference.

1

In recent years there have been a number of research approaches that have been aimed at the interrelationships between fertility and various dimensions of what one might call personal welfare. Such matters as maternal health, education, nutrition, and changes in income distribution are now generally acknowledged as factors that both influence and are influenced by population growth. The attempt at Wingspread was to pick up from that theme but to look at a number of other societal factors that also influence or are influenced by population growth.

The topics selected for inclusion in the conference, primarily because they have been neglected for India, were social interaction and religion; the family; law and legal change; communications; and the planning and provision of services. In each of these five areas, a paper was assigned to one of the participants, for the purpose of either summarizing the existing literature on the relationships between the topic and population variables or to provoke discussion on such relationships. It should be pointed out that most of the papers presented to the conference were intended by their authors as speculative or provocative exercises in areas where there has been a paucity of data or thought on the subject, rather than finished pieces of scholarly work in areas that have been well-researched.

The two major difficulties that the conference participants struggled with throughout are ones that are familiar to anyone who has tried to view India's population from a macroscopic perspective. A country of 600 million people, currently adding 13 or more million people (another Australia) each year, cannot be readily compared with less populous nations, with the result that the models and ratios and proportions that economists and demographers have devised for other societies are frequently thrown out of kilter by the sheer size and diversity of the subcontinent. John Lewis, in his introductory remarks as conference chairman, emphasized the all too frequent lack of recognition that India is a multistate federal system, containing within it a population that is in many respects as varied and as large as all of Africa and Latin America put together. Comparisons between India and, say, Taiwan, therefore, make little sense, although comparisons between Taiwan and one of India's smaller states, say Punjab, might be useful. Second, the sheer size and diversity of India's population causes it to be extremely problem-generating at the same time that a rather rapid rate of population growth makes population-related variables the most critical variables in the whole development puzzle. When population-related factors are perceived as major links in a chain of variables that affect a number of social and political relationships, in a country of India's dimensions, it becomes exceedingly difficult simply to understand them, or to maintain a balanced perspective on their relative meaning and importance.

⌐The urgency of this matter of understanding the response of Indian society to population change, however, is made clear in Chapters
2 and 3,⌐by John Cool and Lawrence A. Veit. As John Cool points
out, on the basis of data gathered from a project called "Second India," sponsored by the Ford Foundation, two-thirds of the world at
the beginning of the next century is likely to be Asian, and it is projected that two-thirds of the Asians living then will be under 35 years
of age. Indians, obviously, will make up a major portion of this
Asian population. The thoughts and actions of what Cool calls these
"majority shareholders in the world" will inevitably be shaped by the
ways in which they are molded by religious, community, and family
institutions, as well as by the values and processes that are carried
by such institutions, and yet there is little evidence that the social
sciences have yet been much aware of the range of issues that would
enable us to understand the responses of such institutions to population growth. In the absence of reliable data, one can lay out a number
of possible scenarios that might take place in India and Asia, but it
would seem that a more rational course than one that simply speaks
of futuristic scenarios would be one that seeks to understand forces
presently at work. In John Cool's words:

> [The] defense of a hopeful view is the basic humanist
> credo that the human community in India, as else-
> where, has the capacity to learn from the past, to
> anticipate the future, to apply experience to the res-
> olution of current and future difficulties and, through
> time, to improve the human condition. To start
> from any alternative set of premises could be to ab-
> dicate before the event. *

While it is clear that the principal determinant of India's response to population change will come from India's own social institutions, it is also certain that this response will have major repercussions for the international community. The wide range of effects back
and forth, with India's population affecting and being affected by international affairs, is the subject of Chapter 3. As the UN Population
Conference at Bucharest in 1974 demonstrated, there is very little international consensus on what population parameters constitute a
"good society," with the result that there is at least as much international disagreement about a proper national response to demographic

---

*Since this essay is intended as a summary of the conference,
all quotations are taken directly from the papers and discussion presented in this volume.

variables as there is intranational disagreement about the proper response of individuals, families, communities, and institutions. Population-related problems, such as the distribution of resources between
the developed and developing countries, environmental conservation,
pollution, environmental degradation, and so forth, will inevitably
cause regional tensions and strains, ultimately affecting the larger international order. Some of these strains and tensions have already
been evident in the as yet low-key discontinuities between Indian and
U.S. perceptions of the nature of "the population problem"; others,
such as those reflected in the Bangladesh crisis of 1971, as Veit points
out, illustrate the complex way in which demographic factors can combine with other variables in determining the course of human affairs.

From the Indian side, the question of the way in which the society has responded to population change is almost invariably colored
by the legacies of colonialism and the nationalist convictions of India's
leadership that have resulted from the colonial experience and its aftermath. This point was driven home in some of the more eloquent
statements at the conference by Asok Mitra, former secretary to the
president of India. Professor Mitra spoke of the "overhang of history," resulting from the situation where, at the end of a colonial
regime, "a country is left the poorer in the quality of its manpower
and in the quality of both its agricultural and industrial products."
With this as his starting point, Professor Mitra's approach to the
question of how India has responded to population growth is one that
includes within its purview the reasons why indigenous Indian entrepreneurs were not more numerous and active, the causes of the inability of India to develop more fully its cash crops, and the factors
that have brought about a situation where industrial and ancillary activities in India are still secondary phenomena despite India's considerable human, mineral, and other resources.

Between 1947 and 1974, Professor Mitra points out, there has
been what he calls a "second industrial revolution" in the West, which
has achieved "immeasurably more than did the first industrial revolution of 1775-1850 . . . an almost magical improvement in levels of
living in Europe and the North American continent." This "second
industrial revolution," from Mitra's perspective,

> has been achieved in the last 25 years through the
> use of raw materials and other mineral resources
> from the underdeveloped countries, obtained at
> prices that are far more exploitative than those
> found in the colonial period 1775-1850. . . . In re-
> turn, the underdeveloped countries have received
> very little by way of plant, machinery, or techni-
> cal know-how, and wherever these have been re-

ceived, they too had to be obtained at exorbitant
prices.

Under these circumstances, Mitra argues, it is not surprising
that India has seemed relatively slow in responding to population
growth. He sees the need for greater efforts in many fields of research and development and the more intensive use of such things as
fertilizer, irrigation water, and electrical power, if Indian society is
to have the kind of economic base necessary for coping with population growth in the decades ahead. But this creates a dilemma so far
as he is concerned, if only because international net transfers would
seem necessary to achieve this economic base while past international
aid programs have, on the whole, been unsatisfactory. The question
of aid, in Asok Mitra's formulation, "reminds one of a line in a Tagore
poem which says that a jeweled necklace is an embarrassment: "It
cannot be worn because it hurts; it cannot be torn because that too
hurts."

Another manifestation of the differing perspectives between Indians and Americans on questions of population growth was expressed
by Beba Varadachar, when he argued that population increase in the
villages he has studied is often a "solution to a problem" whereas
outsiders keep coming into the village and saying that population increase is itself the problem. From the point of view of the villagers
he has studied, says Varadachar, "the problem is existence, survival;
it is gathering wood or making cowdung cakes or trying to beat the
next man in the litigation cycle, or whatever." Most Westerners,
and particularly scholars, Varadachar argues, "have been almost
brainwashed into thinking about population as a problem in terms of
fertility." Reflecting the thinking of many intellectuals in the underdeveloped countries, Varadachar makes the plea that we learn to think
of population-related variables in social terms, from the vantage
point of the villager rather than the activist centrally located policy-
maker.

A third manifestation of the differing perspectives between Indians and Americans on questions of population growth was alluded to
by Krishan Bhatia, when he observed that the seeming reluctance of
Indian leadership to perceive rapid population growth in crisis
terms, as has often been urged on India by Westerners, is at least in
part a result of a psychological predisposition on the part of Indians
to refuse to be herded into a Western conceptualization of a problem.
In Bhatia's words:

Left to ourselves we might have agreed that it is a
serious problem, and that we ought to do something
about it. But frequent rubbing in of the idea by use

of superlatives, and the distressing language that one
hears in reference to India's population problem,
creates a certain amount of resistance on the part of
top Indian leaders. For example, when the Bucharest
conference was held, some of the newspaper items in
the Western press for some weeks before the conference gave one the general impression—perhaps a bit
oversimplified—that the world's population and resource crisis was a function primarily of India and
Bangladesh. The gist of many stories was that if
these two countries could do something about population and stop copulating, everything would be all right.
. . . That kind of approach has created a certain
amount of resistance to accepting or recognizing the
problem of population in India.

SOCIETAL AND RELIGIOUS ADAPTATIONS

Granted the diversity and complexity of India, it is perhaps not
surprising that David Mandelbaum finds, in Chapter 4, a series of
contradictory forces pulling in different directions. He identifies
three principal contradictory pulls.

1. The first is a recognition by "the great majority of men and
women in India" that "contraception by modern means is possible and
that their government urgently wants each child-bearing couple to
limit the number of its children to two or three," side by side with a
predominant feeling, both in urban and rural areas, that "a large number of thriving children is . . . a great good."

2. Mandelbaum finds that there are a number of traditional
motivations for controlling fertility, primarily the advantages to infant and mother of spacing preganancies and the shame of being a
pregnant grandmother, both of which are widely acknowledged even in
India's rural areas. In addition, the traditional ban on widow remarriage has had the effect of lowering fertility, as has the recent rise
in the average age at which girls start marital sex relations. At the
same time, however, Mandelbaum finds that such motivations for fertility control seem to be most prevalent among those segments of society that are better off economically and in terms of status. Mandelbaum notes, for example, that the common inclination of couples impoverished by the partitioning of their family lands is still "to continue
to try to have many sons, in the hope that the wage labor of some may
augment the family's income, and, if things turn out well, the pooled
income of all may be enough to support some education for at least
one boy."

3. A third set of contradictory pulls are those that have to do with the rise and fall of social groups, again both in economic terms and in terms of status. Contrary to the popular notion that everything seems to have got worse in India, Mandelbaum finds that some villages have prospered during this century, and particularly during the past three decades, while others have suffered decline. Similarly within villages, some families and subcaste groups are unquestionably better off now than they were a few decades ago, while the positions of other families and subcastes have unquestionably deteriorated. As Mandelbaum and others remarked on a number of occasions at the conference, the gap between the better off and the worse off in India is widening, and this undoubtedly has much to do with pressures on land, food, clothing, and shelter that result from population increase. At the same time, however, the widening of this gap is seldom perceived by villagers themselves as a population phenomenon. As Mandelbaum explains, "the effects of population growth tend to be interwoven with other kinds of changes, and obscured by them."

The one consistent correlation that seems to flow through the literature, and through the comments of this volume's contributors, is the decline of fertility in instances where infant mortality has been reduced and where there is a high degree of education at all levels. Usually these two factors are found in close association one with the other. Quoting from a study by Gopinathan Nair, conducted in 1974, Mandelbaum attributes the significant decline of the birthrate in Kerala over the past 10 years to the presence of these two factors, although he is quick to emphasize that Kerala is unusual in this regard. In most of India neither Primary Health Centres nor educational systems are nearly as well-developed as they are in Kerala. In this context, however, Mandelbaum singles out the need for research on the dynamics of the relationship between fertility control and education. In his words,

> Among the many gaps in our knowledge of the social
> aspects of fertility control in India, one that merits
> very high priority for research is an examination,
> through a series of different approaches, of what
> real effect the school experience has had on the later
> life patterns of those who have attended schools of
> various kinds and at different levels.

The need for further research with regard to other matters, and especially on the question of the desirability of children and sons, was emphasized by Joseph Elder and Milton Singer. Professor Elder expresses his reservations with the currently popular notion that

large numbers of children are either wanted or are accepted as "God's
Will" as follows:

> The patent fact that so many children born were not
> wanted, or were not planned—perhaps explained af-
> ter the fact by reference to fate—should in no way
> lead us to believe that this was seen in anticipation
> as something deemed by fate. It may, after the
> fact, be seen as God's gift, or as fate, or it may be
> explained in that way. But it is also seen as a bad
> break, and people are, very often, unhappy that they
> have had another child.

In support of Professor Elder's plea for more research on this subject, Singer reports that many of his urban interviewees, in studies
he has conducted in Madras, would speak of the advantages of having
many sons at the same time that they in fact had limited their families
when given access to modern contraceptive techniques. Singer suggests that "there are many other factors [in addition to value prefer-
ences] that influence these decisions and influence fertility as well,
and probably most of them are still unknown to us."

With regard to other matters, Mandelbaum notes the continued
importance of family, caste, and kin relations, in both rural and urban areas, but he also points to ways in which traditional Indian institutions have changed in response to population growth and other variables. If the effects of population growth tend to be interwoven with
other kinds of changes in such a way as to obscure their importance
to villagers, this seems to be the case for anthropologists as well.
In making his case for more research on the general topic, Mandelbaum reports that there are "relatively few notices in the literature
of the relation between population growth and social interaction or
religious practice."

From those few references and studies that are available, Professor Mandelbaum concludes that there are ways in which population
growth has at least played a part in bringing about changes in India's
basic social institutions. Changing agricultural practices and technology, which are direct responses to population growth, have led
in some cases to a deterioration of jajmani relationships, a series of
patron-client ties based on filial and fraternal solidarity rather than
cash payment for the performance of services. At least in one instance, in Punjab, the field labor provided by daughters has become
more valued than before, in response to agricultural practices.
While the evidence is rather spotty and incomplete, it would also
seem that, in general, strains within the joint family, and within and
between subcastes, have intensified with population growth. Mandel-

baum details a number of cases where there has taken place what he
calls a loss of the sense of "moral community" that has been so important in securing cooperation among rival segments of India's complex social structure; he also argues that "through much of India, the
institutions of village and government have been pushed beyond their
effective carrying capacity, partly because of the larger number of
people who are expected to participate."

Indicative of this loss of a sense of "moral community" is the
way in which a number of villages have given up a variety of religious
rituals and ceremonies, at least in part a response to "the weight of
greater numbers of people, either within the village or pressing into
it from outside." In most instances, perhaps, the increasing disuse
of village religious rituals and ceremonies is being replaced with
such things as more large-scale pilgrimages to major pilgrimage centers or participation in wider regional and linguistic associations, often based on caste. Joseph Elder speculated that the rather striking
growth of a pilgrimage site that he had studied in detail was one result of this phenomenon.

What Professor Mandelbaum saw as a loss of a sense of "moral
community" Professor Varadachar prefers to call "moral or value
stretch." Both agree that there had been no sharp break in India's
social patterns such as one might find in China or in other Sinic societies in this century. Both also agree that there had been considerable adaptation and change in basic Indian social institutions in response to population pressures, a point reinforced by Professor A.
M. Shah. Commenting on this, Irene Tinker and Milton Singer suggest that one might conceive of the overall situation in India in terms
of a series of cultural lags, with some portions of Indian society responding much more quickly than others. If this were the case, then
one could argue that population growth and a severe disorientation
of resources had, in Irene Tinker's words, thrown society "somewhat
out of kilter in almost every field," thus producing a state of affairs
that often appeared in the popular literature on India as a series of
contradictions.

Perhaps the most striking response to population growth has
been the way in which pressures on village lands have been cushioned
by adaptive societal institutions without a significant acceleration of
migration into the cities. A. M. Shah suggested that one of the most
basic changes taking place in India's rural areas in response to population growth was a change in settlement patterns, with people (particularly poor people) moving farther and farther away from the old village clusters, which were generally built near the most fertile land.
In addition, Professor Shah observed that more and more village
homes are now two- and three-story structures, in contrast to the
older one-story huts that have dominated the Indian rural landscape
in the past.

For whatever reason, India's rate of urban growth is much smaller than that found generally in Africa, Latin America, or other parts of Asia. To quote Robert Cassen: "The villages are what is growing. The urban areas in India are not expanding all that rapidly." This could in part be explained by what Ashish Bose has called the "push-back" factor, having to do with the undesirability of Indian cities when viewed from the eyes of villagers, or it could be a result of a series of more complex explanations that were discussed in the last session of the conference and will be taken up at a later point in this chapter. In any case, the subject of rural-urban relationships in response to population-related variables is another field where a number of intensive research efforts seem warranted.

To say that there have not been mass migrations to India's urban areas on a scale comparable to those found elsewhere is not to say that there are no links between city, town, and village. Indeed, both the number and intensity of rural-urban linkages seem to be growing rapidly, as pressures on land and resources inside the village require that more and more people go outside the village for services, for economic gain, or for employment. Rather than a mass migration to urban areas, however, what these pressures seem to have generated are a series of goings and comings between people who have both rural and urban ties. Professor Mandelbaum, for example, found some evidence of an increasing number of "share families" that own relatively small plots of land in the rural areas while many of the male members of the family work in factories or in menial jobs in the city during a portion of the year. As pressure on land intensifies, the number of such families seem inevitably to grow. In these cases the family attempts to keep its village land, on which it can at least grow food crops in times of economic distress, thus guaranteeing a certain minimum level of living. Unfortunately, as Mandelbaum points out, members of "share families" are usually neither good farmers nor good factory workers, since their city jobs often detract from their ability to pay much attention to the land while their growing of crops takes them away from their urban jobs for considerable portions of the year.

Milton Singer, an anthropologist who has worked primarily in India's urban areas, is convinced that linkage patterns between India's rural and urban areas reflect a key adaptation to population growth as well as other facets of modern life. On the basis of his own study of 19 industrialists from Madras, many of whom had been born or brought up in a village or small town, and all of whom maintained some ties with the village, Singer concluded that such people "represent in a way the trend of the future, the pace-setters; by looking at them we may find some reason for hope and perhaps a less cataclysmic future." At Wingspread, Singer reported his con-

clusion, based on his previous studies, that a "coexistence of traditional attitudes and modern features" was "more or less a standard
condition, not a temporary condition" among a variety of different
groups in India. With regard to population-related variables, as well
as other modern forces, Singer emphasized that many groups in India are "people with ancient cultures who are adapting and coping
with tremendous modern problems."

For Singer, as for Varadachar, at least part of the key to understanding how people in India have adapted to population increase
is greater appreciation of religious beliefs. Singer suggests that
such things as reinterpretations of traditional Hindu ideas, as well
as Gandhian notions of duty and right, have played major roles. The
assertions by one of Singer's interviewees, that "poverty anywhere
is a danger everywhere" and that "if he can't help the poor he at least
tries not to do them any harm" are examples that he used to show the
manner in which Gandhi's version of nonviolence and ahimsa had been
interpreted by one modern Hindu to cope, at least psychologically,
with population growth and other modern pressures.

If Singer has been sufficiently impressed with adaptation and
change in response to population variables, Morris Carstairs is, in
his own words, "a doomster." For Carstairs, the key variables are
the geometrical progression of population, contrasted with the much
slower growth of food supplies, the lack of preconditions in India for
a population control program, and the factionalism of Indian social
life. As a result of increased pressures on land and resources, in
Carstairs' view, "the stage is set for social upheavals of a destructive nature," not unlike episodes in European history where "there
were sudden natural disasters or very rapid periods of social change
(sometimes accelerated by natural catastrophes like famines, floods,
or outbreaks of plague) in which whole groups of people found themselves deprived of their customary support and security." Carstairs
foresees the coming into being, after a period of relative anarchy
arising essentially from population pressures, of a rather ineffective
and temporary police state or military dictatorship in India, for as
long as a generation.

The difficulty that participants had in accepting the position of
Morris Carstairs was perhaps best articulated by Robert Cassen,
when he said that "although we feel that some crisis is impending,
we cannot see, and nothing that anybody has written can identify,
where it is going to run into some culminating upheaval. It is just
not visible. [What] we can see [are] all kinds of stresses and strains
and all sorts of responses to these positive and negative forces."

If most participants at Wingspread were not as convinced as
Carstairs that some great upheaval or catastrophe was in store for
India, they were in general agreement that societal adjustment and

adaptation to population variables was essential if catastrophe is to
be averted. If there was any consensus on the direction in which the
society had to move, it was, in the words of John Mellor, a direction
in which "the mass of the people [would have] some sense of control
of their destiny," or, in Cassen's words, "the community itself
[would feel] responsible for its own numbers." In the eyes of some
participants, Indian society has already shifted considerably in this
direction; in the eyes of others, the shift has not been drastic or pervasive enough.

FAMILY RESPONSES TO POPULATION CHANGE

The relationship between a sense of control of one's destiny and
a family's decision as to the number of children it will have was the
principal focus of Rama Mehta's paper and the discussion of it at the
conference (Chapter 5). Mehta began with the observation that the
idea of limiting family size was prevalent even in the preindependence
period among families that had had extensive contacts with British
Indian administrative personnel. In attempting to explain the presence of this idea in the preindependence period and the rapid extension of the idea among white-collar families after 1947, Mehta reached
the conclusion that the key variables have to do with family structure
and orientations toward tradition and modernity. Her intensive interviews with 100 middle-class women, conducted during the course of
previous research, led her to the hypothesis that nuclear family
structures encourage fewer children, primarily because of the attitudes and activities of the mother, and that further encouragement
for smaller families is provided by such matters as the education
and employment of the mother, as well as knowledge and acceptance
of legal rights designed to make the mother and daughter equal with
the father and son in such matters as divorce, inheritance, and
adoption. Among the small group of women that Mehta interviewed,
she found that:

> The greatest change between the pre- and postinde-
> pendence eras can be described in terms of a
> transformation in the status of women, and their
> values regarding extended family responsibilities.
> While the former group viewed itself as subordi-
> nate to men and did not have the confidence or
> courage to defy conventional prejudices or their
> husbands' authority over them, the modern edu-
> cated Indian woman is more assured in her status
> as a separate identity. She has become more of an
> individual in her own right.

Having become more of an individual in her own right, Mehta argues, the modern educated Indian woman no longer looks to her extended family, caste, and kin groups as exclusive sources for fulfillment. This means that she no longer needs to subscribe to the logic or rationale of these traditional social institutions, with the result that the determination of the number of children that she will have becomes a matter almost entirely determined by her own wishes, usually in consultation with her husband. Since she is encouraged—by her modern ideas, her education, and her employment—to seek greater independence and fulfillment for herself outside the family, she is usually inclined to have fewer children. Moreover, the greater security that she has gained—from her education, employment, and legal rights—makes her less dependent on her grown sons in her old age. All of these factors, then, serve to diminish the desire among modern urban middle-class Indian mothers for large numbers of children, particularly sons.

By way of comparison, Mehta points out that the same set of factors is not found among blue-collar families. Blue-collar families, Mehta suggests, are still oriented primarily to caste and subcaste and extended kin relationships. Instead of spending their money on education, therefore, blue-collar families are inclined to spend it on ritualistic observances (marriages and other ceremonies) in a manner that will enhance their status within their traditional social groups. Women in blue-collar families still seek fulfillment primarily through extended family, they are not generally employed outside the home, they are usually uneducated, and they are not often even conscious of the legal rights that have been made available to them. Since this is not usually a matter of money or wealth—Mehta argues that blue-collar incomes are in most cases equivalent to the incomes of white-collar workers in India—she suggests that a change in attitudes and orientations among blue-collar workers is necessary, if average family size among this segment of society is to be reduced. Moreover, she suggests that, since blue-collar workers usually have closer linkages with the rural areas than do white-collar workers, changes in values and orientations among blue-collar families could produce a "multiplier effect" in the Indian countryside.

Aside from his methodological reservations about Mehta's findings, Professor Elder questioned a number of Mehta's observations, including those having to do with the relative equality of incomes for blue- and white-collar families, the access of blue-collar families to educational opportunities, and the possibilities for producing a "multiplier effect." However, Elder was in general agreement with Mehta with regard to the importance of education, employment, and legal rights for women, viewing them as factors that could provide some incentive for reduced family size. For Elder, however, the activist strategy that made most sense was one that appealed directly to rural families, as well as blue-collar and white-collar urban groups, but the key question for him was, "What is in it for them if they limit or reduce the size of their families?"

In response to Mehta's paper and Professor Elder's comments on it, Professor A. M. Shah concurred with the judgment of Mehta that a significant shift in behavior had occurred in urban middle-class families in India. However, like Elder, Shah did not account for this shift in terms of family structures. The most important changes, Shah argued, were those that involved feelings of greater equality between husband and wife and the willingness of husband and wife to discuss topics that were previously not discussed, including (1) whether the size of the family should be limited or not, and (2) questions concerning the desirability of sons versus daughters. Professor Shah also observed a continuing marked contrast between urban and rural attitudes. For example, he pointed out that "Urban middle-class couples may want both a daughter and a son, but if they do not have a son, they do not make too much fuss about it. Such a fuss is still made in the rural areas."

With regard to the rural areas, however, Professor Shah reported a number of observations that he had made that indicated that some change is taking place. For example, the question of limiting family size, Shah finds, is frequently and avidly discussed by villagers, and cheap literature on the subject is read and sought out. Two aspects of the family-size question seem especially prominent in village conversations, according to Professor Shah, one being expressed in the worries of many husbands about the health of the wife after a number of children and pregnancies, the second having to do with the consequences for the division of property of various kinds of family composition. Pending further research on such matters, one might conclude from Professor Shah's remarks that villagers are at least asking the question that Professor Elder considered central—that is, "What is in it for them if they limit or reduce the size of their families?"

Extrapolations from this discussion, by John Cool, produced the speculation that a fundamental change in the character of marriage as an institution might be taking place in India, as well as "an altered pattern of demands after the fundamental procreation and child-rearing functions have been served." Referring to the relationship between a sense of control of one's destiny and a willingness to limit the size of families, Cool conceived of the possibility that very significant changes might be taking place in this regard as well, without much reference being made to them in the literature and without much research being done on them. In his words:

> I suspect (although we have not had enough time to
> measure this and I don't think anybody is looking at
> it very carefully) that the capacity of women in In-
> dia, both in the urban middle classes and increas-
> ingly in rural areas, to regulate unwanted concep-
> tion, will result in an enormous cumulative impact
> on their self-esteem and their attitudes toward
> themselves and their bodily functions. This, I sus-
> pect, will have an enormous impact on the family
> structure and the role that women are prepared and
> permitted to play in society 30 years hence.

While none of the participants at Wingspread explicitly questioned the possibility that such a fundamental shift may be occurring,
many of them did express reservations about the extent and pace of
change in family relationships. Phillips Talbot, for example, referred to various kinds of research findings that might lead one to the
conclusion that the functions of jatis and lineages have in many ways
been reinforced by population growth, thus raising the possibility that
the traditional reasons for large family size might remain prevalent
for some time. In a more specific reference along the same lines,
A. M. Shah pointed out that the aged in India look increasingly to their
caste and subcaste, or to a variety of traditional sources associated
with pilgrimage sites, for security in their later years, thus presumably strengthening the importance of traditional family and kinship
arrangements.

On a somewhat different note, Professor Mandelbaum pointed
out that village women generally are not inclined to take advantage of
inheritance laws and other legal rights because such action tends to
alienate them from their brothers, thus converting their brothers
from chief allies to competitors. As things now stand, the brother of
a village woman is her main support outside her husband's family, and
his goodwill is considered crucial for her security. One of the other
results of the usual brother-sister relationship in India, Mandelbaum
points out, is the constant worry among village women who have only
daughters: "How can this daughter get along well in later life if she
has no brothers?" Another result of this relationship is the common
feeling, reported by Rama Mehta, that if large sums of money have
to be spent on a daughter for education and a dowry, and if she is
eventually going to make her home with another family anyhow, then
she should not receive an inheritance.

For a variety of other reasons as well, it is clear that the
force of the legal enactments providing equal rights for men and women has thus far been diluted. As Marc Galanter pointed out in a
series of remarks that will be developed at some length in the next

section of this chapter, one of the major effects of population growth has been simultaneously to increase the amount of legislation being enacted and to make that legislation more passive, in such a manner that only those who have sufficient resources can effectively make use of the provisions of the law. Mehta herself concurred with this assessment as it applies to present-day India when she stated that the effect of legislation designed to provide equal rights for men and women had thus far been limited by the time and costs involved and by the lack of alternatives available to women outside the family. In her words, "The process of law remains a complicated process, and an expensive process, and [a woman] may win in the court but be bereft otherwise."

In all of these matters, of course, it is clear that women in the poorest segments of Indian society are the most disadvantaged, whether this be in relation to legal rights, education, or employment. However, as Milton Singer pointed out, on the basis of comparative studies done by Oscar Lewis, India's poor villagers and urban slum-dwellers do not have a "culture of poverty" in the same sense as the poor in Mexico, Puerto Rico, and New York. To Singer, this means that India's poor "do not get demoralized and alienated in the same way as the people whom Oscar Lewis characterizes as having a 'culture of poverty' . . . they are not very successful in improving their living standards not because they have a culture of poverty but because they are poor." One of the possibilities that flows from this is that, if India's poor do not have a "culture of poverty," it may be that they could more readily gain what John Mellor called "some sense of control of their destiny" or at least the sense of responsibility for their own numbers that Robert Cassen referred to, without a quantum increase in their standards of living. That thought, and a further thought by John Cool—that "the human family and small community have exhibited an enormous absorptive capacity"—perhaps provide the basis for a more hopeful perspective on the adaptations of poorer Indian families to population growth. Lacking very much research on the topic, as was clear from the discussion at Wingspread, these are two areas that seem worth exploring.

POPULATION GROWTH AND LAW

The position of the poor in India was very much at the center of attention during the discussion of law and population change. The focus for this discussion was a detailed speculative comment by Marc Galanter (Chapter 6) in which he argued that a number of pressures on legal systems in large democratic societies, while not necessarily being created by population growth were, nevertheless, amplified by

such growth. Galanter started from the assumption that scarcity and
conflict, at least in the Indian setting, increase as the population ex-
pands. This leads to more "business" for the legal system, but, because of scarcity, the capacity of legal institutions to respond to the
greater demands placed on them does not correspondingly improve.
The result is a series of overloaded institutions, resulting in delay
and "extraordinary bypasses around the delay," as well as a tendency
for the legal system to be quite passive, throwing the burden of assembling cases on the user. Within the legal system, then, real advantage
is conferred on those who are most capable and who have the most resources, while many decisions that previously might have been included within the purview of legal institutions begin to be made elsewhere, again usually by the most advantaged.

A second series of consequences of population growth in the Indian setting, Galanter suggested, were triggered by the tendency for
government to make more law, if only because rapid population growth
produces a situation dominated by friction and conflict, in which the
government "cannot depend on the market to allocate scarce resources."
Granted the commitments of the present Indian government, law is
invariably based on egalitarian themes. But this creates what Galanter calls "a major paradox" since "there is more law with an egalitarian tone to it and yet more unequal results from the law's use."
Professor Galanter mentioned land reform laws, village house site
regulations, the Untouchability Offences Act, and inheritance laws
as examples of "laws that on their face and in their intent are egalitarian [but] turn out to have very different results."

A third linkage between population growth and law that Galanter
identified was also expressed in terms of a paradox. In this case,
scarcity, friction, and conflict mean that the government has less
tangible rewards to distribute, while, at the same time, more organized discontent is clamoring for more things. The result is, in Galanter's formulation, that government depends more and more on symbolic and ceremonial legislation as a source of legitimacy, since
"passing laws is one of the least expensive things that governments
can do, at least in the short run." The consequences of this, Galanter argues, are that (1) those who are relatively advantaged can "use
their initiative to prod the government and get the laws that favor them
enforced" and (2) the development of a system for allocating responsibilities to officials to decide which of the things on the agenda will get
done. Covert allocation of responsibilities leads both to corruption
and to "a massive delegation of control to various local powerholders
who acquire vast decision-making power under these circumstances."

Professor Galanter refers to these three linkages that he described as paradoxes, resulting in shortages of control, equality, and
legitimacy, respectively. These, he suggests, are the "fault lines"

of any democratic system, but such fault lines become especially
strained under conditions of rapid population growth in already
crowded conditions. Professor Galanter was quick to point out that
his comments did not necessarily imply "a picture of breakdown," although it was clear from his remarks that the usual suggestions for
minimizing the impact of stress caused by them—he himself mentioned
political decentralization, relinquishment of equality commitments,
suppression of conflict, and the revival of Hindu law—implied changes
that were at best terribly difficult to effect in present-day India.

Professor Galanter's comments provoked a good deal of heated
discussion at the conference. P. M. Beliappa, a member of the Indian Administrative Service, reacted by detailing his impression that
"law responds to the needs of society and if there is a need that has
been generated by society, it is sanctified by law, not the other way
round." Referring to his understanding of the way the Indian government operates, Beliappa said, "We certainly do not adopt a piece of
legislation and then expect society to respond to it."

Beliappa, therefore, chose not to emphasize the ceremonial
and symbolic aspects of law, or the paradoxes that Galanter had mentioned, but instead stressed "the dynamics that have resulted from
legal changes in response to population growth." The most fundamental change, from Beliappa's perspective, was the provision of equal
rights to men and women, which, he argued, was responsible for a
fragmentation of property. Fragmentation in the rural areas, Beliappa pointed out, had been further encouraged by the abolition of
zamindari legislation and various land reform acts. Land reform,
when coupled with legislation giving additional rights to tenants, was,
for Beliappa, in large part responsible for a decline in absentee landlordism. In the cities and towns, fragmentation of property, along
with other social and political factors, had produced what Beliappa
called "unviable domestic units" and "all the evil consequences of
growing urbanization."

In defense of Galanter, a number of the conference participants
pointed to the ceremonial and symbolic aspects of recent legislation
concerned with population-related matters, and they also indicated
a variety of ways in which this legislation has favored certain segments and classes of society despite its egalitarian tone. Perhaps
the most detailed discussion of a specific law was that which focused
on the Medical Termination of Pregnancy Act (MTPA), so named,
Bhupen Mukerjee emphasized, in order to avoid the use of the controversial word "abortion." Professor Mukerjee also noted that government spokesmen in India had stated that the MTPA "has nothing to do
with population at all." (The law permits abortion up to the seventh
month of pregnancy when performed in hospitals with the permission
of at least two doctors). Galanter showed the relative lack of effect
of the abortion law for the mass of the population, despite estimates

that something like one in every seven pregnancies in India is terminated by abortions, the vast majority being performed by village midwives. In Galanter's words:

> Those few middle-class people who could not man-
> age previously to get a doctor willing to perform an
> abortion now have the benefit [from the new law] of
> being able to do that. For the 15 million every year
> —or whatever the number—who get abortions from
> village midwives, the act did exactly nothing because
> it left this type of abortion still stigmatized as ille-
> gal and still unregulated. The government can now
> say we have legalized abortion and that's a major
> progressive step in population policy . . . but the
> government has done nothing about the really mas-
> sive problem of illegal abortions in the countryside.

In defense of Beliappa, Anrudh Jain suggested that laws like the
MTPA were at least facilitative, in the sense that abortion services
could not "be provided overnight" and obviously could not be provided
on a large scale in the absence of legislation making them legal.
Along somewhat the same lines, Krishan Bhatia spoke of the usefulness of a symbolic law, "in the sense that it stimulates movements
in a certain desirable manner . . . even if it does not immediately
solve the problem." Similarly, Asok Mitra argued that, "even if the
MTPA has not been able to embrace the whole of the population in
terms of implementation at this point in time, yet [it creates] a climate for the enforcement of the rule of law and you can fight over it."

With regard to other recent legislative enactments, A. M. Shah
described the manner in which the Anti-Dowry Act was intended only
for the upper castes, among which the practice of dowry is widespread.
For the vast majority of Indians, who follow the radically different
practice of bride-price, the act had no meaning. David Mandelbaum
made the case that legislation raising the legal age of girls at marriage (to 14 in 1929 and 15 in 1956) has had no beneficial effect on
fertility control and, if extended, "might well be harmful." Mandelbaum's argument is as follows:

> In the first place, the age of girls at marriage does
> not begin to have significant effect on their total fer-
> tility until that age is about 20. If a new law stipu-
> lated the minimum age of girls at marriage to be 20,
> there undoubtedly would be many evasions of such a
> law; it would be exceedingly difficult, perhaps impos-
> sible, to enforce. But it would also give the village

> enemies of a family another way of waging the power
> struggle by bringing a man to the courts on the
> grounds that he had arranged a marriage for his
> daughter at an illegally young age. Litigation and
> prosecution would increase the load on a legal system
> that is already overburdened and waste scarce re-
> sources in litigation.

Finally, Robert Cassen detailed some of the legal aspects of tax legislation that have prevented the Indian government from collecting something like 5 billion rupees, now tied up in tax arrears cases in the
courts, despite the obvious need for government revenues. For Cassen, this paradox could be explained by factors that Marc Galanter had
described.

A slightly different kind of support for Galanter's position was
introduced by John Lewis, when he interpreted it as a case for decentralization, even though this might mean "passing decision-making into
the hands of the least disturbed elites, who are likely to be least compassionate in their dealings with the poor." Lewis argued strenuously
for decentralization in the Indian context, to deal with some of the
problems Galanter had identified, but, in order to "shore up the equity
situation for the poor," Lewis also argued for centralized leadership
in "strengthening the poor to bargain more effectively in the local
arenas." In one of the more controversial statements made at the conference, Professor Lewis outlined his position as follows:

> We should be expecting and indeed hoping for more
> violence—more class violence really—in the villages.
> It would be part of the reformers' aim in various
> ways, by helping to organize politicoeconomic orga-
> nizations of the poor and by trying to weaken the de-
> pendency mechanisms through which the village
> elites keep the poor subservient, to generate greater
> capacity in the poor to compete for resources in the
> local arena. We could expect this to lead for some
> time to quite a lot more violence in the countryside,
> although hopefully contained within some kind of more
> or less orderly frame. I think that, if you see pov-
> erty at least in part as a joint product of population
> and population growth, then you can say that one ef-
> fect would be, through this sequence, to increase
> violence and conflict in the countryside—in a way that
> I would regard as constructive.

While Asok Mitra disagreed with Lewis about the pressing need for decentralization, he was in general agreement with the necessity for the Indian government to "go hammer and tongs against many of the customary laws," which he saw as "entirely laws of privilege." Mitra also agreed with Lewis that some of the most encouraging benefits for the poor were visible in precisely those states (West Bengal and Kerala, for example) that had witnessed some of the most radical and violent political movements, although the connections between the goals of the radical movements and the benefits derived by the poor, as Mitra pointed out, are "rather complex things." The complexity of the decentralization and equities issues was also alluded to by P. M. Beliappa in his interventions.

One of the ways in which both the decentralization and equities issues were discussed in more concrete terms was with reference to a statistical presentation by Galanter, in which he pointed out that civil litigation on a per capita basis had dropped from 147 per 10,000 in undivided India in 1931 to something like 47 per 10,000 for the same area in 1961, while criminal cases were about 50 per 10,000 in 1911 and 77 per 10,000 in 1961. Galanter himself explained this rapid rise in the incidence of criminal cases as possibly a function of population change, since most crimes are committed by males between the ages of 15 and 20, an age cadre that has obviously been expanding disproportionately to the rest of the population during the past few decades. Other participants, however, sought alternative explanations. John Cool suggested the possibility that the rise in the crime rate was simply a function of better record-keeping, while he explained the relative decline in the amount of civil litigation by referring to the disadvantages to the poor resulting from such things as the cost of "bringing cases," the distances involved in going to court several times in a system known for its delays, and the complexity of the legal procedures that have been introduced in India in modern times. Professor Mandelbaum related the decrease in civil litigation to the villagers' conception of such litigation, as "a means of fighting your enemies of the other factions," as well as a means for securing justice. Mandelbaum speculated that, since other village arenas (principally the voting arena) have now become the foci for struggles between factions, the functional need for civil litigation in the village context may have been diluted. As regards the increase in criminal litigation, Mandelbaum hypothesized that this may be indicative of the weakening of the village sense of community, meaning that villagers could no longer keep the police out of local disputes and settle criminal matters themselves.

COMMUNICATIONS AND POPULATION GROWTH

At one point during the discussion on law, Milton Singer said that Marc Galanter's description of the Indian legal system reminded him (Singer) of William James's definition of democracy, this being "a system of government in which people holler and the government tries to do something to silence them, and after it has acted another group hollers and as a result the government tries to do something about that, and so on ad infinitum." With regard to communications, the question that provoked the bulk of the discussion at Wingspread was the extent to which central, regional, and local leadership in India had responded to population growth by "hollering" up or down. The comments during this discussion were directed at a statement by Bryant Kearl, in which he described the development of the communications media in India as being almost exclusively concerned with the national and regional levels, even when attempts are made to localize or decentralize the system. In Kearl's view, the concept that seems to be prevalent in the minds of media leaders in India is that of a transmission belt, onto which you can feed messages and convey them out to the populace. At the local level, however, people in India have understandably fortified themselves against national messages, since local leaders still conceive of communications in quite traditional terms. The result, Kearl argues, is to create something of a communications void between national and local levels.

Population growth, Professor Kearl suggested, was at least in part responsible for this situation, since large-scale populations had produced the economies of scale that have made national media networks almost imperative. Moreover, the communications technology and management practices that have been developed in response to the growth of population worldwide has made such networks possible. In this view, then, the Indian communications media have been shaped in large part by the fact that they were developed in the 20th century, a period of time when global forces in communications were pushing in the direction of nationalized and centralized control. By way of contrast, those communications systems that developed in the 19th century and earlier (the example Kearl used was the United States) had developed in local communities, staffed by local people, in response to local needs.

During the rest of this century, one might expect somewhat of a convergence between the communications systems of India and the West, since, in Professor Kearl's words, "there are all sorts of forces in our system that are pushing toward centralization, and there are all sorts of forces in the Indian system that are pushing toward decentralization." Kearl's concern in this context was the adoption of policies that might facilitate the development of radio and televi-

sion stations, and newspapers, in such a way that initiative for establishing and running the media would rest with local people in local
communities, publishing or broadcasting whatever pressures in the
local community forced them to carry. Such policies, Kearl pointed
out, might help produce the situation that Robert Cassen had described
as imperative, where people in local communities felt some responsibility for their numbers. When commenting on the diversity of India,
and such consequences of population increase as the likely growth of
20 new cities of multimillion dimensions or the growth of 150 concentrated population centers of 100,000 or more people during the next
30 years, Kearl stated, "I cannot believe that All-India Radio, no
matter how much it decentralizes, can perform [these functions].
. . . I can't believe that the traveling postman or markets or pilgrimages or weddings, or whatever else one finds traditionally, can perform [these functions]."

    In Chapter 7, Promilla Kalhan indeed conceives of communica-
tions in India as essentially a one-way flow. "In a situation where
educational facilities are limited," she argues, "the mass media acts
as educational instruments while being dependent on levels of education for their effectiveness." Rather than focus on the development
of local communications efforts, therefore, Kalhan suggests that India's response to population growth had to be based, as it is, on further national development of such things as the educational system,
primary health centers, changes in ideas about sex and the status of
women, a more appropriate contraceptive device, and a general increase in standards of living. The mass media, in Kalhan's view,
can only play a limited and temporary role in the absence of "development in its widest sense." Granted the limitations of the mass media,
however, Kalhan argues that India's communications effort thus far,
particularly in disseminating family-planning messages, "has not
been as ineffective as some would make it out to be."

    Krishan Bhatia provided a third perspective on the relationship
between population growth and communications when he took the position that, in population-related matters especially, "India's conception of what it is about is lacking." Bhatia suggested that the source
of India's failure to respond adequately to the challenges of population increase was the inability or unwillingess of India's top leadership "to make up its mind as to how serious the population problem
is." The inadequacy of the response of India's societal leaders,
Bhatia suggested, "will unavoidably be reflected in the media."
When commenting on Bryant Kearl's pleas for more far-sighted communications policies that would encourage local initiative in developing the media, Bhatia was, therefore, quite pessimistic. The gist
of his response to Kearl's formulation was stated as follows:

> I don't think there is any sort of realization in Delhi
> that a few years from now such and such a develop-
> ment might take place and we should now go about
> meeting it. Should we increase the production of
> newsprint? Should we denationalize some of the
> broadcast media? I don't think any serious thought
> has so far been given to such questions. Like most
> governments anywhere, the Indian government will
> be drawn into some kind of a policy decision by eco-
> nomic forces and compulsions.

Milton Singer took exception to both Krishan Bhatia's pessimism
and Bryant Kearl's characterization of the communications flow in India as essentially a one-way "conveyor belt" when he said that "obviously the hollering goes from the bottom up and also from the top
down." Professor Singer felt the need, in a society as complex as
India's, for study of a variety of different kinds of communications
processes, which cannot be translated into a uniform modern idiom
or language or conceptualized only in terms of formal communications
media networks. Examples of some of the informal means of communication that various participants considered important in this regard are public meetings and religious discourses; such figures as
the postman, ticket collectors on buses, construction workers, and
itinerant salesmen and service people; institutions like the increasing
number of village cafes, family planning exhibits, and weddings; and
popular Bombay movies and educational films. While no conclusions
were reached as to the roles that each of these have played in response
to population variables, there were a number of suggestions as to how
one might gain greater understanding of the communications process
in the subcontinent by focusing on them.

At the other end of the communications spectrum, there was
some discussion of the potential roles of television and radio as they
relate to population variables. Both Robert Cassen and John Lewis
questioned the appropriateness of television as a principal medium
of communications for India, partly on the grounds that television
encourages perceptions of communications on the "holler-down"
rather than the "holler-up" side of the equation. Related drawbacks
of television that were noted had to do with the tendency for this medium to provide global rather than local information, the likelihood
that televised communications would "be in the language of the establishment," the difficulties involved in keeping television sets in good
repair in Indian villages (despite alleged attempts to "ruggedize"
them), and what Cassen called the "rather dubious economics" of establishing a widespread television network in India in the near future,
owing largely to the cost of equipment and the need to import much of

the technology. Further disadvantages of television that were mentioned, particularly when considering its use for such things as family
planning messages beamed to large audiences in a village setting,
had to do with the small size of the screen and the likelihood that the
bulk of the messages that could be produced for it would be repetitive
slogans on taped film.

The development of radio, on the other hand, was considered
by several conference participants to be desirable, particularly in a
situation dominated by the phenomenon of rapid population increase,
for a number of different reasons. Since small transistor radios can
now be produced entirely in India without additional inputs, the economics of this medium in a situation of scarcity seem favorable.
Professor Lewis also argued that "a very little gadget that belongs to
the villager himself, which he can turn off at will, is in some respects
much less threatening and interesting." Most important, the possibility of establishing local radio stations, broadcasting in local languages, seems more likely feasible in the near future than such stations for television, since radio stations and sending equipment involve considerably smaller capital costs and can be produced indigenously. Again, the thrust of the conversation at Wingspread seemed
to veer round to finding ways for local communities to gain some measure of control over their own destinies.

PLANNING AND THE PROVISION OF SERVICES

Perhaps the archetype of a city that has lost control of its own
destiny because of population growth is Calcutta, which was the subject of Asok Mitra's paper (Chapter 8), stimulating discussion for the
last session at Wingspread. Mitra showed how the planning of services in Calcutta has been based on Western models of development,
with the consequence that projects and funds have been concentrated
in the core areas of the city. At the same time, the city's poor, including large numbers of international migrants, have settled in clusters of "urban villages" spread out around the city, despite the lack
of funds that have been available for the provision of services in these
latter communities. The result is that heavy investment in the core
areas of Calcutta, based on Western models and promoted by those
with political clout, benefit the very few residents of the city who can
get access to them, while the vast majority of the people in the larger
Calcutta metropolitan area are left to fend for themselves. This
creates a severe dilemma. The more development is concentrated
in Calcutta proper, the more Calcutta proper is threatened with the
possibility that it will be overwhelmed with migrants from the surrounding neglected urban and semiurban connurbation. Since greater

successful concentrated development in the core area would attract greater and greater numbers to this area, the urban problems of the core become the more intense the more the plans succeed, thus requiring larger and larger inputs of scarce resources, which in turn leads to further neglect of the already poor "urban villages" surrounding the city.

The resolution of this dilemma, Asok Mitra suggests, might be found in alternative planning models that would invest heavily in services for several clusters of "rural villages" around Calcutta, each with its own unique demographic, social, economic, transportation, and servicing features. In addition, Mitra argues, alternative planning models have to be found that have standards and norms appropriate to the vast majority of the people, "instead of thrusting on them standards and norms of development that are too precious and that are irrelevant, being more suited to highly developed economies." Among the many examples of revised standards and norms provided by Mitra were those having to do with building materials and water supply. In Mitra's words,

> India will have to forget about steel and cement for
> low- and middle-income housing, for steel and ce-
> ment will be scarce, prohibitively expensive, and
> sorely needed for more urgent national purposes.
> Secondly . . . it is becoming increasingly plain that
> a central water supply, as well as sewage, sewerage,
> and drainage systems for the entire Calcutta Metro-
> politan Region, such as has been planned for Calcut-
> ta, are things that the resource traffic will not bear.
> They will have to be broken up into smaller mini-
> systems, designed to bring about self-sufficiency
> for defined geographical spaces of say 10 to 15 square
> miles each; conceived, planned, and executed on
> scales that local resources can maintain and replace.

The relevance of Asok Mitra's approach to the provision of services in the larger Calcutta metropolitan area was extended by Robert Cassen to other parts of India as well. Wherever you look in India, Cassen suggests, you find that the cost of providing services is always far greater than resources will allow, primarily because of the incredible numbers of people involved. Since concentration of funds, particularly on the basis of Western models, leads invariably to the kinds of dilemmas that Asok Mitra describes for Calcutta, the only sensible solution, in Cassen's view, is to revise standards and norms to the point where they are more appropriate to the Indian environment. Moreover, Cassen emphasized the importance of providing employment and incomes, in order that people "will be able to find services for themselves." According to Cassen, then, Asok Mitra's suggestions for deconcentrated investment, with more appropriate norms for India, are "just as relevant in rural areas; if you have funds they should be used to provide employment and income for the mass of the people. . . . You only have to do certain very basic things by way of services."

That concentrated investment in a few major cities, and in the core areas of these cities, has been neglectful of the dynamics of population growth during the last few decades was clear from a number of other statements by the participants at the conference. B. R. Deolalikar described how a lack of adequate resources for such investment, in urban areas of 100,000 or less in Gujarat and Maharashtra, has resulted in "a kind of decay" in these cities and a consequent worsening of the standards of living of the urban poor. Asok Mitra estimated that something like 15 billion rupees ($2 billion) has been invested in New Delhi since 1947, a level that cannot be contemplated for most other Indian cities, meaning that New Delhi cannot be a prototype or model of urban development for the rest of the country. John Mellor pointed out that an emphasis on the concentrated development of the core areas of older cities has meant that less attention is paid to agriculture, thus producing a situation where the rural areas cannot contribute to economic growth in smaller towns because of the extent and predominance of rural poverty.

By way of emphasizing the need for new planning models, A. M. Shah stressed the importance of local leadership and the use of local resources in those instances where economic development has taken place in India during the past two or three decades. One of the most neglected areas of research on development, Professor Shah argued, was the role of corporators in large cities, the chairmen of zilla and taluka panchayats in the rural districts, and the leadership of villages and small towns in developmental activities. Shah is himself convinced that, in those cases where there are bright spots in the economy, local leadership has played an extremely important role. In a somewhat similar manner, Asok Mitra suggested that one of the reasons why the core areas of India's cities have recently exhibited a trend of decline of population growth rates has much to do with the emergence of a variety of different local leaders living in "urban villages" outside the central metropolitan regions, who have pursued self-help activities almost in defiance of the heavy government investments being made in the inner city. In addition, of course, the frequent lack of implementation of schemes for the development of the inner city has resulted in a rather common situation where the surrounding semiurban areas seem more desirable by comparison.

Attempts to account for the predominance of inappropriate planning models during the past two decades produced discussion of several different factors. Professors Deolalikar and Shah stressed the role of regional and national political factors that seemed to push planners in the direction of large-scale projects based on technologies developed in the West. Deolalikar also singled out a lack of managerial skills at the local level as a key variable. Almost everyone who spoke on the subject emphasized the need for international transfers in almost all development activities, and the way in which India's dependence on the West for such transfers tends to skew project designs in such a way as to conform rather closely with Western patterns of development. Finally, the need for data and research on local-level planning and resource use, as a prerequisite for inclusion of such factors in policy-making, was emphasized and reemphasized on a number of occasions.

However, while everyone at Wingspread could agree that India had to find its own model of development, both Milton Singer and John Lewis were concerned that this not be interpreted to mean that India and the Western nations have no problems in common. Singer stated his impression that an increasingly large number of people in the United States are becoming disappointed with their own models of urban growth, on the basis of a series of past experiences, particularly in large metropolitan areas. Referring to Mitra's plea for investments in "urban villages," Professor Singer remarked that "many of us living in places like Chicago or New York or Detroit are coming to share similar ideals." In his concluding remarks, Lewis commented on the tendency for both nationalism and a search for the leverage of "poor power" to be in the ascendancy in Asia, while, at the same time, more and more elites in the West are coming around to the position that "the problems that are really overwhelming the world . . . are essentially transnational problems." Granted the increasing consciousness and global influence of Asians, and the simultaneous tendency for Western elites to adopt the "subversive" idea that solutions to problems must be conceived in planetary terms, Lewis sees some realistic hope for future reductions of disparities in income and standards of living.

CONCLUSIONS

While the Wingspread conference was not the kind of meeting where a consensus is sought or reached, it did produce substantial agreement about the nature of India's response to population growth and the ways in which this impinges on policy-making activities. It was useful in other respects as well. Perhaps the most valuable aspect of the conference was the opportunity to see, through the eyes of some of the most informed and thoughtful people concerned with South Asia, the myriad ways in which population growth and movement is entwined with a chain of factors that shape social, political, and economic behavior. While we obviously know much less than we should about the details of specific relationships, and despite well-worn cliches about the complexity of the topic, it was still a remark-able experience to witness the interaction among a group of men and women who come at this complexity from many different angles.

One essential point of agreement at Wingspread was that India had not yet produced movements of any significance that have as their ultimate goal the rooting out of existing social and cultural values or institutions, as has been the case in China. A second such point is that Indian society has obviously been disturbed by population growth and other modern forces, to such an extent that it is, in various for-mulations, somewhat off balance, out of kilter, or faced with a series of contradictions. From the perspective of the "doomsters," socie-tal institutions and values have been thrown so drastically off balance by population change that some massive catastrophe or tragedy seems inevitable, if only to restore a new balance. Those with less extreme orientations are impressed with the adaptability and resiliency of the Indian population and would like at least to reserve judgment about the course of future adjustments.

No one at Wingspread, to my knowledge, felt that the response of Indian society to population growth had been sufficiently adequate that one could adopt a sanguine attitude about future developments. There is simply too much intensive poverty, among too many people, for that. Yet, it was also generally agreed that the response of peo-ple in the fields and on the roads and footpaths of the subcontinent was often severely circumscribed by factors beyond their control. So long as society is structured in such a way that local communities and individuals have so little stake in controlling their numbers, at-tempts to change them otherwise are likely to be unsatisfactory. So long as India remains very heavily dependent on the Western world in international trade and other monetary matters, Indian leaders are unlikely to be able to induce changes and adaptations that would, in a realistic manner, generate greater responsibility among local commu-nities and local power-holders.

If all of this seems to reinforce the sinking feeling of hopeless-ness and circularity that one often gets when discussing population themes in South Asia, it is at least refreshing to report that Wing-spread was, on the whole, an upbeat experience. In thinking about the reasons for this, it seems to me that there are two explanations. The first has to do with the emphasis in the conference on what has already been accomplished, and the almost unanimous agreement

that, with or without international aid, India is increasingly becoming
oriented toward self-help activity. Asok Mitra perhaps expressed
this facet of the conference discussion best when he said, "There is
no way but to proceed. . . . Everybody gets tired of giving alms, and
charity has its limits. . . . To pull oneself up by one's bootstraps
gives one a sense of fulfillment and a certain contentment, as also an
appreciation of the art of the practicable."

The second facet of the conference that was encouraging was the
constant reference to the large numbers of options that are available
to India and the way in which so many different individuals and organizations are searching for the proper combination of options in response to this most baffling of human situations. Toward the end of
the conference, John Mellor articulated the frustration that many of
us have had on this score, when he referred to the wish that "there
were not quite so many possibilities, because any one of them might
well create enormous problems." A breezier, related thought,
which also flows from the possibilities presented by the existence of
so many different options, was, again, expressed by Asok Mitra:
"One cannot just sit down and contemplate doom forever. One lives
in hope and keeps on trying. If one area of thought exhausts itself
one must go to another while one is alive."

2

THE DYNAMICS
OF INDIAN
POPULATION GROWTH
John Cool

The forces generated by the expansion of modern thought during the last four centuries—and especially by ideology, nationalism, and technology during the last 150 years—ensure that the next three decades will be a period of tumultuous change in India, in Asia, and in the world. Population growth and concomitant changes will be among the major factors affecting the shape of the future. Demographic dynamics foreordain the advent of a "Second India," a doubling of India's current population by early in the next century. Yet population change is only one among a number of simultaneous and related factors that will affect the future. Rapid population growth itself is, in a broader sense, the product of other dynamics. Variables such as productivity; the distribution of power; control over land, resources, and capital; levels of health and education; patterns of social stratification; and cultural attitudes toward collective enterprise and individual achievement will play significant roles in determining the effects of population change upon Indian society.

But Indian society cannot be considered in isolation from the broader processes of change currently affecting Asia and the world. The system of political and military alliances, power blocs, and trade arrangements that have afforded a precarious order to the world for the past 30 years are currently being dismantled. It is not yet clear what pattern of arrangements will take their place. It is clear that the ground rules for the new political and economic order will be significantly different. Between rich and poor, industrial and agrarian, and even between socialist and capitalist, distinctions will be blurred and adversary relationships altered.

Yet, without a more comprehensive model of the emerging international order, it is not practical to speculate concerning the nature of future interactions between nations. It is, however, impor-

tant that we recognize that such interactions exist and that they will
profoundly affect other projections and conjectures regarding the future. For it may be that those outside India who are concerned with
the unfolding of future events within India and with the implications of
those events for the rest of the human community will have the capacity, in the decade just ahead, to participate in and positively shape
the new international order in ways that will make it more equitable.
This, in turn, may substantially increase the options available to Indian leaders as they seek to meet the challenges of domestic change
and population increase.

PROJECTIONS OF CHANGE

    To give order to thought about the broad shape of Indian social
and cultural responses resulting from population change, it is also
necessary to think of the nature of the world within which the Second
India will emerge.* It is likely to be, in the early years of the next
century, a world with more than 7 billion inhabitants. On present
form, it looks as though two-thirds of the earth's population will then
be Asian and that two-thirds of those Asians will be under 35 years
of age. Thus, the patterns of interaction that will shape the Second
India's relations with the world will be colored by the reality that the
majority shareholders in that world will be young Asians. And these
young Asians are unlikely to be silent or powerless to articulate
their preferences. For them, the traditional values of religion, language, community, and family will remain important, although perhaps less so than for their parents. They are likely to be more urban, more literate, more skilled, and more aware of their options
and their power than their predecessors. They may also be impatient, frustrated, militant, disciplined, and nationalistic. And the
national governments of most of them will possess advanced nuclear
weapons and sophisticated delivery systems.
    The leaders of the Second India may have to their north a China
of 1.3 billion, to the west a Pakistan of 150 million, and to the east
a Bangladesh of 170 million. Asia may also include 260 million In-
donesians, 150 million Japanese, and 90 million Filipinos. It is difficult to conjecture what the political orientation of the major national,
religious, ideological, and ethnic groups within Asia will be in 35

---

    *All projections in this chapter are derived from the "Second
India" project currently being sponsored by the Ford Foundation. For
some of the preliminary findings of this project see J. P. Ambannavar,
Long-Term Prospects of Population Growth and Labour Force in India (Bombay: Second India Studies, University of Bombay, August 1974).

years. Some observers, noting the trend away from open political systems as the frustrations inherent in achieving significant per capita increases in well-being become apparent, are inclined toward the view that democracy will not survive the next decades in Asia. Therefore, it is possible that India, if it chooses to continue to work toward secular and democratic solutions to the problems of equity, modernization, and effective government, will find that she is increasingly isolated—or at any rate distinguished—from her Asian neighbors. As we consider the effects of population change, it is important to recognize the pressures, domestic as well as external, that may work upon the Indian body politic during the next three decades to move it by degrees away from openness and the forms of democratic process toward increasingly closed, authoritarian patterns.

We cannot predict the effects of systematic changes in the basic value orientation of Asian society upon India or upon the role of India within Asia during the next 30 years. Yet we must consider how the possible move from open to closed, perhaps military, regimes will affect the attitudes and values of Asian youth—and of Indians yet to be born in this century. How will these as yet unborn Asian youth regard the West—and especially the United States—when they assume positions of commanding influence in India and throughout Asia during the first quarter of the 21st century? How will the experience of their parents and their national governments in this generation affect their attitudes? How will their teachers, their textbooks, their national newspapers, radio, and television condition them to regard the non-Asian world?

For Europe, America, and the West in general inherit a legacy in Asia—and in India especially—of four centuries of domination and exploitation. A generation of postcolonial development, with some highly motivated technical assistance, and timely food aid (but regrettably inadequate efforts at concessional transfers of capital and resources) has done something to erase that bitter heritage. But often, in its place, a new relationship, equally uncomfortable because it is based upon inequalities and special interests, has arisen. Partly because the interest of the West in Asia has been so often stated in terms of security and narrow national interest; too often because it was conveyed with a sense of technological superiority that engendered resentment—the pattern of relationships that has emerged between 1947 and 1974 is not the ideal model for future development. To define and foster a more equitable and enduring model is a matter demanding urgent attention as we seek a more just world order.

First, however, let us consider the reality of India. Her population, now 600 million, continues to grow at a rapid rate. For the past three decades, that rate of growth has been accelerating. Since Independence, India has added to its population more than the total current population of the Soviet Union. In absolute terms, the incre-

increase in population is likely to rise from the current level
illion annually to over 16 million annually by the end of the
next decade. This rate will not begin to decline until the early part
of the 21st century. While all projections are fraught with uncertainty, there is reason to suppose that, barring widespread famine, pan-
demic, nuclear warfare, or communal and civil disorder on an unprecedented scale, India's 1971 population of about 550 million will have
doubled before the end of the first decade of the next century. Recent
Second India projections suggest that this doubling may occur by A.D.
2007.

The dynamics of past, current, and anticipated growth are complex and are not as fully understood as we might wish. Yet they are
not shrouded in mystery. Generally the rapid growth of the past 50
years is attributed to the dramatic decline in the death rate and the
increase in life expectancy brought about by the more effective public
health measures that have been extended across the world during the
past 60 years. The partially completed demographic transition,
wherein initially high birth- and death rates—historically resulting in
approximate population equilibrium—were destablized by rapid declines in death rates without accompanying declines in the birthrate,
provides the basic explanation of current growth. Improved nutrition,
reductions in subfecundity and sterility, suppression of female infanticide, relaxation of restrictions on widow remarriage, altered migration and settlement patterns, and other factors have affected growth,
but the heart of the matter is that the death rate has dropped and life
expectancy at birth has increased while the birthrate has remained
high. In the decade 1911-21 the average annual death rate in India
was 47.2 and life expectancy at birth was 20.1 years. By the decade
1961-71, the annual average death rate had been reduced to 18.6 and
life expectancy at birth had increased to 45.5 years. During this
same interval, the birthrate declined from an annual average rate of
48.1 to an estimated 39 per 1,000.

What is it that sustains the high birthrate? Most important, perhaps, is the fact that thousands of years of Indian experience have
shaped cultural values and social institutions, which encourage the
survival of the family and the community through high fertility. In
an era when life expectancy at birth was 20 years, as it was in India
until the 1920s, this required early marriage, early child-bearing,
and nearly as many children as were biologically feasible. This high
fertility pattern remains deeply embedded in cultural attitudes and
practices. It is supported by religion and by the network of pro-natalist kinship and community pressures and obligations. And, in contemporary India, family and community, more than anything else, continue
to give meaning, purpose, and direction to the lives of the Indian people, especially those in rural areas where fertility remains highest.

While traditional Indian society is strongly pro-natalist and its
values and reinforcing institutions continue to work to socialize most
of the population to adopt attitudes calculated to encourage high fertility, it must be recognized that there were always controls over un-
bridled reproduction. Most significant among these is the pattern of
rules that regulate marriage according to kinship, caste, religion,
and astrological compatibility as well as social, educational, and economic status. Prohibition upon widow remarriage, female infanticide,
and abortion as well as abstinence and traditional contraceptives afforded additional checks upon population growth. But the great anxiety of the culture was not with overpopulation but with survival. There
was widespread fear of domination, enslavement, or extinction by
more powerful neighbors. There was, and is, real fear that not
enough children would survive to cultivate the lands and defend its
boundaries in times of adversity. Children, and especially sons,
were strong arms and strong backs. The marginal costs of an additional child were seen as being greatly outweighed by the economic
and social benefits. Even today, when other forms of saving are simply not open to rural people, a large family is seen as a happy family
—notwithstanding governmental admonitions to the contrary.

The dynamic of future population growth is therefore rooted in
traditional values, current economic and social reality, and in the
demographic fact that there are more than 110 million girls under
15 years of age today, most of whom are being socialized to perceive
that fulfillment of their potential is contingent upon their performance
as wives and mothers. They are likely to marry early and produce
large families. Probably less than 1 percent of them will pass
through their child-bearing years without being married. It is predictable that they will, on the average, have more than four live births
each by the time they complete their child-bearing years in the early
part of the next century. Their mothers are currently reproducing
at a rate that will result in their total completed fertility being more
than 5.5 live births each. Notwithstanding the future effectiveness
of family planning measures, the momentum of growth inherent in
the very large size of these younger female age cohorts appears to
make inevitable the doubling of India's 1971 population within the next
35 years. Hence the need to think affirmatively about the requirements of the "Second India" that must be planned and created during
that time.

It may be argued that we simply do not know enough about total
processes of social and cultural response to identify to isolate the
unique consequences of population change. Yet it is clear that among
the major factors that will shape the future of Indian society, population growth will be of vital importance. While it could be misleading
to imply that population change is more significant than, in fact, the

warrants, it would be equally wrong to suggest that it is not
riable.

is recognized that basic inequities in control over resources,
lly agricultural lands, rigid hierarchies that enforce social
stratification, unequal access to education, widespread illiteracy, inadequate capital, poor skill training, and a pattern of cultural rewards
that penalize initiative and enterprise will all affect the future substantially. Therefore, while we attempt to isolate population change
for special consideration, we do not imply that other aspects of social
and economic process demand less urgent attention. We must consider
the separate parts but deal systematically with the whole.

The parameters of the "Second India" are slowly coming into
focus. A series of studies currently being conducted by Indian scholars and institutions should provide the framework for more organized
speculation concerning the shape and magnitude of anticipated opportunities, problems, and critical choices and the policy and program
options that lie ahead. Certain patterns already seem evident. Urban
growth will certainly continue at a rate faster than overall population
growth. Initial studies suggest that almost one-third of all Indians
will live in urban centers in the Second India—more than 350 million
as contrasted with the 110 million currently in cities. The pattern
of future urbanization is not yet clear. Major metropolitan areas continue to grow, even as levels of service appear to decline. Urban
planners appear too often to underestimate the relative attractiveness
of city life as perceived by rural peoples. And yet much future urbanization may not involve migration to existing cities, for, as population
doubles, many market towns and bazaars are likely to—willy nilly—
become urban places, without piped water, closed sewers, adequate
power, zoning, planning, or effective governance.

To provide productive employment to even one member of each
urban household may tax the ingenuity of the planners, for while the
overall labor force is likely to increase from 227 million to 465 million, the urban labor force will grow from 36 million to 123 million.
Net new additions to the labor force, now estimated at 4.8 million annually, will increase each year until early in the next century. At
the time of the Second India in 2007, the annual increase will exceed
7.5 million. Given the very large numbers who fail to find employment today, these enormous net inflows into the labor force constitute
a problem of staggering magnitude. Nor can they be easily "turned
off," for, like the mothers of the next generation, the new entrants
into the labor force for the period up to 1990 have already been born.

Free and universal primary education remains the goal of Indian educators. Enormous progress in this direction has been made
in the first quarter-century of independence. Since 1950, the enroll-
ment rate for boys of primary age (6 to 11 years) has increased from

59.8 percent to 93 percent, and for girls from 24.6 percent to 57 percent. Impressive gains have also been made at middle and higher school levels. Yet the projected increases in the size of school-age populations require that educational planners fundamentally reassess their goals and methods in relation to national priorities and limited national resources. The number of primary schoolchildren in the Second India will be 113 million; the total number of school-age children (6 to 17 years) will increase from 158 million to 266 million. Given the reality that, in absolute numbers, the pool of illiteracy continues to increase and that even at the highest skill levels less than half of the graduates from the educational system find ready employment today, there would seem to be urgent need critically to assess future options and strategies.

It is vitally important that policy-makers systematically study public health, agriculture, food, housing, water, energy, transportation, communication, industry, and other developmental and social sectors in light of anticipated population growth. Major sectoral studies being undertaken in the Second India series represent an initial attempt to provide Indian leaders with basic data. When completed, they should give an in-depth assessment of our understanding of the interrelationship between continued rapid population growth and selected areas of Indian life. They will also reveal both the strengths and weaknesses of the available data and the limits of the conceptual tools currently available to analyze complex interactions through future time. Most important, they will have served to engage the intellectual attention of many of India's best minds in the organized study of the implications of continued rapid population growth and the options available to policy-makers as they seek to move toward a preferred alternative future.

Beyond the assessment of resource constraints and of the relationship between current governmental goals and future demand levels, there are other critical areas that deserve thoughtful analysis, since these too will profoundly affect both developmental and political options. These lie in the area of behavioral change—in individual and group responses—which are likely to result from changes in the size, distribution, and composition of India's population in the decades ahead. They are areas in which the instruments of measurement are imprecise, where theory and methodology do not, as yet, seem to have great power to illuminate and inform. They are also areas where too little work has been done.

Yet it may be argued that it is in precisely these areas that many crucial changes are likely to occur. It is of the greatest importance to those who seek to understand the future of Indian society to measure in a better manner than heretofore the changes that are already in process as a result of the past 30 years of sustained rapid

growth as a base from which to assess the probable unfolding of future social and cultural changes. Unfortunately, there is little evidence that Indian scholars in the social sciences are yet seized by
this range of issues. The impact of crowding upon individual behavior, upon the family and the community, seems to be treated incidentally, if at all. There has been all too much emphasis upon family
planning knowledge, attitude, and practice surveys and almost no in-
novative experimental or observational research on the first-order
problems of human accommodation and behavioral adjustment to population growth. The focus remains on the determinants of such growth
rather than the consequences. This may be a defensible family planning research strategy, although it may be argued that one of the most
critical determinants of fertility is increased understanding of the implications of such growth for the individual and for his family and
community. It is not, however, a sound population policy research
approach.

How will family structure be affected by growth? How will the
role of women change in the Second India? How will individual and
group self-esteem be affected if life chances are so limited that the
prospects for meaningful recognition or employment in a respected
craft or skill are essentially nil? What patterns of accommodation
to crowding and perceived deprivation are likely to emerge? How
will political behavior be affected? Given changes in communal composition, what tensions are likely to arise? What policy options may
be open to alleviate these tensions? Is it possible to link more effectively the consequences of individual fertility behavior to societal
change and establish feedback to the individual in ways calculated to
provide greater motivation for fertility limitation? Many related
questions arise. While some of them may not be researchable with
present instruments, many others are clearly both susceptible and
deserving of organized study.

While it is possible that some of this important work can be
aided by scholars from outside India, it is imperative that the major
responsibility for conduct of such studies be carried by Indian institutions and researchers. One would hope that government, the scholarly community, and the Indian Council of Social Science Research
might attach special importance to the design, financing, and conduct
of a coordinated series of studies on various critical consequences of
population growth and its implications for Indian society.

At the level of the individual, the reproductive couple, the family, and the community, it seems clear that there are a range of researchable hypotheses deserving attention. Understanding of these
might facilitate and accelerate the transition to low fertility. At the
level of the nation and of the international system, it is less clear
that systematic research by social scientists is feasible. On the

other hand, it is at this level that events are likely to move most
rapidly, for the future seems unwilling to await a clear understanding
of the present. It is also at these levels that the leadership is urgently seeking to comprehend and anticipate the consequences of current growth patterns. But at these levels, we have neither a well-
tested body of theory nor the methodology and detailed data essential
to permit construction of relevant, comprehensive models.

ALTERNATIVE SCENARIOS

In the absence of either solid hypothesis or detailed data, it
may nevertheless be acceptable to speculate concerning possible alternative scenarios for the next 35 years so as to construct a framework
for the consideration of our options. At the national level, a number
of themes that have been discussed should be examined. First, the
"doomsday scenario" predicated upon the collapse of the existing order as the pressures on internal organizational capacity and resources
mount; as development targets become increasingly illusory; as corruption and nepotism increase; and as the social and economic inequities become increasingly difficult to paper over with political rhetoric.
We have seen the passage of that era when the citizens had buoyant
confidence in the capacity of government to control events effectively
—or even ameliorate them. During the past decade some have observed a decline in self-assurance and confidence among both seasoned
administrators and political leaders responsible for developmental
programs. Political leadership rarely conveys or inspires genuine
commitment in this cynical age. The mood is one of self-doubt and
low expectations rather than the optimism of the 1950s. In such a
situation, some conjecture that during the next decade the institutions
of Indian society will be strained to the breaking point and that political will will be so eroded that those in positions of authority will be
paralyzed. In this view, Indian leadership will lack the vision and
decisiveness to take timely and effective action. Should this occur,
it is hypothesized that collapse will occur through a gradual process
that will be cloaked in the garb of constitutionality and democratic
process. The authority of the center will be weakened; the federal
system will be compromised. States will become increasingly more
powerful and more numerous as competing local interests exert pressure to fragment and obtain "a more just share" of a static or shrink-
ing economic pie. The doomsdayers marshal Malthusian arguments
that make this scenario credible, noting that many resource lines
intersect with future population growth during the next 20 years and
that the failures in performance and achievement during the past decade already mark the beginning of "the decline and fall." They ob-

serve, correctly, that it is truly difficult to see how mortal men will find their way, given the limits of present organizational discipline and capacity.

Should the doomsday scenario prove a reasonable projection for the decade ahead, there are at least four follow-on subscenarios that require examination. First, it is possible that reaction from militant ideological and political groups, either to the left or right, could arrest the deterioration, impose an authoritarian regime, initiate fundamental reform, mobilize political support, and/or suppress overt opposition. Some suggest that only such a junta could manage to hold the body politic together long enough to restore self-esteem, root out corruption, eliminate the grosser social and economic inequities, and begin anew to build a progressive, though closed, society. One obvious difficulty is that the basic problems, both those arising from greatly increased population and from other origins, do not readily go away even under authoritarian command. Short of massive blood-letting and forcible control of fertility, there is, as we have seen, no quick means of braking population growth. The horrifying policy option of genocide may not, of course, be wholly excluded.

Second, it is possible that, as a modification of the doomsday scenario, foreign powers could attempt intervention in behalf of ideological, economic, or perceived security interests and that this could lead to escalation of conflict resulting in local or regional warfare. An appeal on behalf of the large Muslim community would be difficult for Islam to resist if it appeared that (1) India was on the brink of anarchy and internal collapse and (2) communal strife endangered the lives of a persecuted religious minority. The oil-rich Gulf States, Iran, the Soviet Union, China, and the United States all have traditionally been thought of as having special interests, some of which might tempt them to become involved in support of internal factions, with unpredictable consequences.

Third, on the brink of collapse, India could use its technological capacity, especially in the nuclear field, as a bargaining counter to negotiate for international resources to meet domestic crises. In the event that, at that time, India possessed a capacity to deliver nuclear weaponry, it is not inconceivable that beleaguered political or military leaders could justify to themselves the implicit or explicit threat of nuclear blackmail—if they saw that as essential to obtain the concessional transfers of food or fuel required to ensure survival.

Last, it is possible that, at some point after a prolonged slide away from a centrally dominated federal system, a new equilibrium might be achieved between a national regime and more effective state administrations. Corrective adjustments, which would bring government closer to the reality of the states and disaggregate the basic problems might, in time, restore confidence and turn around the declining economic situation.

In any of these subscenarios, the probability seems high that, at least initially, levels of services, including food production and distribution, health, and family planning would decline or even that the services would be suspended for a period. In such a period the horrifying specter is that population growth might be effectively braked by a dramatic increase in the death rate, through disease, famine, and possibly civil disorder.

A second scenario could involve "muddling through," essentially along present lines, always riding close to the brittle edge, with government being forced, always a little too late, to do the "needful" to cope and to accommodate the new reality that is upon them. The same interest groups would continue to protect their narrow advantage, the same rhetoric would be articulated concerning reform and equity, the same patterns of exploitation would pervade, but somehow under increasing pressure from a restless populace the authorities at all levels would manage, as they have done these past 25 years, to keep the machinery of the state together, operating at the minimum level required for survival. There would be increasing civil disorder and increasingly authoritarian quelling of such disorder, but the forms of due process and of democratic participation would be maintained. While the general situation would deteriorate, it would never become so bad as to demand or permit a revolutionary break with the past. Not much might be done, things might get worse, but the patience, apathy, and resilience of the people would make it possible for things to come out all right.

The "optimistic scenario" begins with the basic belief that, notwithstanding rapid population growth, the inequities of the social and economic order, and the slow pace of development, the problems of India are within the power of thoughtful, energetic mortals to overcome. In this view, population per se is not a negative point. This scenario is what one would like to consider the "realist-rationalist" unfolding of events, which counts heavily upon the emergence from within India of a new generation of enlightened and highly motivated young leaders who will shape from the experience of the past a blend of Gandhian philosophy, modern social thought, and economic programs appropriate to the needs of the Second India. There are among the university students of today small numbers who give promise of accepting this charge and providing the enlightened leadership required.

A crucial question is whether the system, "the establishment," and the events of the next decade will provide sufficient scope to permit the nonviolent transfer of effective control to this group. In some states of the Indian Union, we have already seen that the restiveness of youth, in a society where nearly 60 percent of the total population is under 25 years of age, is a force that political leadership must recognize and accommodate. That the "under-30s" have not yet evolved

a cohesive political strategy or organization of their own should not
be seen as surprising in a traditionally age-graded society. What is
of interest is the inability of the major political parties effectively to
attract the allegiance of younger people and the surprising capacity
of poorly organized youth significantly to affect the political process.
The New Society movement in Gujarat, with its concern for rooting
out corruption and nepotism and its emphasis upon programs designed
to diminish the inequalities apparent in Indian life, may be a harbinger
of this new force. If the educated youth of today can be mobilized to
serve the nation and lead the people to overcome the nation's systemic
difficulties, if the young scientists and engineers can be afforded an
environment where they are not frustrated and where new ideas are
not resisted, it may be possible to harness creatively the enormous
skill and energy that they represent and to discipline democratically
and focus their efforts on the priority tasks ahead of the nation. To
do this may require the generation of an ideological or spiritual commitment currently absent, for the youth of today are not likely to be
captured by old slogans.

    The achievement of this optimistic scenario also presupposes
the establishment of a more equitable international economic order,
a change in the terms of trade and transfers of resources as a matter
of right and routine from rich to poor rather than as a part of linked
aid arrangements.

    Realistically, the optimistic scenario seems somewhat improb-
able at present, for the world is caught in a backlash of psychic fatigue and developmental disillusionment. It may, nonetheless, be
psychologically imperative that we construct a positive alternative to
the doomsday scenario, since mankind requires ideal objectives, no
matter how unattainable they may appear.

    It is not easy, however, to write the optimistic scenario. That
task must be worked out "in the doing," and the "doing" must be Indian. Some points, however, seem clear. To achieve an increasing
level of well-being for the less advantaged within Indian society will
require a willingness on the part of the more advantaged to forgo
some of the benefits their privileged position has assured them in
the past. Where the top 10 percent control one-third of the disposable
income—while the lowest 30 percent have less than one-eighth—there
will be the roots of continued and increasing tension. To complicate
matters, the educated young, although to a lesser degree than the
educated of this generation, have their origins in, and family ties to,
privilege. One should not, therefore, underestimate the complexity
and tenacity of the problems that must be overcome. Nor should we
undervalue the capacity of the human species to respond to challenge.

THE HUMAN DYNAMIC

Demographic imperatives give urgency to the human dilemma. The problems in India are of a different order of magnitude than man has known in the past. But they are not beyond the power of human resolution. And that resolution can begin in Indian minds. It can begin with a clearer appreciation of the true condition of the human community in India and in the world—with the internalization in the minds of scholars and leaders of more relevant and comprehensive models of external reality. For while science, technology, resources, organization, and management offer important aids to overcoming the problems of food production, equitable distribution of well-being, employment, housing, and the other challenges that accompany population change, the crucial variable remains man himself. And in India for the past quarter-century there has been a lamentable tendency—not unique among foreigners—to undervalue the capacities and achievements of Indian leadership, the resilience of her disaggregated agrarian economy, the strengths of community and family, and the tenacity and ingenuity of the Indian people.

What is argued here in defense of a hopeful view is the basic humanist credo that the human community in India, as elsewhere, has the capacity to learn from the past, to anticipate the future, to apply experience to the resolution of current and future difficulties, and, through time, to improve the human condition. To start from any alternative set of premises could be to abdicate before the event.

It seems certain that the times ahead for India, Asia, and the human community will be fraught with uncertainty. No easy way out is evident. Even with the energy of youth and the wisdom of the past, problems of the complexity and scale of those confronting India are not likely to give way easily. Indeed, we would do well to accept that solutions to some problems will have to await future generations. But if we will use the time we now have to seek improved understanding of our condition in order that Indian leaders and policy-makers can work toward the rational allocation of intellect and resources to resolve the priority conflicts and problems that affect human survival, there need be no despair.

There are, worldwide, some hopeful signs. An emerging concern for the global environment, for population policy, for food and energy—all of these initiatives during a period of less than five years—signal increasing recognition of the interdependence of the human community. But conferences and international agreements will not solve internal Indian problems, and governments must afford tangible evidence of both concern and capacity. The rapid increase of India's

population makes this increasingly difficult. Indeed, government now
finds itself on the horns of a terrible dilemma. After more than 20
years of effort to shake the backward rural peoples out of their leth-
argy and to instill in them a sense of their own capacity to effect meaningful change through individual and community initiative, those responsible for governmental programs now find themselves doubting
that capacity in themselves and in government. While the poorest of
the poor are only now awakening to the attractions of "the revolution
of rising expectations," the leadership, the educated, and the urban
middle class are caught in the anguish of inflation, a leveling off of
living standards and a crisis of confidence that is characterized as
"the revolution of falling expectations." This role reversal could
have disastrous consequences if it results in an extended leadership
vacuum. On the other hand, the awakening of the masses in India
could be the key to the future. For without their active engagement
in the process of building the Second India, the optimistic scenario
will remain a dream without a blueprint. That blueprint and the political will, resources, and energy to implement it must come largely
from within India. The energy and commitment can only come from
the people.

What happens in India during the remainder of this century is
of great importance both to India and to the human community. Those
who are concerned with the survival of man and of those uniquely human values that have made possible the emergence of civilizations in
India and elsewhere have a stake in understanding, anticipating, and
ameliorating the negative consequences of population growth in India.
For the essential dynamic of Indian population growth is the human
dynamic. In it is both cause for concern and cause for limited optimism about the prospect for human betterment in India and in the
world.

3

INDIA'S
POPULATION AND
INTERNATIONAL AFFAIRS
Lawrence A. Veit

The international situation of the 1970s is quite unlike that of previous generations. This is not to say that peaceful resolution of conflicts is no longer a serious concern of statesmen. But concern for issues of Realpolitik has been joined—some would say surpassed— by attention to the new sets of issues raised by the changing ways in which individuals of various countries relate to one another. Because of the communications and technological revolutions of the past century, a complex of new and vital interdependencies has developed, linking nations and people who hitherto were relatively independent from one another.

It has become the platitude of our generation to say that man's welfare is now threatened by resource scarcity and ecological change, caused by a thoughtless and unwise exploitation of nature's limited bounties. Moreover, it has become a commonplace in developing countries—and sometimes in the rich—to say that welfare disparities among rich and poor countries, and between the rich and poor in most countries, are generating social tensions that undermine the stability of nations and the tolerances of the international order.

To describe these observations as platitudes and commonplaces is not to belittle them. Indeed, these ideas are expressed so often because in the minds of the speakers and many of the listeners they contain more than a grain of truth. What they have in common, which makes them germane to our concern, is that in both instances population size and growth are significant—if not the most important—determinants of our world order. Without attempting to be precise about the critical time frame and role of world population growth that would so strain the fabric of our society as to make a radical change in our relations to one another and the natural environment a necessity, one can say it is clear that global population growth has proceeded at a rate that makes it an urgent issue for the international community. It is also clear that the situation in particular nations is more difficult than in others.

From the floors of the UN General Assembly and the Lok Sabha (India's Lower House of Parliament) to the fields of Gujarat and the New York offices of women's liberation organizations, decisions and actions that will affect both India's population and the content of foreign affairs are being taken daily. Illustrative is the decision of a Punjabi girl and her family to see to it that, in marked contrast to her mother's experience, she stay in school through the college level. Such decisions, which are being made with increasing regularity, relate not only to a purely domestic change in India but to a number of foreign considerations such as the international popularity of the women's liberation movement and her family's new wealth. These in turn reflect the input of foreign technology and resources in the Green Revolution. Incidentally, because of this education, the Punjabi girl will probably marry at an older age and bear fewer children than most women in her society.[1]

We could give endless examples of how population affects—and is affected by—international affairs. What is needed, however, is a more rigorous frame in which to specify the wide range of such effects, from which a coherent overview of the importance of population to international affairs can be gleaned. This is more easily said than done, however, because, except when it is the dependent variable, population almost never stands alone as the cause of events affecting human relations. Indeed, neither a catalog of population-related factors nor the synthesis of how these relate is easily obtained. The list of factors is long, and the interlinkages are many. Moreover, population effects often are simultaneously obscure and basic to other social variables. For example, the character, size, and rate of change of populations is regarded sometimes as the objective and at other times as the instrument of public policy and private action. Finally, as demonstrated by the debate at the UN Population Conference at Bucharest in 1974, there is very little international consensus on what population parameters constitute a "good society." Intranational disagreement about the significance of demographic variables often is just as vitriolic as that among nations.

In writing about population and international affairs, there is not only a remarkable lack of agreement on the issues taken separately, but a near absence of literature directly probing the connections between these two factors. Much of what follows herein, therefore, is preordained to be both tentative and controversial. It also will be full of gaps, and, to some readers, certain passages will appear downright wrong-headed. To the extent that this is background material, the views expressed herein are not of major significance, and we do not plan to allocate a block of time for discussing them. The purpose is to highlight the relevance of our meeting, to raise major issues that are pertinent to, but might not otherwise be made explicit at the sessions we have planned, and to suggest areas where additional research would be helpful.

THE SETTING

It has become popular in the 1970s for some observers to talk of the world order, global interdependence, and transnational relations as though the significance of national sovereignty has been unalterably diminished, to imply that unless the world is beset by some unanticipated shock, the role of national governments will continue to recede. There is an element of truth in this perception, but there remain many activities, such as foreign trade policy, in which persons cannot act alone but require the presence of institutions—national or international. Our experience to date is that only marginal amounts of sovereignty have been yielded to international institutions or abandoned to nonofficial actors. Thus, we may have to make do with national authorities for some time to come. Paradoxically, the growth of nonofficial transnational relations creates a demand for official intervention. Demographic factors have proved to be among the more important concerns of the international community. As individuals in one part of the world are increasingly affected by the behavior of persons living elsewhere, they are certain to become increasingly sensitive to events abroad and seek to affect them through various actions. Moreover, as we have noted, 20th-century technology gives nations and individuals both the information about events abroad and the capacity for changing them.

In most of what follows, the focus is on the behavior of governments rather than individuals. This does not do full justice either to the processes whereby government policies are decided or to the special role that individual persons play in international exchanges. Although these subjects are not discussed here in detail, it bears emphasis that Indian and foreign stereotypes, slogans, and images relating to demographic variables—and also perceptions of how each believe the other to view the situation—are of great importance in determining the interaction of Indians and outsiders.

The juxtaposition of a new discovery, what Lester Brown calls the "world without borders," and the enduring fact of national sovereignty, imparts a special character to the consideration of India's population and world affairs. This is a subject of substantial academic interest because it pertains to a cross-section of the humanities and social sciences, including history, economics, political science, and so forth. But it also has normative content, which arises at meta-physical as well as practical levels. Stated more dramatically, population and population-related questions of social adjustment, economic growth, human development, and international peace are a burning issue of our time. They pervade the economic, political, and humanitarian aspects of our lives. As distance in time and space continues to grow shorter, the international aspects of local demographic situations continue to grow in significance. Population-related problems, such as the division of currently produced resources between the so-called developed and developing countries, environmental pollution, and so forth, are bound to cause regional clashes, in many cases affecting the larger international community.

The obvious statement that population has economic, political, and humanitarian implications does less than full justice to the complex interrelations among these. The 1971 crisis in South Asia and its aftermath, for example, involved all of these factors. Economically, it arose because Bengali Hindus were landowners, and many of them therefore chose to remain in East Pakistan after Partition, because of East Bengal's resentment that it received less than a fair share of national Pakistani economic benefits, and for a variety of other reasons. Politically, the timing of the crisis and the nature of India's reaction can be explained by Islamabad's unwillingness to recognize the democratic force of East Bengal's superior population numbers and India's concern that the 10 million people (mainly Hindus) who emigrated from East Bengal return quickly and not disrupt its already precarious demographic balance. Morally, it involved not only such issues as income disparities between East and West Pakistan and the right of India to interfere in the affairs of a troubled neighbor, but the international community's response to the suffering of the people of the new Bangladesh.

The 1971 South Asian crisis is illustrative of how demographic factors combine with other variables in determining the course of human affairs. Thus, whereas the following sections of this chapter are directed to political, economic, and humanitarian factors, respectively, it must be recognized that this categorization is done merely for presentational reasons and that it has only limited resemblance to reality. Finally, it bears emphasis that demographic factors cannot be considered in a vacuum. The relationship of population to resource availability, for example, is a critical factor in determining a nation's economic position, but the favorable economic experience of some countries with few resources (Japan) and unfavorable experience of others that are richly endowed (Indonesia) suggest that the semiintangible and institutional elements that we lump under the heading of "development" are also critical.

This is true not only for physical resources, but for ideas, culture, and social style. Moreover, essentially domestic characteristics usually are reflected in a nation's foreign affairs just as foreign considerations affect domestic policy. It is not surprising, for example, that the Gandhian notion of village-level self-sufficiency is reflected internationally in India's decision to emphasize the autarkic strategy of import substitution rather than the interdependent approach of export promotion. The rationale for India to adopt a Gandhian approach to its socioeconomic system has been undercut to a considerable degree by counterarguments related to India's large size and the preponderance of population as an economic resource compared to other factors of production. Because of its size, India has had the option of building large factories to take advantage of economies of scale and specialization in production. Moreover, Ricardian considerations of comparative advantage (the value to India of trading labor-intensive goods that it produces for the capital-intensive products of others) have reduced the weight of Gandhian arguments insofar as balance-of-payments considerations are of importance to India. Thus, in what follows, it often will be necessary to link population and international affairs through a variety of other variables.

ECONOMIC FACTORS

The Malthusian idea that population would expand to keep living standards of the masses close to the subsistence level has been belied by the experience of many countries during the past several centuries. But although Malthusian reasoning has not proved to have universal application, it is not without its merits; for some nations, including India, the multiplication of population has tended to follow uncomfortably close on the heels of GNP growth. Moreover, through a series of developments unforeseen by the classical philosophers, economic expansion globally has proceeded so fast, and with so little regard for the environment, that even though their population growth rates are low—sometimes even below the replacement level—the world's wealthier nations are now threatened with a possible need to reduce their consumption of materials.

The impact of India's large and rapidly growing population on its economic strength and rate of development is neither fully understood nor a total mystery. According to the pioneering work of Ansley J. Coale and Edgar M. Hoover, rapid population growth hinders development by raising the "dependency ratio" (the proportion of the total population deemed outside the work force either because of youth or old age). Moreover, it (1) reduces the amount of national income that might otherwise be available for savings and investment and (2) diverts a large portion of new investment into replicating existing economic and social facilities for the benefit of larger numbers rather than deepening and broadening the capital stock for the creation of higher per capita incomes.[2]

There also are certain"diseconomies of scale" that directly link the economics of population size with foreign affairs. Among these are the relatively low per capita aid receipts of India compared to other countries. This factor is grossly overstated in much of the literature, but even after adjustments are made for (1) the greater year-to-year regularity with which foreign aid has been provided to India, (2) the higher proportion of economic to military aid, and (3) the better financial terms India has received, it is still clear that, compared to other developing states, India has been handicapped by its large size. Similarly, options open to smaller nations, such as achieving comfortable balance-of-payments positions by specializing in the export of a limited number of items, have not been available to India. Regrettably, India has not always been able to enjoy some of the offsetting options that are open only to large countries. For instance, because of demographic factors, India has not fully exploited economies of scale through long production runs. In practice the Indian government has found it necessary to take note of the nation's internal diversity in order to satisfy all major claimants.[3]

In addition, and related to the population growth rate and its absolute size, are certain economic characteristics of the people. In particular, the balance between population and natural resources (land, climate, mineral reserves, and so forth) determines India's potential for production and trade in the immediate period and distant future. It is hardly profound to observe that it is the combination of India's large population and underdeveloped natural resources that produces the current widespread poverty. It is the same combination that suggests that for the foreseeable future India should concentrate on developing its natural resources (which are quite substantial for a number of minerals), exporting labor-intensive goods, and exchanging these for capital-intensive products and strategic commodities produced abroad. It is the existence in India of underutilized and inefficiently utilized labor and natural resources—and the potential for mobilizing these to improve the global economic situation—that color foreign economic assistance as part of a global development effort rather than a merely humanitarian gesture.

Since the inception of planning, and earlier, India's principal economic goals—growth, social justice, and self-reliance—have featured human welfare and the need to improve the living standards of its poorest people along with other objectives. The intensity of the new Indian government's concern for achieving economic progress was of a much higher magnitude than that of the administration during the colonial period. The gradual recognition of how difficult it is to achieve development eventually led India to seek outside assistance and substantial foreign aid, which began as a balance-of-payments rescue operation in 1958, only to become an integral part of India's Third Five-Year Plan (1961-66). India's international economic relations suffered a setback following its 1966 devaluation. The intimacy that India and aid-donor governments had developed in the late 1950s and early 1960s because of their common concern about the Indian economy was unable to withstand the mutual disappointments of the postdevaluation period, albeit the aid relationship continued to be important. Indeed, International Bank for Reconstruction and Development (IBRD) President Robert McNamara's sense of egalite, expressed first in his concern for the world's poorest 25 nations and later in his desire to have the World Bank Group more carefully focus its programs on the poorer people in developing countries, is indicative of the hold that population has in international affairs and the serious linkage between foreign aid and domestic economic management.

Foreign aid, however, is not the only facet of the population-foreign affairs relationship; in fact, it may not even be the most important. In UNCTAD and elsewhere, India has taken the position, along with many other developing countries, that the current international economic system does not serve equally the interests of all nations. India's concern has been that commercial practices and institutional arrangements discriminate against the poor countries. For instance, at the procedural level, India objects to systems of weighted voting. Substantively, it has taken the position that any system that is so inegalitarian as to permit the 6 percent of the world's population that is American to use one-third of the global resources consumed each year is highly unfair.

India has proposed various measures to rectify this situation, including international policies to improve its export prospects, assure it adequate and reasonably priced supplies of petroleum and fertilizer, link the distribution of Special Drawing Rights (SDRs) in the International Monetary Fund (IMF) to developmental needs, and so forth. In 1972 when Prime Minister Indira Gandhi attended the United Nations' special session on the environment, she tended toward the position that the world suffered from excessive resource use by the West rather than excessive population in India and elsewhere. (Indeed, there are some Indians, including Western-educated economists, who regard population growth as having a net positive effect on economic development.)[4] Implied in Gandhi's posture was the threat that India would not be able to treat population control or environmental preservation as feasible goals unless a greater effort was made to eliminate poverty and that, as part of this effort, there should be a more egalitarian sharing of international production.[5]

This policy outlook appeared to have been moderated somewhat when at the UN Conference on Population in Bucharest in 1974 India's minister for Health and Family Planning, Karan Singh, was no less adamant about the need for Western countries to help developing countries and to share their wealth in the spirit of "one world for all," but in his presentation there was not the slightest hint of the militant threat to ignore population growth if the West did not comply with developing country demands.

In a 1974 speech in New Delhi Singh noted, "The optimum size of population for any country inevitably depends on a number of economic and social variables." Although he went on to say, "It is indisputable that, in the present situation, the high rate of population growth in India is definitely acting as a negative factor in her economic growth," he rejected the one-sided interpretation of how poverty and population are causally linked. "We do not, therefore, subscribe to the view that overpopulation is the main cause of our poverty."[6]

While more convinced than Singh of the significance of demographic variables as determinants of social conditions, I agree with his thesis that welfare is a key factor in determining fertility. This view is strongly supported by a number of studies, including a recent book, Human Fertility in India, by David Mandelbaum, which concludes that the joint family system, religion, and urbanization are not the critical variables affecting child-bearing behavior. According to Mandelbaum, the significant factors tending to lower birthrates are higher education and greater affluence.[7] It is not clear how important it is that, in contrast to the other variables, these are both goals and symptoms of development. Nonetheless, to the extent that Mandelbaum is correct, it is fair to assume that major foreign efforts to aid India's development will help India to achieve a better demographic balance.

We must be wary of this conclusion, however, because foreign assistance efforts in India to date do not appear to have substantially changed the proportion of the population living below what India regards as the subsistence level (the figure remains at about 40 percent).[8] Would poverty be even more widespread in the absence of foreign assistance? Has outside aid merely perpetuated Indian poverty among a slightly larger population? Regrettably, economists and other social scientists are in near total disagreement on such questions and, consequently, when they are addressed at the political level, decisive views and action are less common than divisive debate. Understandably, this tends to have a negative effect, both on a range of domestic economic policies as well as on India's relations with other countries.

POLITICAL FACTORS

The importance of demography to international political—as distinct from economic and humanitarian—relations is cited more often than it is made explicit; social scientists are far from any definitive view on this subject. In part this is because demographic factors are central to most political situations; because they invariably are present along with other variables; and because population-related factors tend to have an effect over time rather than at any particular instant.[9] As in the case of economic factors, it is not only population size and the growth rate that are important but also a variety of demographic factors. For instance, differential population growth rates among nations and among regional or other subnational groups can affect international affairs by (1) altering economic relationships within nations, (2) changing power, bargaining, and prestige relationships among nations, and (3) causing migration, which in turn affects international relationships. The example of such factors at work to which we have referred previously is the 1971 South Asian crisis.

There is a considerable body of literature touching on how the ambiguous force of Lebensraum permeates international attitudes and motivates foreign policy. Although this has generally been inspired by the behavior of Japan and Western countries, there is no reason to doubt that Lebensraum has been a factor in Asia and elsewhere. According to Ainslee Embree, there is enough historical evidence to support the view that India has traditionally followed an expansionist foreign policy. In particular, his research and analysis of India's 19th-century foreign policy suggests that "the foreign relations of the government of India, despite ultimate control by Great Britain, expressed needs and interests rooted in the subcontinent, and that the content and style of this diplomacy was a formative legacy for modern India." Embree does not deny that Indian imperialism in the 19th century reflected Britain's imperialism, but he shows that an indigenous Indian expansionism was also at work during the period.[10] In pondering the validity of this thesis and its applicability for the future, it is necessary to examine motives. Was Indian expansionism intentional and based on motives of national defense and territorial aggrandizement? Or was it "involuntary" in the sense that it was dictated by growing domestic tensions caused by population growth?

Related to the idea of Lebensraum is the equally ambiguous geopolitical notion that large countries count for more than small ones. The word "large" in this case is a composite measure of geographic size, population numbers, and economic wealth. This concept partly explains the West's post-World War II concern that "democratic" India

prove m ore durable and develop faster than "totalitarian" China.
Lebensraum and geopolitics are undoubtedly important, but to understand their significance we must try to be more concrete about how
population factors affect aggression and cooperation—both domestic
and international.

The phrase "local Leviathan" was coined by Samuel Huntington
because it is ideally suited to describe the political-economic situation of countries such as India, Brazil, and Nigeria.[11] Due to its
overall strength, in which its large population is both a positive and
a negative factor, India dominates South Asian affairs. It has much
less impact on Asian affairs generally and still less impact on world
events. The substance of its local power is reflected in a variety of
policies: military involvement in the cases of Kashmir and Bangladesh; patronage in the cases of Nepal and Sri Lanka; and political ab-
sorption in the case of Sikkim. The limitations on its international
power can be read, first, from its inability to compel other developing nations, including members of the Economic Commission for Asia
and the Far East (ECAFE) and the Gulf states, to adopt its positions
on a number of issues, and second, from its status as the subject of
patronage by the great powers and other wealthy nations. The role
of population in this spectrum of foreign relationships is that India's
large size permits it to dominate regional affairs. Beyond South
Asia, however, India's poverty and population-related weaknesses owing to its religious, regional, and other diversities, while no bar to active diplomacy, constitute a major constraint on its options and on the
effectiveness of its actions.

There are at least three major tangencies between population
and political strength as they affect foreign affairs. First, there is
the psychological, sometimes subconscious, weight of social egalite.
We are accustomed to believing that large nations should occupy an
important place in international affairs, and, to some degree, the
fact that we think this way makes it so. The notions of international
democracy, one-man/one-vote irrespective of national boundaries,
and an income tax levied by the United Nations are indicative of how
egalite enters into our thinking. Clearly, egalite must be regarded
as a moral and economic consideration as well as a political force.
Because of its ambiguous nature, its impact on foreign affairs is difficult to assess.

Second, international power is sometimes calculated as a function of population numbers per se. A nation's bargaining and bullying
position is affected by its demography, and those with large—but not
necessarily fast-growing—populations have options that are not available to smaller countries. This is true for international warfare,
where, despite its poverty, India has been able to dominate if not bi-
furcate and otherwise seriously affect the political situations of its

neighbors. It is particularly true in the defensive sense that because of India's large population, there are few, if any, outside nations with the capacity to defeat India militarily and occupy its soil. In short, even with India's near subsistence economy the nation has pockets of wealth large enough that they can be combined with noneconomic power factors to create a reasonably forceful foreign policy.

Third, a nation's power is determined not only by its domestic economic resources but also by its political cohesion. Both of these factors are conditioned by the size and growth rate of population. At its current stage of development, India has an imbalance between the amount of usable resources and the number of people claiming a share of them. Moreover, its social and political systems are weakened by competing claims of powerful special-interest groups, rapid and unplanned urbanization, large and conspicuous income disparities, and similar factors. Both India and other nations recognize that, in the absence of a more intensive development of its resources and more effectual political and economic management, the capacity to use India's population as a constructive force in international affairs is reduced, as is the scope for an effective Indian foreign policy.

The outstanding feature of India in 1974, therefore, is not the way in which demographic forces are driving it directly to international aggression or cooperation, but the impact of population on the texture of its domestic political and economic situation. This factor, while only of indirect concern to foreign countries, is nonetheless of great significance to them and to India's foreign relations. As recognized by India's First Five-Year Plan and subsequent Plans, one direct consequence of population growth is to reduce the potential for improving per capita incomes. The resulting intense competition for economic resources can lead to political problems among the states, between state and central governments, and at other levels of society. It can also lead to violence. There is no direct and invariant relationship between these developments and international affairs, but it is not unreasonable to speculate that domestic turbulence will one day spill over and cause international problems. The precise scenario for its doing so is uncertain, but we can identify India's dissatisfaction with the terms of international trade and emigration of its people as among the factors that could someday elicit international terrorism or economically hostile acts.[12] The threat of such remote but undesirable developments is bound to have an impact on how other countries view and treat India and how India regards itself in developing its foreign policies.

In short, to the extent that the current imbalance between India's population and the supportive resource and institutional base is exacerbated, there is a danger that internal violence will become internationalized. Immigration from India may appear to be a lower order of concern, but it is a sensitive issue and one that already confronts India and the West. In formulating responsible immigration policies, Western nations cannot help but be mindful of the demographic characteristics of the countries from which they are receiving people. And there is perhaps no factor so likely to deter them from adopting liberal immigration policies than the specter of mushrooming population in countries like India. The politics of international immigration is an intriguing but lengthy story. Suffice it to say here that, as illustrated by the confusion of events in 1972 when Idi Amin decided to expel most of the British passport-holding Asians living in Uganda, international migration can have foreign affairs repercussions that go well beyond the immediate lives of migrant peoples.

HUMANITARIAN FACTORS

Although students of international affairs tend to concentrate on socioeconomic variables, ethical concerns can be just as compelling to action. They are less tangible, however, and if there is not more controversy over what constitutes moral objectives in foreign affairs, there certainly is greater debate over how humanitarian results can be achieved.

Ethical relationships are not easy to define, largely because there is no universal agreement on what is moral. For instance, the same Western society that has embraced the morality of the "white man's burden" has alternately supported foreign aid programs and ideas about leaving developing countries alone to preserve their "cultural authenticity." The common feature of these responses is a hardy strand of moral concern for the human condition and the development of individual human beings. This concern has often been overlooked, misunderstood, and overadvertised, but it nonetheless has deeply affected the way Indians and other nationals view each other.

Morality is often used to camouflage hard political and economic policies and, on some occasions, arguments of Realpolitik are used to cloak policies affecting genuine humanitarian concerns. Thus, U.S. interest in India in the 1950s and 1960s was as concerned with containing communism as it was with promoting development. Moreover, actions taken in the name of morality may have unintended and undesirable consequences—moral or otherwise—or they may fail to achieve their stated purpose. The practical questions that ethical concern raises is illustrated by the way in which the outpouring of humanitarian spirit experienced during the Kennedy years was later subject to reversal in response to a changing world situation. Less certain now of our approach to international problems, former Senator William Fulbright was recently moved to say that India "would have been better served if we had let them alone and forced them to face up to their own political and economic problems."[13]

There is a natural tendency for moral concern to focus on problems that are dramatic, immediately at hand (close to home in time and space), and subject to change by outside forces. Earlier I referred to the communications and technological revolutions of the 20th century, which are bringing the lives of geographically remote peoples into new and closer relationships. These developments, combined with the explosion of wealth in a number of countries and the increasing disparity between rich and poor nations (or at least increasing sensitivity to disparities) have expanded the potential for moral relationships between India and other nations. In postulating a gradually increasing moral tie between the peoples of rich and poor nations, however, one must be wary because even if a trend can be discerned, it is only gradual and is bound to be obscured by cyclical changes.

Despite all of these qualifications, it is clear that India's population size, its rate of increase, and its poverty have made it a focus of global moral interest. On the one hand, it has attracted sympathetic attention from foreigners who wish to improve Indian conditions. On the other hand, it has alienated those who thought that solving India's problems would be an easy matter and those who are frightened by the prospect of intimate relations with any country as poor and populous as India. There is still another group that is put off by India's situation, those concerned with the amorality—or immorality, depending on one's viewpoint—of income disparities within India and of other forms of social injustice.

Finally, as suggested earlier, it is an essentially moral argument that India and other developing countries make when they insist on more attention to population in the division of the world resources, in votes in the International Monetary Fund, and so forth. Such arguments are fundamentally constructive insofar as they reject the Marxian view that imperialist exploitation is inevitable. They even go so far as to suggest that "have" nations can be made to understand why sharing with the "have-nots" is in the mutual interest. Nonetheless, India's view of the morality of international resource-sharing and the desired shape of world order sometimes differs so sharply from that of the United States and other "have" nations that it will only be through the exercise of good diplomacy and some compromises by both sides that sharp conflicts will be avoided in future international discussions.

POPULATION AND FOREIGN AFFAIRS

In the final analysis, the effort to separate population considerations from other policy variables is particularly useful because it
provides new perspectives on how population and other societal forces
affect one another. It adds to our understanding of how demographic
factors pervade economic, political, and humanitarian relationships
and how their significance varies depending on a variety of historical,
functional, and other factors. It also helps to show how, when one
policy interest coincides with others, it is more likely to be achieved
than when it conflicts. Indeed, when objectives are at variance, re-
sultant policies are likely to shortchange one if not both of them.

In concluding, there are several key questions that command attention. How would India's foreign policies be different if the size
and growth rate of its population were higher? What if they were
lower? How would a higher or lower population size and growth rate
affect other countries' policies toward India? Assuming higher or
lower Indian population size and growth, how would respective foreign
policies interact? In posing these questions I do not mean to imply
that there is any feasible way to shrink the size of India's population,
but in thinking of the future it is necessary to recognize that a current
lower rate of increase will result in a smaller population than would
otherwise be the case. This is significant, if in a particular period,
both population size and the growth rate have an impact on development
and foreign affairs.

My view, based on arguments presented all too sketchily in the
preceding pages, coincides with those who believe that a more moder-
ate population growth rate would gradually cause India to become a
stronger nation, politically and economically. To some readers this
will appear to be stating the obvious, but for others, like Subramaniam
Swamy, it will be seen as wrong-headed. Be that as it may, I would
expect that, when translated into that ambiguous equation that defines
"national strength," the gain from higher per capita national income
would exceed any loss in total income and that a net political benefit
would be reaped from a reduction in the disintegrative tension attributable to demographic strains.

In the first instance, this increase in discretionary economic
and political capital would permit India to strengthen its international
position by increasing its spending not on economic investment but on
military and foreign aid programs and also by reducing its dependence
on foreign assistance inflows. A more significant dimension of this
argument is that although increasing domestic strength would not inevitably make India a better world citizen, given India's concern for
social justice, democracy, and nonviolence, there is considerable
likelihood that this is what would happen. The international reaction

to an easier state of affairs in India might range from displeasure to strong approval. Pakistan and China, which have a record of antagonism toward India, might be either indifferent or hostile to growing Indian strength. In contrast, so long as the Soviet Union is seeking to build anti-Chinese alliances in Asia, it would probably welcome a stronger India.

The Western nations also would be pleased, but for a rather different set of geopolitical, economic, and humanitarian reasons. Some people might be concerned that added strength would encourage India to play the "local Leviathan" to a greater extent than in the past, but the balance-of-power equation in South Asia is such that any major change from the present boundaries does not appear likely. If the nation comprising 14 percent of the world's population were to change status, from problem area to strong point, this would be an event of major international significance. It would not only relieve anxiety about the welfare of the peoples of South Asia but also allow the world to refocus its energies on other problem areas.

What if India's population growth rate were to accelerate? According to our logic, this would weaken India, exacerbate domestic and international income disparities, heighten violence, and increase the existing imbalance between the Indian people and the physical and institutional resources at their command. Under these circumstances, the focus of India's foreign policies might narrow and public policy might become more concentrated on domestic issues, but this is not necessarily the case. Another possibility is that India would lash out with a high-risk foreign policy aimed at forcing foreign attention and aid for solving its domestic problems. Such disruptive behavior might be fostered by a government but could also occur in the form of private terrorism such as has become so prevalent in the 1970s as a result of frustrated elements in the Middle East. The chances are that an Indian population spiraling out of control would lead many nations to adopt a siege psychology in the sense that they would seek to isolate themselves from India's hardships by further increasing their barriers to the immigration of Indian people, discriminating against imports of goods produced with cheap Indian labor, and so forth.

A weaker and hence more rudderless India would invite others to treat it as an object rather than subject in foreign affairs. There might be occasions when others would seek to take economic or political advantage of its weakness, but it is likely that the great powers and China would abandon it to its own devices and that its South Asian neighbors would be too weak to challenge it on any major issue. In short, I suspect that the domestic disruption caused by persistent high population growth rates would cause a crisis and change in India's situation well before any foreign power intervened deeply in its domestic affairs. The costs of such a crisis, however, would not be a matter of indifference to the international community, particularly if they involved the demise of democratic and related humanitarian values. This suggests that there might be some foreign intervention to prevent a crisis, but, in view of the very questionable results of interventions—economic and military—during the 1960s, there can be no certainty that foreigners would help or that their actions would substantially change the situation.

Up to this point, I have avoided population control as a specific issue in foreign affairs. Sovereign borders pose a certain constraint insofar as it is widely felt that the people of one nation have a right to tell one another how to behave but not to impose their will on citizens of foreign countries. Nonetheless, the question arises as to what course the United States and other countries should follow if they do not agree with India's demographic policies. Because the question cannot be posed with any degree of precision, the answer must be somewhat vague. It is especially difficult to speculate whether, in the face of an Indian population policy with which they disagreed, foreign countries would better serve their objectives in India by withdrawing support or by taking no notice. In contrast, if foreign governments agree with India's population policies, there is a great deal they can do to help India reduce its fertility rate. Recalling Mandelbaum's findings that the population growth rate is most affected by rising affluence and education, we can see that the unique contribution of foreign governments would be to adopt political and economic policies conducive to raising the pace of development in India.

To some degree, this whole discussion of lower or higher population growth rates is artificial because the demographic experience that was acceptable in the 1960s may prove unpalatable in the 1970s. The urgent need of our day is for Indians and others to increase their recognition of the domestic and international dimensions of India's demographic situation; to formulate policies to coordinate their objectives when they coincide; and to compromise them for their mutual benefit when they conflict. The alternative, nations pursuing their narrow self-interests without regard for the longer-run repercussions in space and time, is already too much with us to be perpetuated, much less intensified.

NOTES

1. For a review of the much neglected but unique position of women, see Adrienne Germain, Some Aspects of the Roles of Women in Population and Development, UN Document ESA/SDHA/AC.5/3/Add. 1, February 13, 1973 (mimeographed).

2. Ansley J. Coale and Edgar M. Hoover, Population Growth and Economic Development in Low Income Countries: A Case Study of India's Prospects (Princeton, N.J.: Princeton University Press, 1958).

3. Alan S. Manne, ed., Investments for Capacity Expansion: Size, Location, and Time-Phasing (London: Allen and Unwin, 1967), p. 146.

4. For the economic rationale of how rapid population growth could speed development by increasing the size of the labor force and increasing production through a demand-pull effect, see Subramaniam Swamy, Indian Economic Planning: An Alternative Approach (Delhi: Vikas Publications, 1971).

5. Marcus F. Franda, "Mrs. Gandhi Goes to Stockholm: A Survey of India's Policies and Non-Policies on Population and the Environment," American Universities Fieldstaff Reports, South Asia Series 16, 10 (August 1972).

6. From an adaptation of the minister's inaugural address at the National Symposium on Labour and Population Policies in New Delhi, April 15, 1974.

7. David G. Mandelbaum, Human Fertility in India (Berkeley: University of California Press, 1974), pp. 57-59.

8. V. M. Dandekar and Nilakantha Rath, "Poverty in India: Dimensions and Trends," Economic and Political Weekly (Bombay), January 2 and 9, 1971.

9. See Nazli Choucri, Population Dynamics and International Violence: Propositions, Insights, and Evidence (Cambridge, Mass.: Massachusetts Institute of Technology, Center for International Studies, 1973).

10. Ainslie T. Embree, "The Diplomacy of Dependency: Content and Style in Nineteenth Century Foreign Relations in India," unpublished paper presented at the Conference on Leadership, School of Oriental and African Studies, London, March 1974.

11. Samuel P. Huntington, "The Change to Change, Modernization, Development and Politics," Comparative Politics 3, 3 (April 1971).

12. Hedley Bull, "Violence and Development," in Development Today, ed. Robert E. Hunter and John E. Rielly (New York: Praeger Publishers, 1972), pp. 99-115.

13. U.S. Congress, Congressional Record-Senate, February 7, 1974, p. 15422.

CHAPTER

4

SOME EFFECTS OF
POPULATION GROWTH
IN INDIA ON SOCIAL
INTERACTION AND RELIGION
David G. Mandelbaum

By now the great majority of men and women in India know that contraception by modern means is possible and that their government urgently wants each child-bearing couple to limit the number of its children to two or three. The Family Planning Programme's educational efforts have been vigorous and pervasive; even in remote hamlets, its emblems can be seen prominently posted. But these urgings are not as persuasive as they might be because frequently they are not congruent with the strong needs and desires of those being urged.[1]

A large number of thriving children is still considered to be a great good by many. This is true among urban people as well as villagers; our focus in this chapter is on villagers, who make up some 80 percent of India's people. A young woman typically conceives of no desirable role for herself other than that of wife-mother, and in the early months of her marriage her great fear is that she may turn out to be a barren woman. When she does become pregnant, her relief and joy are matched by the beaming approval of her husband and his kin and of her natal family. During her pregnancy, she usually basks under solicitous treatment, gets better food than before, and enjoys the experience enough to want to repeat it more than once or twice again.[2] A young wife commonly feels that the best security, for whatever fate her later years may bring, lies in having a number of grown sons. Most of the religious rites in which she participates include her prayers for a large, healthy family.

A village man, too, generally feels that he can attain full manly stature and best guarantee security for his later years by having a large family, preferably of sons. When the children are younger, they cost little and can soon begin to add to the family's potential income if only by herding animals or collecting dung and twigs for fuel. If they go to school they cost more, but they are also building up the family's potential capital for the future. And grown sons are a man's best support when he needs help most, whether during the harvest, or in case of illness, or in the confrontations of village fights and feuds. An underlying purpose of his religious participation, whatever his affiliation and rituals may be, is to assure him that something of himself will continue beyond his own mortal span, and sons are the principal props for such assurance.

A good many observers have described the reasons why many people in India want to have large families; I have tried to summarize the effective motivations elsewhere and have also discussed the traditional motivations that people in India had, and still have, for controlling their fertility.[3] These are principally the advantages to infant and mother of spacing pregnancies and the shame of being a pregnant grandmother.

Many people believe that the health of a mother and of her nursing child are hurt if the woman becomes pregnant again before the child is weaned. In almost all groups in India, a married couple abstains from intercourse for some time after parturition. The length of the taboo period varies among groups from a few months to two or three years. It varies also by individual couples who may or may not observe their group's preferred period of abstention. In one study done in Bombay City, 53 percent of 1,105 women who had borne children during January–March 1965 later reported that they had abstained for a longer period than that stipulated by their caste or religious group. It may well be that they did so, although the study did not explore the possibility in detail, so that they might postpone their next pregnancy.[4] Both among villagers and townspeople, the deliberate spacing of pregnancies is considered desirable, especially if the infant survives its first weeks of life.

A very powerful motive for averting pregnancy, particularly among women of the higher wealth and status levels, is the unseemliness, even the disgrace, of bearing a child while one's other children have already become parents or are soon to do so. A principal factor in the lower fertility rates of these women over the whole of the reproductive period is that they stop having children sooner than do women of poorer and lower status. They have done so long before modern contraceptives became available, partly because they may have felt that they had enough children, and partly because of the shame of having it known that they continued having sex relations in their later, matronly years, say in their mid-30s and early 40s.[5]

Fertility has been traditionally controlled in other ways as well. The ban on widow remarriage among those of the "twice-born" categories was one method; its effect in lowering fertility has greatly declined in recent years. More important now is the rise in recent decades of the average age of girls at the start of marital sex rela-

tions. This average age, among some groups, has reached to about
20, which is high enough to lower the average number of children born
if other forces are also involved in lowering fertility rates.[6]

True, the Family Planning Programme's educational campaigns
have heightened the awareness of villagers that there are too many
people on too little land for the nation's welfare and perhaps even for
their own children's good. They can see for themselves such confir-
mation as that there are increasingly more people searching for de-
creasingly fewer bits of wood and dung for fuel. And without enough
fuel to cook the meal, a family may go hungry even if there is grain
for the pot.

Most notably does the increase become apparent when the father
of several sons dies and after a time the divisive pressures within the
joint family build up enough to impel the brothers to partition the family land among them. Then each brother may be left with an acreage
precariously small to support his own wife and children. But the common inclination of a couple thus impoverished is to continue to try to
have many sons, in the hope that the wage labor of some may augment
the family's income, and, if things turn out well, the pooled income
of all may be enough to support some education for at least one boy.
Having at least one in the family with some education is a good way,
and sometimes the only way, to improve a family's economic lot and
social status. There is also a broader rationale for having as many
children as possible, that in the competition among groups in the village or in the regularly recurrent contests through the ballot box, it
is always advantageous to have as many of one's own social kind as
possible.

This is not to say that the Family Planning Programme's efforts
have been fruitless. The necessary informational and administrative
foundations have been laid, and calculations of the cost-benefit ratio
of expenditures on the Programme conclude that even with its limited
success so far, these outlays have already saved the nation much
greater sums in future expenditures.[7] But the individual man or woman is naturally more concerned about his own and his family's future,
and that concern disposes many to ignore official advice concerning
the number of children they should have.

This inclination is all the stronger because the effects of population growth tend to be interwoven with other kinds of changes and
obscured by them. The overall consequences of excessive population
growth are more apparent to planners than to parents. These effects
intensify other constraints on development of all sorts, constraints
that would be considerable even without the added burden of too many
births. Because the pressure of increasing numbers exerts a gradual
tidal influence, because it often is a strong background factor rather
than a vivid foreground event, even close observers of Indian life have

tended to gloss over this force with a sentence or two in their analyses. Some comprehensive accounts of villages whose populations have increased greatly during the years in which they were being studied fail to focus directly on this fact and its consequences. A general survey of the peoples of South Asia written by an anthropologist, Clarence Maloney, concludes with a chapter on population. Maloney notes that "Criticism has been leveled against anthropologists, and justly, that though there have been scores of village studies, few have paid much attention to demographic factors, in spite of the statistical data available on many areas for a century."[8] While the statistical data are often difficult to use, it is true that there are relatively few notices in the literature of the relation between population growth and social interaction or religious practice. So the comments I make on these subjects can only be exploratory until better data and analyses become available.

ECONOMIC CONSEQUENCES OF POPULATION GROWTH

Whatever other consequences may follow from a steep and steady increase in population, certain economic imperatives cannot be avoided, which, in turn, affect social relations. More people need more food, more clothing, more of all the other basic life necessities. Nowadays the amount of land under cultivation cannot be significantly increased, certainly not enough to keep pace with the current rate of population increase, and so additional food can be produced only by more intensive and productive cultivation of the land already being worked. Thus in one village of Bulandshahr district of western Uttar Pradesh, the population has grown from 451 in 1863 (when the village records begin) to about 1,500 in the 1971 census. During the past 110 years, as Gilbert Etienne has analyzed the records and his own field data, these villagers have continuously improved their agricultural technology, until by 1972 practically all the cultivated land was under tube-well irrigation and many of the cultivators were talking knowledgeably about the uses of various kinds of chemical fertilizers. Some of the village men have found outside employment (45 in 1963) in city and government jobs and in the army. Most of those who do get outside employment are from the higher and wealthier groups whose education and family contacts smooth their way. But among the 70 landless families, fewer have been able to move out, and, the author notes, the improvement in their real living standard, while agricultural production rose greatly, has been small.

House sites have encroached on farm land: In 1889 some 2 percent of the village area was devoted to house and household use; in

1960 about 6 percent was so occupied. Further, there are no lands
for pasture or lying fallow any longer, so the number of milk cows has
decreased. The number of draft oxen, however, has gone up because
each family wants its own yoke, no matter how small its holding and
how inefficient it is to underwork a pair of costly oxen. Sharing a
pair requires more sustained cooperative effort than can be mustered
in this village. So also with tube-wells. It would be more efficient
to have deeper and fewer tube-wells, but, as Etienne describes the
cultivators of this area, they are first-class agriculturalists but also
"first-class quarrelsome people," so "jointly owned tube-wells are
out of the question."[9] In other villages, jointly managed tube-wells
are maintained, but such management is not easy because of each member's fragile confidence in getting his fair share of the water.[10]

A similar development has gone on in a Bangladesh village near
Comilla that has been studied by S. A. Quadir.[11] There the population
has increased from 140 to 426 in 1960. There also, technological improvements have increased yield, and there are fewer cows and more
oxen. There was less cultivable land available in 1960, not only because of more house sites but also because the number of plots has
doubled since 1899 so that an additional 3 percent of the total village
land was taken up by uncultivated boundary strips. Quadir writes
that the average family had less than enough to eat during the two
months before harvest.

These villagers and most landowning cultivators in the countries
of South Asia are thus strongly motivated to increase the yield of
their lands. But this demands modern irrigation and other inputs such
as improved varieties of seeds, chemical fertilizers, pesticides.
These inputs require the cultivator to raise capital and to obtain credit. Some of this can be facilitated by the government; the greater
part of the necessary capital most farmers must raise from their own
surplus, if any, or from private sources. Those who have small
holdings have little or no surplus and are less able to obtain credit to
invest in a tube-well or even in sufficient fertilizer.

Once a family's land is reduced to a certain minimum—perhaps
two to three acres in some circumstances, a bit less or more in
others—then its members are on a slippery slope toward losing more
or all of their land. If there should be two or three bad monsoons in
succession, or a lengthy illness, or several costly marriages, they
have no surplus to tide them over the thin times. They must borrow
money at high interest and, frequently, must eventually sell off their
land, the most precious, most valuable, readily salable commodity
that the typical landowner-cultivator can have. A villager I have
known for over 35 years found himself in such a predicament. His
difficulties began when, after his wife bore him a son, she produced
five daughters in succession. By the time the fifth came along he knew

that his middle-range holding would not yield enough for five dowries
of a size suitable to uphold his family's prestige. So he gambled by
borrowing large sums to lease more land and cultivated his own and
the leased land in an intensive (and costly) way in the hope of rich
harvests that would provide suitable dowries. But as luck would have
it, he gambled at the wrong time, when the rains were light and
plant disease was heavy. He was compelled to sell all but a sliver of
his land to pay his debts. He did later have a bit of luck after he succeeded in marrying his first daughter quite suitably. She turned out
to be barren, and so her husband took her next younger sister as a
second wife without asking for a second dowry. One of my friend's
brothers became a successful merchant and helped with the subsequent
marriages and dowries. His own education and standing in his village
has enabled him to avoid the dependence and humiliation of sinking
from a landowner to a wage laborer, as has happened to others.

Tribal peoples have been especially vulnerable to the loss of
their land to creditors.[12] But in many parts of India as well as in
tribal areas, the absolute numbers and proportion of landless laborers seem to have been increasing, while despite governmental efforts for land reform and land redistribution those families who have
the greater holdings, or those who are for other reasons relatively
affluent, have been able to maintain or even increase the amount of
land they own.[13]

Most of those who are at the lowest levels of the caste hierarchy
in a locality are also in the lowest economic stratum, as landless agricultural laborers. More and more villagers are falling into that
category as former smallholders who now have no land or even tenancy
opportunities. Some are artisans whose crafts have become obsolete
or whose numbers have become too large for all of them to find employment in their traditional occupation. It is families of these kinds
who in 1961 constituted an estimated 154 million to 210 million living
"in abject poverty, or at a level of Rs 200 ($26) per capita per year."[14]
They are the 40 percent of the rural population who, in Dandekar and
Rath's analysis, are not able to afford an average daily diet of 2,250
calories, the bare minimum for adequate nutrition under Indian conditions.[15]

In the fierce competition for livelihood and status that characterizes many an Indian village, those who have land have power. A
landowner commonly feels that if he is to protect what he has, he and
his compeers must exercise social and political dominance in the village and, if possible, in the wider political divisions as well. Even
within a jati (the endogamous social unit, sometimes called subcaste),
those of its families in a region who are wealthy are likely to inter-
marry with others of their economic and educational standing. They
tend to relegate their poverty-stricken jati fellows to inferior roles

in their society and economy. They may try to help them through special charities, through their caste associations, by sending favors
their way. But sometimes such wealthier people are reluctant to
hire laborers of their own jati lest such workers challenge control by
their jati peers or lest the status of the whole jati be jeopardized if
some in it have to accept work more menial than is in the jati's tradition.

As in most of the less developed countries (and not infrequently
in developed ones as well), the more affluent are able to strengthen
their economic position while the economic gap between them and the
poor steadily widens. This is not because the affluent are necessarily
immoral, evil-intentioned, or irreligious but rather because they necessarily feel compelled to advance their individual and group interests
within the social environment in which they live, lest they sink into
the mire—quite literally so in the case of field laborers stooping to
transplant seedlings in the muck. The richer families can afford
the critical social investment of education for their children, and the
watershed in education is crossed when a family can educate a child
to the point where the youngster can speak and read English, the language that allows access to national and international networks.
Their education, in turn, influences the educated to have fewer children than do uneducated folk, and they are less likely to pass on to
their children a dismal consignment of poverty.

The wealthier can also afford to invest in interpersonal relations. They commonly maintain more kinship relations than do poorer
people because they can stage lavish ceremonies to which many are
invited, and they can accept invitations that entail costly gifts. A
larger outreach of kin means more supporters in case of need and also
provides more opportunities for contacts with influential officials,
professionals, and businessmen. Their wider social horizons further
assist the affluent in such critical matters as obtaining scarce supplies, getting a hearing for a license, promoting jobs for their clients,
and securing effective attorneys in their law suits.

A good many of the landless, uneducated poor have been further
bereft of what influence they could wield on their landowning patrons
in the traditional patron-client, jajmani relation. This system involves the exchange of services, from that of priest to that of sweeper,
for a share of the patron's crop at harvest as well as other perquisites.
A family of one of the lower jatis in a locality, say ironworkers,
would provide their services to a set of cultivating landowners. Should
the ironworkers have a serious complaint against their patrons, their
council might declare a boycott, which would often induce the patrons
to come to terms with their blacksmith associates. But now landowners need pay little heed to a blacksmiths' boycott since they commonly
can buy the utensils in town and get the repair work done by the piece

rather than as part of a complex, long-term relationship. Yet a landowner who lives in his ancestral village may be reluctant to abrogate
all the traditional ties. There still are advantages for him in keeping
up a modicum of them; such ties are useful for ritual purposes, in
factional disputes, and when extra labor is much needed during harvest.[16] But the landless poor commonly feel that they have even less
leverage on the patrons than their fathers had, and, while caste relations are generally still significant in a village, some of the poorer
families are turning to modern political sources of influence in the
hope that their votes and governmental sympathy for their plight will
send some favors toward them.

IN THE WAKE OF THE "GREEN REVOLUTION"

The social and economic disparities between the landed and the
landless in a locality have been further increased recently in those
places where the stepped-up intensification of agricultural technology
has successfully been applied, the areas in which the so-called Green
Revolution has been achieved.[17] Landowners are reluctant to lease
land to tenants, partly because they can earn more under the new technology by managing all their own lands, partly because they do not
want a tenant, under the new land tenure legislation of some states,
to acquire some rights in a plot by tilling it for several years in succession. Sharecroppers may get a third rather than the former half
of the crop because, with greater expenses for cultivation, the landowner takes a third for himself and deducts another third for his increased expenses. Those who have only a little land also tend to be
disadvantaged. Even where government officials, by legal duty or
personal empathy, are motivated to help the small holder, such a
small holder usually does not have enough education to fill out the
numerous forms required in order to obtain subsidized supplies nor
does he have the money and know-how to push the completed forms
through the necessary bureaucratic channels. A more affluent or better-educated cultivator does not have an easy task in doing so, but
given some enterprise and perseverance he can usually succeed in
maintaining the flow of credit, seeds, water, fertilizer, pesticides,
transport, and labor essential in order to produce the higher yields
of wheat or rice. An agricultural laborer can only concentrate on getting work enough to feed himself and his family and, perhaps, to pay
something on the debts he has almost invariably incurred.

A landowner who puts in a cash crop like sugarcane is able, in
some localities, as Joan Mencher notes for Chingleput district of
Tamil Nadu, to avoid some of the most important of his former dealings with laborers. He and his family may manage the work on the

crop with little extra labor during growing phases. At harvest, he formerly had to compete with other landowners for workers and so had to pay higher wages at harvest time. By the same token, the workers counted on their income during harvest to carry them through a part of the year. Now the management of a large sugar mill sometimes buys the standing crop and then deploys its lorries to round up labor from distant villages or from towns. Mill employees oversee the cutting of the crop, and the landowner need have no direct relations with the laborers. [18]

An incidental effect of the greater importance to a cultivator, in at least one village of the Punjab, of the labor provided by his family is that a daughter's contribution there tends to be more valued than before. This has persuaded cultivating landowners to postpone the age at which their daughters are married to an average in 1969 of 20.6 years, an older age for a girl's marriage than is their own ideal and enough to lower the average fertility during her child-bearing years. [19] The economic incentive to keep a daughter at work for her natal family as long as possible is clear enough. What is not so clear is why parents in this area apparently do not feel the traditional dread, or feel it much less keenly than before, of having a nubile, unwed daughter in the house, vulnerable to acts that might impugn the family's honor or, more likely, to damaging rumors of such happenings, whether true or not.

Beyond his own village, a cultivator finds advantage in establishing cordial relations with elected and administrative officials. This is nothing new, but these relations have become increasingly important. The wealthier try to do so because officials can facilitate or obstruct their applications for permits or credit or subsidies. The poor want to do so because the influence of their collective vote is one of the few means of leverage they have on the critical machinery of government.

Once a cultivator has embarked on the newer, more sophisticated, and more productive kinds of agriculture, he tends to be drawn inextricably into a network of wider relations. He has to maintain continuous contact with the wider market and governmental research facilities if he is to maintain the higher crop yields and maintain his family's standard of living. The new plant varieties tend to be more vulnerable to disease than are the older lower-yielding varieties; they must have ample water and fertilizers to make cultivation profitable. Both water (or electricity for the pumps) and fertilizer have been in short supply from time to time, and sufficient supplies may be obtainable only through special influence. The more efficient cultivators cannot rest on their laurels of past production and merely repeat, as was feasible for centuries past, the cultivating pattern that was profitable in past seasons. That pattern must be continually revised, bolstered, adapted to the now ever changing conditions, whether of the natural environment or plant pathology, of social relations or political-economic forces, in order that it may suffice for the ever growing number of mouths to be fed.

TWO VILLAGES OF KARNATAKA, 1955-70

These general economic trends are illustrated in specific detail by a fine study of two villages of Mandya district of Karnataka (Mysore) State. In 1954-56, T. Scarlett Epstein studied and compared the villages she calls Wangala and Dalena. The two were quite similar until the 1930s, both being dominated—numerically, socially, and economically—by members of the "Peasant" (Okkaliga) caste, none of whom was a large-scale landowner. Then the canals of a major irrigation project reached Wangala while Dalena's lands remained "dry" because of topographic reasons, though there were villages whose lands had become "wet" all about them. The villagers of Wangala could now profit handsomely from a cash crop, sugarcane; their plantings were much assisted by the state-owned sugar mill in Mandya town, which provided management services, supplies, and guidance and which purchased much of the crop. Thus relieved of many tasks, the farmers of Wangala had mainly to work hard in their fields and so increase their income. Since there was little incentive for them to venture away from the village, their traditional social and political organization remained much the same as it has been.

The Dalena villagers, by contrast, had to go outside their village to make economic gains if they were to keep up at all with the burgeoning prosperity of more fortunate cultivators in nearby villages. Dalena landowners tried a variety of ventures, including setting up rice mills, getting work in town, and acting as middlemen and tradesmen. This kind of economic reorientation led to changes in the village organization, particularly to the cutting off of most of the former jajmani relations, especially in the close, multiple ties between families of landless Adi-Karnatikas (AKs, Harijans) and families of Okkaliga landowners.

Such was the situation in 1954-56 as described by Epstein.[20] In 1970, she was able to revisit both villages for five weeks at the invitation of a team from the University of Nurnberg who had been studying the same villages. Using some of their data as well as her own, Epstein worte an account of the two villages as observed 15 years after her first study of them. Population growth in both had been substantial during those 15 years. Dalena had grown from 707 to 1,072, an increase of 51 percent; Wangala's numbers rose from 958 to 1,603, an increase of 67 percent. There had been some immigration into

Wangala, a little into Dalena; the natural increase had averaged at
least 2.5 percent a year. Although the villagers had experienced other
forces for change, the weight of greater numbers of people has directly or indirectly affected some of the basic elements of life in the
two villages.[21]

One manifest consequence is that the average size of landholding has decreased despite a considerable (60 percent) expansion of
cultivable land in Wangala, mainly through extension of the canals,
and despite the diligent acquisition by some Dalena landowners of wet
lands in other villages. The average holding among Dalena's landowning households has declined from 4.9 to 3.7 acres, in Wangala
from 3.1 to 2.7 acres though the proportion of wet landholdings has
increased in both villages.[22] Some 24 percent of the Wangala wet
lands were owned by outsiders in 1970, mainly from Mandya town.
The Wangala decline was more than made up for by higher yields, the
increase for paddy during the 15 years being nearly 50 percent, so
that Wangala as a village (though not all within it) produces a basic
food surplus. Dalena suffers a deficiency in the food its people produce on the village lands. Both villages were greatly advantaged in
agricultural production when Mandya district was chosen in 1962 to
be one of the districts (usually the one with the most promising agricultural potential in each state) to be included in the national Intensive
Agricultural Development Programme. The villagers under this program received a package of special advantages, including improved
irrigation, the services of a village-level adviser, reduced rates for
hiring bulldozers and tractors, and easier loans from village coopera-
tives.

Even though they have been thus favored by governmental agencies and encouraged to diversify their crops, the farmers of both villages continue to place highest priority on growing food for their families. A Wangala cultivator can earn enough from an acre of sugarcane to buy about twice as much paddy as he can grow on it, yet not
one of them has put all his land into cash crops. All prefer to make
sure first that their land yields enough for their family's food needs,
and only then may the rest of their holding be put into a cash crop.[23]
In continuing to be subsistence-centered, they are not lacking in fore-
sight. Epstein estimates that the population of Wangala will double in
about 25 years (only 3 of a sample of 72 Wangala men "felt decidedly
positive" about family planning), so that much more of their land will
soon have to be planted in subsistence crops and they will have less
paddy and sugarcane to sell out of the village.[24]

All in Wangala and Dalena are concerned about their supply of
food, but not all can get enough food for even a minimal diet adequate
for health. Epstein notes in her concluding chapter, "I have shown
that social inequality in these two villages had continued almost un-

changed while economic differentiation has considerably increased
during the past fifteen years: the poor have become poorer not only
relatively but also absolutely."[25] Her first impression on walking
through the two villages after an absence of 15 years was that of considerable improvements in the caste sections, fine new houses, electricity, a new school, new wells, new cafes, and new machinery.
But the poor section where the AKs live looked "poorer and more dilapidated" in Wangala; in Dalena there was still the huddle of small,
dilapidated, thatched huts with their residents wearing the same kind
of tatters and scraps they had worn earlier. In 1970 there were 44
households of AKs in Wangala, 21 in Dalena.

When she came to calculate the calorie intake of individual AKs,
she found one, reasonably typical Dalena man to have about 1,680
calories per day, and another AK man, Malla of Wangala, who owns
a half acre of wet land, to have about 1,960 calories per day. Malla
had experienced the marked lowering in standard of living that is common among the poor and the poorest in these villages. The income of
Malla's household from wages had dropped about 70 percent at 1955
prices; he and his family must now eat more of the coarser grain,
ragi, than rice and they have had to reduce consumption expenditures
by about two-thirds on clothes, cigarettes, betel, and even on such
household items as pots and pans.[26] At that, the Wangala AKs are
better off than are the 23 households of Voddas in the village. These
people are migrants, presumably pushed by hunger from their Tamil
village, where, as stonecutters by caste occupation, they lived in the
main caste section. In Wangala they are ranked even below the local
Untouchables, who do not permit them to draw water from the Harijan
well. The calories available per day as calculated for one of their
men amount to no more than 1,500, only two-thirds of the minimal
2,250 calories cited by Dandekar and Rath (1971) as necessary for
health.

The pinch of too many workers seeking too few jobs is shown in
the work statistics for Dalena. Its male working population rose
from 199 in 1955 to 300 in 1970. The work of only about 50 of the 300
is needed to cultivate the village lands for most of the year. This fact
and the relatively low productivity of the Dalena unirrigated lands
makes outside work a "dire necessity" for many Dalena residents.[27]
But work opportunities in or out of the village are scarce, and men
and women from Dalena, along with many others like them, wander
endlessly through town and villages, searching, searching, for work
just to stave off their own and their families' hunger. Epstein discusses the general situation in the final section of her report. "As we
have seen, the supply of labour in agriculture has increased much
more than the demand for it. This has led to a reduction in real wages
which was facilitated by inflation." As for population increase, out of

a sample of 116 Dalena men and women, no more than 20 percent "felt decidedly positive" about family planning; the author assumes a similar condition for South Asia generally. "Since we must expect population increase and inflation to continue in South India in the near future, real agricultural wages will continue to fall until they reach bare subsistence levels, unless drastic steps are taken to prevent a further deterioriation in the standard of living of the poorest landless labourers."[28]

Those Dalena residents who must seek outside work include not only the 12 households of Harijans but also a good many of the dominant farmer jati, since some 43 percent of their 196 households do not have enough land "to meet their basic requirements."[29] The plight of this growing cohort is revealed in Epstein's comment that while agricultural productivity and crop prices have considerably increased, "My own data for Mandya region indicate that the real daily wage rates have been about halved between 1955 and 1970 while employment per labourer has also declined."[30] Moreover, the average labor input per acre of cane has been reduced about 10 percent because cane farmers have learned how to rationalize cultivation better (not, so far, because of increased mechanization), and they now employ more female workers than they used to because females are paid at only half the male wage rate.[31]

Under these conditions, it is no wonder that the Harijans of Dalena envy those of a village like Wangala where more of the traditional patron-client relations have been preserved. A Wangala Harijan who is obligated to a landowner under the traditional arrangements has, at least, a certain minimum social security. His patron will not let his servant's family starve so long as the landowner has enough to feed his own family and a bit more. In return, the patron has first priority on the laborer's work, services, and support. Wangala landowners do employ workers at peak labor demand periods of the agricultural cycle, and they say that such hired workers are more efficient than the indigenous AKs since their employment depends on their immediate performance. But the Okkaliga landowner also gains from the traditional relationship, partly because it ensures that he commands labor that is reliably, even if not very efficiently, available. And because most of the people of Wangala still comprise a moral community in the traditional sense, he feels some social and moral obligations to his Harijan servants and, indeed, needs them to perform certain essential ritual services, especially in life-cycle rituals.

Both sides stand to gain in other ways as well. Thus, when new wet lands became available in Wangala through the extension of canals, certain plots were reserved for sale to local Harijans at much reduced prices.[32] Malla's patron bought 1.25 acres in Malla's name. He ad-

vanced the money, saw to all the arrangements, and so added a
precious acre to his holdings at a low cost. Malla received a quarter-
acre for himself, which, together with the quarter-acre he had previously owned, gave him more food-producing resources than he could
otherwise have had. Without his patron's intervention he could not
have managed to get the quarter-acre even though he knew that theo-
retically he could have earned enough by cultivating an acre of sugarcane for a year or two to repay the cost of the land. And he might
have borrowed the money under the favorable loan terms provided by
government agencies for AKs. But he also knew that he probably
would have needed Rs. 150 to procure the required official signature.
And, he said jokingly to Epstein, if he had had that much cash available
to smooth the way to a loan ". . . I would not have needed the loan at
all!"[33]

The AKs of Wangala are not allowed to sit beside men of higher
caste status in the village cafes, as those of Dalena can now do, and
their one gesture, during Epstein's first visit, toward breaking a customary taboo failed ignominiously and has not been tried again. But
in continuing to provide traditional ritual services and in accepting
traditional symbols of inferiority, they are less vulnerable to hunger
than are the freer, but more precariously situated AKs of Dalena.

Men of both villages who are in the middle stratum of their society and whose income is about enough to feed and clothe their families adequately by local standards also find themselves in a tightening
economic bind, particularly if they rear to manhood the number of
sons they continue to want. Jagegowda of Wangala is described as a
representative person in this middle category. "As with so many
others of his kind, the increase in the size of his family has depressed
his standard of living."[34] He has four sons, each of the two older
sons is married, and in 1970 each had two children. The 12 individuals lived together as a joint family on a landholding of three wet acres and half a dry acre. Jagegowda had had to sell some land to meet
the marriage expenses for his eldest son (marriage customs have now
changed, as we shall note later, so that the parents of the bride bear
the heaviest expenses rather than the former Okkaliga custom of having the parents of the groom do so). As his affairs stood in 1970, he
just about managed to make ends meet. He and his family ate a less
varied diet than they did in 1955 and used more of the cheaper, coarser
grains. The daily calorie intake for a working male of the family had
declined from an average of 2,430 to 2,240 calories, but they still
grew enough sugarcane to provide money for some clothes, utensils,
and other essential cash purchases.

In 1970, however, the usual divisive pressures within a joint
family were building up in Jagegowda's family to a degree that made
sharp economic losses for all its members quite likely. The two mar-

ried sons (and probably their wives as well) were not happy about
continuing to live in a joint family and wanted to separate and partition the family lands. Jagegowda's arguments that they will all be
worse independently are true, but he seemed "too weak a person" to
withstand his sons' demands much longer.[35] After the land is partitioned, Jagegowda and each of his sons will fall from the category of
Okkaliga households in Wangala who have sufficient land to meet their
requirements (70 percent of the 228 households) and become part of
those who must seek other income because they cannot make their
living only from their lands. Obviously, more than 30 percent of the
Okkaliga households will find themselves in this bind in the future;
43 percent of the Okkaliga households in Dalena were already in that
category in 1970.

Members of the dominant caste group of the area have better
chances of getting employment than do Harijans because job-seekers
of that group have access to a network of jati fellows sympathetic to
their difficulties and inclined to favor one of their own if they can.
Thus of 26 Dalena men who commute to work in Mandya town daily,
20 are Okkaligas, 5 are of artisan groups, and one is a Harijan.

But no landowning cultivator in either village prefers to work
in a factory. He would rather have the "free and easy" life of the
village cultivator than the disciplined routine of the town factory. If
he has any land at all in his village, he holds on to it and, if possible,
cultivates it himself. Such men are neither good farmers nor efficient factory workers. The demands of cultivation make them leave
their work in town for long periods; they commonly miss opportunities
for job promotion and usually remain at the level of unskilled workers.
Yet they cannot manage their land continuously enough to be efficient
farmers.[36] Being poor farmers, they rarely can get a foothold toward becoming full-scale cultivators again.

For one thing, they cannot get the necessary credit. Cooperative credit institutions have greatly aided some of the farmers of these
villages. "However, co-operative credit, like so many other types
of external aid offered to cultivators, helps the wealthiest most and
the poorest least." The richer a man becomes, the more credit-
worthy he is, and the poorer he becomes, the less credit he can get
even under the relatively liberal terms that have been established in
the area. In all, Epstein concludes, "The fate of these Peasant middle-
farmers is largely determined by the rate of increase in the size of
their families: the more rapid the increase, the quicker the decline
in their economic status."[37] So a small holder's good luck in raising
several sons may eventually lead to bad luck for his grandsons when
they come to inherit tiny bits of land or none at all.

THOSE WHO HAVE PROSPERED

Yet a good many of the landowning families in each village, in Wangala amounting to perhaps half the village population, are not caught in so tight a demographic-economic squeeze. Their standard of living has risen; they eat more and more varied food. Wangala's farmers produced enough of the staples of millet and rice in 1955 to afford a daily per capita supply of 1,920 calories, had there been equal division of these crops among all men, women, and children in the villages. By 1970, the yield was enough to raise that figure to 2,650 calories available; though as we have seen, many families lived on far less than that average availability.[38] The more prosperous families enjoy the amenities of electricity, radios, better houses, more wells, better schooling opportunities, and more shops and cafes.

As the population has grown and village economy has become more complex, the cafes have become important centers for information and communication. There was only one small cafe in Wangala in 1955; there were six in 1970 and another for Harijans. These are the places where men (not women) come to meet fellow villagers and outsiders, where news and gossip are exchanged. Gossip in such villages, as elsewhere in the world, not only amuses, titillates, occasionally shocks, but also tests and reinforces the values of society. Further, since village agriculture is now so closely dependent on wider market conditions and on governmental activities, news about such matters is an important adjunct to profitable cultivation. The cafes in Wangala serve enough cups of tea and coffee for an average daily consumption per caste man (above the Harijan level) of one and one-half cups. Some men regularly have three or four cups a day, which means, Epstein tells, that they spend at least a couple of hours each day chatting in a village cafe.[39] The customers in the busiest cafe in Wangala are about half men of the village and half outsiders. The cafe for Harijans is little used by them, partly because they are less able to afford the hot drinks and snacks, and partly because they have less need to keep abreast of the news and gossip.

There are 34 radios in Wangala. The broadcasts are generally of little interest to the villagers although some men listen keenly to the programs about agricultural activities, as those that advise when to plant a particular crop.

Dalena supports four cafes. Those Dalena men who do business in cattle trading or other ventures conduct their negotiations in them. The more enterprising and wealthy men in Dalena are always on the lookout for an opportunity to buy irrigated land, and so they spend a good deal of their time outside the village, visiting relatives, sitting in cafes, in the hope of hearing of a possible transaction.

Some of the Dalena men who have been forced by lack of sufficient land to work outside the village maintain "share families"with
their brothers who are still full-time cultivators. As we have noted,
the wage-earners hold on to whatever land they have in the village
and participate actively in the village social system. Each brother
lives separately with his wife and children; one set may live in town,
the other in Dalena. All share their incomes as well as their expenditures. It is a mutually advantageous arrangement, the frictions of
joint residence are avoided, the wage-earner shares in the yield of
the land, and the cultivator obtains the cash needed for household expenditures.[40] An exception is the AK who has a job in town but has
no land in Dalena. He seems to have cut his village ties completely
and has no contact with his brother who still lives in the village.[41]
For him, there is neither the pull of land nor the attraction of village
society to take him back to Dalena.

At the upper economic level in both villages are the enterprising,
able men who have succeeded in amassing land, wealth, and prestige
above their fellow villagers. Two representative examples of these
village "magnates" are given by Epstein. Tugowda of Wangala had
two sons and two daughters in 1955; his holdings were six wet acres
and one dry. By 1970, his elder son was married, had three children,
and continued to live in the parental household. The younger son was
a student at the University of Mysore; the two daughters were married;
one of them and her child had rejoined her father's household. Tugowda's landholding had increased by 13 irrigated acres; his annual income
had almost trebled. The family had a fairly good average daily diet
in 1955 (2,700 calories per adult male); it was better in 1970 (2,980
calories per adult male), but as with the other wealthier villagers,
Tugowda did not spend much of his surplus on items of personal consumption. He rather built up his capital, not only by investing in land,
but also in animals, machinery, a large new house, and in making
loans. He also enlarged his social capital, by lavish weddings for
his daughters, by building a village shrine and contributing to the
building of a large pilgrimage temple, and in the education of his
younger son. The weddings and the religious expenditures enhance
his standing in traditional ways; by his son's education he makes provision in the modern sector.

His counterpart in Dalena, Lingowda, had three sons in 1955 and
owned five acres of dry land in Dalena and six of wet in neighboring
villages. In 1970 his family had grown to five sons, the elder married
with one child. Lingowda had acquired four more irrigated acres,
and his income had almost doubled. He too has increased his capital
investment more than his consumption expenditures. He operates a
rice mill, a cane-crusher, and a tube-well and pump set. His special
investments, however, do not run to temples and ceremonies. His

eldest son failed to get an engineering degree, but Lingowda made
another large investment in him by financing his successful campaign
as a candidate on the Taluk board of elections. Like other villagers
of Dalena, Lingowda has had to become involved in extra-village relations. By helping his son achieve a formal position in the regional
political structure, Lingowda achieves greater opportunities for
friendly contacts with administrative officials and with farmers of irrigated villages. [42]

Both these "magnates" live in joint families. Both steadily increased their wealth because, for one reason, they were able to keep
their grown sons content to maintain the family estate undivided. Two
of the men who were magnates in Wangala in 1955 failed in this. One
of them was the chief moneylender of the village, feared by many who
were in debt to him. But his lands had to be equally partitioned between himself and his four sons, all were the poorer for it, and "he
disappeared from the village economic scene."[43] Many sons can indeed be a powerful asset to a family's prosperity, provided they can
be persuaded to work and share together when they grow up. But if a
wealthy father cannot hold his sons together in the joint family enterprise, he may suffer a "social death" before his physical demise. [44]

If a father can afford the expense of secondary or higher education and a son has the ability to pass examinations, there is little
question as to whether to give the boy as much education as he can
manage and as the family's purse can support. In 1955 there was not
a single person in Wangala who was literate in English. By 1970, the
village had produced five university graduates, and there were five
more undergraduates. All were Okkaligas except for one undergrad-
uate AK. Though special high school scholarships are available for
Harijans, they provide too little assistance to be of marked help for a
poor family. The one AK youth whose family did manage to keep him
through high school won a university scholarship sufficient for his
needs. [45] Educating a son not only opens the possibility of a better
career for him but also provides his family with a potential link to the
potent spheres of officialdom and modern business. Such links can be
major advantages in village society where intense social and economic
competition, long a basic fact of life, has been further heightened by
the increase in numbers of people. Yet parents in these villages recognize some drawbacks also. Graduates, unlike their less educated
neighbors who get town employment, are likely "to sever their ties
with the village completely and, becoming contemptuous of village
ways of life, will try to become full-fledged townsmen."[46] The one
exception in Wangala to the prevailing brain drain from villages to
cities is a young man who did manage to get a university degree but
was such a poor student that he still cannot speak or understand spoken
English. He has returned to live in the village, and his higher educa-

tion has widened his interests enough so that he has learned improved, mechanized methods of cultivation and has opened a fertilizer shop. [47]

Educating a son has come to bring another kind of return on the investment in the form of dowries. The traditional marriage custom of the dominant jati in these villages required the bridegroom's family to bear most of the expenses of the wedding and to give a sum to the bride's family because her family was losing a worker and his was gaining one. But about 1965 the richer men in both villages discovered that they could not arrange suitably prestigious matches with educated young men for their daughters unless they paid substantial dowries. They were not too reluctant to do so because dowry payments emulated the custom of the high-status Brahmins of the area. Their girls, moreover, no longer worked in the fields and were not an economic asset. In these villages, there is still very little education for girls. Some of the small holders still practice the old marriage arrangement, but a man who wants to enjoy the lift in his status that comes from a good marriage for his daughters tries to marry her to a young man with some education, and the payment of dowries is becoming more prevalent than the payment of bride wealth. [48] The richer villagers, in adopting the new dowry custom, are continuing the ancient and widespread practice of translating economic gains, which may be transitory for the family and certainly for the mortal individual, into higher social and ritual status, which, in their view, is surely more lasting and important.

WANGALA AND DALENA AS MORAL COMMUNITIES

Both villages have absorbed massive increases in numbers in the 15-year period with certain similar results, as in the decrease in average size of landholding and with certain differences, which stem from the fact that Wangala got canal waters and Dalena did not. The people of Wangala remain more of a moral community, with shared values and identity, than do those of Dalena. Factional alignments are important in both villages, as they are in many Indian villages. In 1955, factional disputes were particularly rife in Wangala because the new economic conditions had enriched certain lineages, whose men then wanted more honored ritual prerogatives than they had previously enjoyed. A particularly bitter struggle broke out over who should perform a certain rite at a village ceremony. The ceremony was not abandoned, as has occurred in other villages under similar disputes; each Wangala side performed its own ceremony until, after a few years, one faction was clearly victorious and the village council decreed that all would again unite in performing the same ceremony. [49]

Lavish wedding feasts are still offered for all the people of
Wangala. The council of lineage elders still runs the village. Jajmani relations are still maintained between a good deal of the landowners and the landless AKs. While the Harijans may not like the
stigma of inferiority that this relationship entails, they like even less
the situation of the Harijans of Dalena, where jajmani relations have
been largely abrogated and the landless have been deprived of even a
minimal social security so that they must endlessly worry about finding work and staving off hunger.

In Dalena the community bonds, the shared ritual and common
values have become more loosened. Dalena landholders have tried
to participate in the formal political structure of the locality but
have been disappointed with that experience. A few of the wealthier
landowners have become so concentrated on economic and political
activities outside the village that they have lost interest in the affairs
of Dalena. But small holders who have had to take outside jobs find
insufficient social and personal satisfactions in the town. They cling
to their village affiliations, even though the ritual unity of Dalena is
probably not as frequently or strongly expressed as once it was.

One such man, Chennu of Dalena, became a mill worker in town
when he was 17, and by 1956 he had already taken on some of the
standard accoutrements of a town-dweller of the time: a bicycle, a
gold watch, a white shirt, and spotlessly clean dhoti. But he also
acted as a spirit medium, a shaman, whose role is of considerable
importance to villagers in search of a cure for their ailments or who
have some other reason for seeking contact with transnatural powers.
He had to give up that calling since he could not keep up the dietary
purity required of a Dalena village shamam while he lived and worked
in town. Yet in 1970 he continued to be very much village-oriented.
He and his brother in the village share income and expenditures; he
visits Dalena frequently and sees himself as a future leader of the
"new progressive movement" in Dalena that would bring about a fusion
of the modern ways of the town and the traditional ways of the village. [50] A fusion is indeed gradually being brought about in both villages, though in different ways, and in this development many of the
villagers must continually cope with the scarcity of land and food,
problems that have become sharper with the increasing numbers of
people in these two villages.

THE RELEVANCE OF RITUAL

One swallow does not a summer make, nor do two villages make
plain a country of over half a million villages. Yet the conditions depicted in Epstein's microscopic examination accord, in general, with

the macroscopic surveys we noted earlier. In his broad, economic appraisal of the "Green Revolution," Wolf Ladejinsky refers to an important factor that has not been much discussed. "Often overlooked technological constraints are educational requirements and co-operative action on the part of village farmers and the community as a whole . . . activities like pest control and water management call for communal effort."[51] We have noted the educational requirement before and shall return to it below. The matter of cooperation within a village, and the lack of it, is commonly of considerable importance in the amount of food that is produced and in the general level of living of its residents. It is much more than a mere technological constraint, for it involves the kind of mutual trust, common sense of identity, and shared purposes and values that underlie not only cooperation in water management and pest control but also a vital range of other factors, such as the effective resolution of conflict, the avoidance of costly litigation, the availability of mutual assistance, and the furthering of common village concerns. Village rituals are still important in Wangala and have practically been abandoned in Dalena.

Traditionally, common causes and cooperation were strengthened by the performance of village religious ceremonies. These rites commanded and expressed the unified effort of the people of a village, and in so doing they strengthened their attitudes and inclination for cooperation in other spheres. This is not to say that village ceremonies eliminate friction and faction but rather that they help the participants to set aside their divisions when the good of all is at stake or when the welfare of the village is threatened as through the incursions of cattle disease or encroachments by outside officials. Among the several factors that have impaired the performance of such all-village rites has been the weight of greater numbers of people, either within the village or pressing into it from outside. Villagers who have forsaken their ceremonies tend also to have a lowered sense of belonging to a moral community, of sharing an identity across caste and class lines that these rites often fostered.

An example of such changes in religious practice is given in Professor G. Obeyesekere's study (1967, 1974) of a small village, a hamlet in the southern province of Sri Lanka (Ceylon).[52] In 1961 it had 289 inhabitants, all of the same caste rank of independent farmer. Until the 1950s all the people of the village had to participate in certain ceremonies that helped to declare and reinforce their sense of group solidarity. One such ceremony was the celebration of the first fruits of the harvest. It culminated in the eating of a communal meal by all the members of the hamlet. A feast, Obeyesekere notes, is a symbol of social solidarity wherever and in whatever context it is given. "Here it expresses the solidarity of the hamlet and helps to affirm its collective unity as a moral community."[53]

By 1961 this ceremony was no longer being performed. The reason was not because of lack of religious belief since certain rituals, such as those organized by individual households for curing and those for exorcism, are still performed, apparently even more often than before. A fundamental reason for the abandonment of the first fruits ceremony, Obeyesekere concludes, is that the hamlet was no longer a homogeneous community. Economic and demographic pressures had altered its previous composition. "Outsiders had settled in the hamlet and citizens of the hamlet owning shares had left it, absentee landowners from outside the village had bought shares from the hamlet estate." Conflict over land and property rights was rife, and "it was not possible for the hamlet to mobilize resources to perform the ritual."[54] The change in the internal cohesion and solidarity of the group led to the breakdown in communal ritual, and this, we may surmise, further loosened the villagers' sense of belonging to an invigorating community.

While village rites were being relinquished, the villagers were increasing their pilgrimages to four main centers outside their district. With improved transportation and other modern facilities now available, these centers are more readily reached than they used to be, and pilgrimages to them have become practically obligatory, almost as much so as the old ceremony of the first fruits had been. The author comments that "the social function of these obligatory pilgrimages is clear. It transfers the individual from the narrow moral community of his village to the larger moral community of Sinhala Buddhists."[55] That sense of a larger community, as currently experienced, excludes other citizens of Ceylon, notably the Hindu Tamils, and the exclusions have raised serious political problems. Sharing a sense of belonging to a wider ethnic group within the nation and opposing other ethnic groups may make for lively political encounters, but it does not replace the sense of community among the farmers of a locality that encourages an increase in agricultural production.

Though the content of such political encounters differs in India, the general pattern of shift in the performance of village ceremonies is similar. The decline of rituals that enhance the villagers' sense of village solidarity tends to inhibit those cooperative efforts that enhance the yield of the land.

Some villagers are quite aware of the bracing effects of common ritual observances and try to maintain ceremonies for all in their village. McKim Marriott has sketched the lives of five farmers of Kishan Garhi, a village of Aligarh district, U.P., that he first studied in 1951-52 and restudied in 1968-69. Many of the Kishan Garhi farmers have taken up the new agricultural technology, have adapted to its requirements, and have prospered. The leading caste groups in the village are Brahmins and Jats. One of the Brahmin farmers whom Mar-

riott calls A.B.D., has built a fine new house in which he likes to
give large feasts for both major factions of Brahmins and for the
lower-ranking groups of the village as well. The Jats did not attend
in 1969 because A.B.D. was sensitive enough to the Barbers' desire
to dissociate themselves from menial tasks that he did not insist that
they remove the Jats' dirty dinner plates, as was sometimes done in
1951. "Although the net effect of A.B.D.'s feasting policies is to reduce caste ranking, A.B.D. nevertheless sees himself as keeping the
community in something like its old, ideal order through his liberal
expenditures."[56]

Another villager, identified as I.A.C., was in 1951 one of the
wealthiest men in the village and one of the greatest givers of village
feasts despite his belonging to the lower-ranking Goatherd caste
group. In 1951, "at the huge feasts given by I.A.C. in the village
area, the twenty-four castes were invited in order and seated with
punctilious regard for all conceivable distinctions of rank." In 1969,
his heir and grandson called A., now owner of a tractor, silos, and
a large dairy herd, also gives feasts but has succeeded in persuading
even some Jats to accept certain changes in the ritual order at his
feasts. "One recent honored guest at A.'s house, seated in the first
feasting line along with Brahmin and Jat ex-landlord notables of the
village, was an untouchable (of leather-worker caste) official, a frequent helpmate of A. in his technological modernization."[57] In the
17 years between Marriott's visits, the village population had increased by 20 percent, considerably less than the national average,
and perhaps this is not unrelated to its leaders' prosperity and ability
to make suitable ritual adaptations.

THE CARRYING CAPACITY OF INSTITUTIONS

Through much of India, the institutions of village and government
have been pushed beyond their effective carrying capacity, partly because of the larger number of people who are expected to participate
in a particular institution. An institution, as we use the term here,
comprises a set of people who share certain premises, arrange themselves into systemic roles, follow specific procedures in order to
achieve certain purposes together. An institution can be overloaded
by being assigned more functions than its personnel and resources
can fulfill or by covering more people than its carrying capacity can
hold, or it may be strained in both ways at once.

We have already noted some ways in which a joint family may be
overcrowded with people. Despite the common ideal of filial and pa-
ternal solidarity, a joint family is eventually partitioned when it comes
to contain too many married couples for comfort. The carrying ca-

pacity of a joint family varies with the personal authority of the parents, the comity of the brothers and their sons, the nature of their livelihood, and the amount of their income. But sooner or later each joint family's carrying capacity breaks down and the component couples separate. There is some indication of a similar process in the regrouping of village factions. It may be that when a faction grows beyond a certain size, say 50 households, it becomes too difficult for its leaders to manage and tends to split. [58]

Some governmental agencies in India are stretched beyond their efficient carrying capacity. Thus a study of rural Primary Health Centres shows that villagers are generally eager to have the advantages of modern medical care but that the system of delivery of modern health services to them through PHCs is overburdened. For the past two decades a network of over 5,000 such centers has been established, each planned to care for a population of 80,000 to 100,000. D. Banerji (1973) has reported on a study of health services in 13 villages across the country that either have a center located in the village or are not far from one. [59] Each of the centers was above average in its staffing and record of service. The research workers lived in each village for three to five months and interviewed residents from all sectors of the village population. The common image of the dispensary that they found these villagers to have was far from a favorable one: "Complaints about medicines, and over-crowding and long waiting are made even against the best of the PHCs studied." But the difficulties are not only those of sheer numbers of patients. They seem as much to be due to deficiencies in personnel and to the cultural and social gap between patient and health worker. The local health worker and the auxiliary nurse-midwife are seen as "meant for special people or for those who can pay for her services." Lady doctors are seen as even more inaccessible. [60] The research findings, as reported by Banerji, show that "workers of rural health and other development agencies generally have a strong distaste for rural life. This distaste is for the entire rural way of life, and not simply for the very poor facilities available there." Hence they keep their distance from the rural folk among whom they work. This apparently common characteristic naturally limits the effectiveness of the Primary Health Centre as an institution. Banerji states that making quantitative additions to the health services or giving "orientation training" will not remedy this deep-seated malady, which requires sweeping changes in the culture of the bureaucracy. [61]

One of the most overloaded of government agencies in India, in the relation of resources to expected results, is the Family Planning Programme. This effort has become, since 1965, the largest and most active program of its kind in the world. In my view, it has been quite successful in taking certain essential preliminary steps, as in its campaigns to let the people know that contraception is possible, in establishing the infrastructure for production and delivery of contraceptive devices, and in building a large agency.[62] But appraisals of the program, whether done by Indians or others, have pointed out serious shortcomings that have so far hampered the program in meeting the goals that have been set for it. One such shortcoming, noted by Prime Minister Indira Gandhi among others, is that workers in the program have been assigned impossibly high quotas if they are to fulfill them properly. The emphasis on "targetry" has induced these workers to use whatever means possible to achieve the assigned number of interuterine device (IUD) insertions or vasectomies, without much consideration for aftercare, the number of quick removals of IUDS, or the advanced age of many of the vasectomized. Planners were naturally eager to accomplish as much as possible, but the targets they set only swamped the program and helped give it a bad name among many of those who needed to be persuaded.[63]

The report by D. Banerji of the study of rural health services makes some of the harshest of the criticisms of the Family Planning Programme (FPP). The image of the family planning workers in rural areas, the report states, is that of "persons who use coercion and other kinds of pressure tactics and offer bribes to entice people to accept vasectomy or tubectomy." Some of the workers make "pathetic entreaties" to village leaders to give them some cases to help them keep their jobs. "To a large section of the villagers, the inverted red triangle and the workers behind this banner invoke a feeling of strong antipathy."[64]

Nor is this program well thought of by health officials. Banerji tells that "a number of directors of health services (in the respective States) drew attention to the very unfavorable impact of the family planning programme on the rural health services." The staffs of the Primary Health Centres were assigned to help meet the FPP targets, and during the preparation for a mass vasectomy camp, "the entire health work comes to a virtual standstill for over four months preceding a mass camp."[65] Some of these officials produced charts to show that outbreaks of smallpox, cholera, and gastroenteritis synchronized with the organization of the mass camps. The recommendations of this study of rural health services urged immediate action to alter the FPP, to stop further waste of resources, to halt the vasectomy camps, to abolish the "target" system.[66] Some part of this severe critique reflects the expectable response of officials of the long-established health services to a new agency charged with a special mission, allotted large resources, given much publicity, and even drawing other government workers away from their normal duties. Such critiques do not, in my view, make enough allowance for the political pressures on legislators and planners to resolve quickly a problem that can only be eased over a span of years.

A more favorable view of the influence of Primary Health Centres, and one that does take a broader time perspective, is given in Gopinathan Nair's analysis (1974), which finds that there has been a continuing decline of the birthrate in Kerala over the past 10 years. [67] Nair attributes the decline to two circumstances that preceded the full deployment of the Family Programme. One was the success of the Primary Health Centres—despite their manifest shortcomings— in reducing infant mortality. The other was the relatively high degree of education at all levels. Both these factors, Nair suggests, enhanced the response in Kerala to the activities of the Family Planning Programme. Better-educated parents are generally more open to adopting family planning measures. Moreover, the lowered infant mortality may have heightened parents' confidence that fewer births in a family could yet provide enough survivors to adulthood for the parents' later economic and social needs. Nair's inferences from the available statistics on primary school enrollments and other aggregate statistics have to be tested by more detailed and controlled observations, but they do suggest that the social-cultural base is no less significant to the outcome of family planning efforts than are the direct efforts themselves.

EDUCATION AND FERTILITY LIMITATION

One promising avenue toward alleviating the population squeeze is through education. Educated people, especially those who have completed elementary schooling or more, regularly produce a smaller average number of children than those with less education. Indeed, the average fertility rate for women goes down quite consistently as the number of years spent in school (except for the very first years) goes up. A greater amount of education and of family income are generally much more significant in lowering fertility than are such other factors as religion, urban residence, or joint family living. [68] There are, however, special difficulties in the critical matter of education for girls if the girls have to go out of their own village for their schooling. There are also difficulties in maintaining an effective proportion of female teachers. [69]

We have noted that many village parents are strongly motivated to educate at least some of their sons if they can afford to do so. When a number of the boys of a jati come to have some modern education, the parents of girls must give their daughters some education also if they are to be able to arrange marriages for them that will be suitable to the family's status and aspirations. Educational facilities in general are overloaded. One demographic consequence of decades of rising population increase is that a large proportion of the total

population is of school age and requires large public expenditures on
even a modest incidence of school enrollments. Cora Du Bois, in
her article "Schooling, Youth, and Modernization in India" (1973),
has summarized some of the educational problems of so large a youth
cohort: "These problems derive in part from the abrupt and sharp
increase in their numbers that has followed the introduction of improved medical practices. It is also obvious that job opportunities
are scarce for those who have more than a primary schooling."[70]
She notes that, in her field studies in Orissa, she has heard parents
complain repeatedly about the inadequacy of the teachers at the primary and secondary levels. The teachers are "wretchedly paid and
overworked," constrained by formal curricula and outside pressures
to pass their students; they are often strangers to, and suspect in,
the communities in which they teach. Their disaffection is rife.
Among college students, Du Bois observes, the bloated numbers in
many colleges makes for great impersonality in teaching. Indian
students, no less than their counterparts in many other countries, often feel that they are anonymous parts of a disrespected mass. Their
feelings of frustration and deprivation lead some of them to lash out
at the college teachers and administrators. "The concerned parental
authority should not be flouted; but the impersonal authority of institutions is fair game."[71]

As against these well-known criticisms of education in India we
should note that the proportion of the population that has had schooling has steadily been rising at every level of education. Even a low-
quality school experience seems to make a difference in the student's
later behavior, though just why and how is not yet clear.[72] We may
recall the example of the young man of Wangala who came back to the
village with a college degree yet was unable to speak the language in
which most of his college courses were given. Had he been a better
student, he might well have left the village and secured a job in a city.
As it turned out, he remained in Wangala (after an interlude away as
a teacher), and his activities there are to the general benefit of his
family and the good of agricultural production in Wangala. Epstein
deplores the dearth of educational opportunities that are directly
relevant to agricultural improvement.[73]

Education, Professor Warren Ilchman properly reminds us in
his worldwide survey of population knowledge and population policies,
is not a thing but a category. "Fertility possibly varies with the
varied activities that are summarized by the noun education. These
are in different combinations in the life experience of different persons, and the combinations are relevant to policy." Moreover, except for the few studies that deal with willingness of respondents to
accept contraceptives, "there is no specification in these studies about
what in education inclines a former student to regulate his or her
fertility."[74]

Among the many gaps in our knowledge of the social aspects of fertility control in India, one that merits very high priority for research is an examination, through a series of different approaches, of what real effect the school experience has had on the later life patterns of those who have attended schools of various kinds and at different levels. One commentator has stated of higher education that "What it does primarily is change the class affiliation of the subject. He now 'belongs' to the urban white collar class where unemployment is far more severe and the costs of upbringing [are] much greater." So the inclination toward lower fertility of those with higher education comes not from any information they may have gained but from the social experience of the educated unemployed.[75] This may be so but has to be tested against good data, and, further, the more significant questions for population policy are about the effects of primary and secondary schooling on those who have studied only to those levels.

Some of the college graduates who do leave their natal village or town find jobs outside their own state. Unskilled workers, too, pushed by the plethora of people in their home place, migrate in quest of work to other states, especially to the larger cities. Hence, the indigenous residents in many parts of the country have come to resent the migrants, both educated and uneducated, as usurping jobs and other income opportunities, which, they believe, should properly fall to them. This resentment has given rise to "nativist" movements and to political parties dedicated to securing job preferences, especially in government, for indigenous residents. Myron Weiner has discussed this growing political problem, noting that at one level of society, interstate and intercultural migration is an integrating force since it brings together men and women of diverse backgrounds to share membership in modern institutions. But at another level, such migration seems threatening to some both economically and culturally. A difficult dilemma faces those who must cope with the problem. According to Myron Weiner, "The process of development tends to stimulate social mobility within the multi-ethnic society as elsewhere, but in such a society mobility is likely to result in interethnic conflict, nativistic reactions, and violent confrontations."[76]

TRENDS IN CITY AND VILLAGE

This and other problems related to population growth tend to be more vividly seen in cities than in villages. The overload on urban facilities, as in transport, housing, schooling, is readily apparent in many Indian cities. What is not clearly known is the difference in response to increasing numbers as between villager and city-dweller. Perhaps the similarities are as important as the differences. Maloney comments that, "in South Asia, cities grow more by natural increase than by in-migration, and in any case the life style of laboring people born in cities is not much different from that of in-migrant laborers."[77]

In a study comparing Lucknow and Kanpur, Harold Gould (1974) has found that people of all classes in both cities, from ricksha wallahs to business tycoons, tend to differentiate between their occupational pursuits, in which they follow the newer, modern ways, and their domestic life in which traditional modes tend to be maintained.[78] Certain trends seem to be more pronounced in cities than in villages. One example is found in Sylvia Vatuk's study (1972) of two middle-class mohallas in Meerut City.[79] Young wives there are much freer, less bound to and by their husband's family than are young wives in their ancestral villages. A wife at home in these two neighborhoods acts more as a village woman does when she visits her natal home.

Concerning religious practices in cities, Milton Singer has described the rising popularity of devotional bhakti cults in Madras City. These provide city residents, especially newcomers of the higher socioeconomic levels, with a congenial, supportive social group in which they gain benign personal relations, as contrasted with the usual impersonality of the job and the frustrating anonymity of city life in general.[80] Whether these trends are common in other Indian cities and whether they are, in part at least, responses to population growth have yet to be documented.

In their study of slum-dwellers in Vijayawada City, K. Ranga Rao and M. S. A. Rao have found that the people at the bottom of the urban social scale there are well-organized and that each slum area is something like a village with its own socioeconomic and political arrangements. The people maintain traditional caste relations though not as rigidly as in the villages. In the work situation, unions and other occupational groups may command their allegiance, but these often overlap with caste groupings, and in domestic arrangements caste organization is still effective.[81]

It is clear that both in city and village, the caste affiliations of most people typically continue to be of considerable importance in their lives. Through their caste relations, they commonly find their most reliable groups for socialization and support. With the aid of caste ties, they can develop advantageous networks. Common interests of economic class, whether of wage worker or merchant or magnate, do unite people under some circumstances and in some places. Perhaps with increasing numbers of people, the advantages to be derived from caste ties will weaken and class interests may become more important.

From the evidence of both macro- and micro-studies, it appears that the population squeeze among villagers (and perhaps among city-dwellers as well) affects the poor most adversely of all. These are

the 30 to 40 percent of villagers who live in abject poverty. As in
Wangala and Dalena, these poor have generally become poorer than
they were a few decades ago, not only relatively, but also, in a good
part of the country, absolutely. The numbers of these poor and their
proportion in the population are growing, both through natural increase
and by the addition of former landowners who have lost their land.
As these ill-nourished people become hungrier still, their productivity declines because of illness and lack of strength, and they are liable to get fewer and fewer opportunities for work. Moreover, the demand for agricultural labor has tended to decline as landowners have
to put more of their land into subsistence crops to feed their own families and as they rationalize the cultivation of cash crops.

The desperate state of these poor, if the Wangala and Dalena
examples are indicative, tends to make them clutch more tightly to
whatever they may have as a means of livelihood. While they may be
open to radical religious movements, they seem now to be in no position to give impetus to radical political movements of right or left.

At the other end of the village economic scale are those like
the successful cultivators sketched by Marriott and the "magnates"
of Wangala and Dalena. These farmers have benefited by the government's efforts and by the new economic opportunities to improve
their standard of living and, even more, to build up their capital assets. Some of their families, however, must cope with the frustrations of hope fulfilled, of having many sons. If the father's authority
and the brothers' amity fails, then each son may find himself inheriting a portion too small for comfort, too little to feed his family adequately. Those of the sons who do well enough in their studies to get
a university degree and move to town, may find themselves without a
job or with one in which the frustration is as great as the pay is small.
The numbers of such people is also growing apace. Not many of them
set up "share families" for social security as do town workers from
Dalena. Not very many can find total satisfaction in a religious movement. They are more inclined to fix their hopes for economic salva-
tion on political solutions. But whatever solutions are sought, at
every level of Indian society, the fundamental problems have been,
and are being, exacerbated by the flood of obstetrical immigrants.

DISCUSSION

Morris Carstairs: One of the striking contributions of this paper is
to draw our attention to the slippery slope on which the smaller cultivator finds himself when his debts tip over a certain scale; when he
finds he can no longer remain a common cultivator and has to join
the growing army of the landless laborers. We are reminded that the

constraints of capital investments—in water, machinery, credit, and fertilizer—limit the capabilities of the Green Revolution.

This meeting is taking place just after the Rome Food Conference of the United Nations and Food and Agricultural Organization (FAO). Consequently, during the last 10 days I have been watching the reports coming out of the Rome conference, and I was particularly impressed by an introductory paper by Barbara Ward in the Economist. She was talking about population increase in general and the factors correlated with a decline in population increase in particular. She says that population control programs have played a minimal role. There are, however, certain identifiable social correlates of population decline. It occurs only when developing countries have attained a certain level of health care and education for the great mass of the population and, more important, when members of local communities have acquired a degree of participatory involvement in local affairs, so that they have a measure of control over the well-being of their families and of their community. There are examples of countries where this has been obtainable to a small degree and of others where it has been obtainable to a large degree. At any rate, these are the preconditions for the establishment of a population program.

David Mandelbaum has reminded us that, in the vast bulk of the territory of India today, these preconditions do not exist. The rewards of having a large family are still much more important than the persuasion of the family planning programmers. David also illustrates what I think most of us know only too well, namely the fact that village life in India is characterized by fierce competition for wealth and status. In that context, the extended kinship members of the jati are indeed protective of their families. When hard times come their protection is particularly valuable. David has reminded us that the jajmani system involves nonjati members and nonfamily members in a relationship that is akin to the responsibility of the wealth toward their employees. Quite a few services are now being paid for in cash in a substitution for the jajmani system.

But again and again one comes across the stumbling block, that the jati and the extended family, though good for their members, are not very good for cooperation. When one looks for efficient collaboration and cooperation, the obstacles of long-standing inheritance disputes and distrust between families and communities take precedence. People are reluctant to share their bullocks. They are reluctant to join together in drilling a deep tube-well and prefer that each family own a shallow tube-well, and thus economic progress is impeded. Economic progress is also impeded by the splintering of landholdings through inheritance, which finally reaches the point where inheritors find it impossible to survive because their share of land is not large enough.

At the same time there is a growth of interest groups; for example in the irrigated village there is a clear example that the wealthy
landholders are becoming stronger. They are a minority, but a tough
minority and a prosperous one. As I read about this in David Mandelbaum's paper I was immediately reminded of the Russian phenomenon
of the kulaks. You remember the kulak was the large landowner who
was seen as an obstacle to both cooperative development of agriculture and to the development of the Marxist economy. The kulaks were
the rural equivalent of the predominantly urban middle classes, people who have a stake in a partly developed society.

Until now the Indian middle class has been a privileged group,
far removed from village life. Because of its higher educational and
economic status its members constitute a strong point in Indian society; and yet they are threatened. They are threatened by this wave
of "obstetrical immigrants" to which David made passing reference.
I suggest that it is this middle class that is most keenly aware of the
impending threat of disaster. The better-off landlords, for their
part, are the most keenly aware of a much closer threat of outbreaks
of local unrest—lootings, burnings, sacking of storage sheds, that
sort of thing. The masses themselves, however, particularly the
landless laborers who are the first to feel the pinch when the rains
fail, are also the first to know when hunger becomes starvation. They
are fearful and bewildered and quick to explode—or so it seems to me,
reading the Indian press.

There have been a number of references recently to the situation in West Bengal in 1943 and to the famine of that year that killed
5 million people. I'd like to suggest that the great difference between
today and 1942-43 is the heightened awareness of the villager. He's
still poor, he's still illiterate, but the ratio and the political activity
of 25 years of independence have very considerably widened his horizons. For example, when I revisit the Rajasthan village that I lived
in in 1950, I find the villagers sitting around the radio listening to
the six o'clock news. This was inconceivable 25 years ago. Of
course, they didn't have a radio in the first place, and they weren't
the least bit interested in the radio or in news of the outer world.

Frankly, I'm a doomster. It seems to me that the threat is
mounting, that catastrophe is on its way. I believed this to be so 20
years ago; already at that time the geometrical progression of population, contrasted with the much slower growth of food supplies, argued
inexorably that something terrible was going to happen. In recent
years I have increasingly become persuaded that this "something terrible" is becoming imminent. In this setting of impending catastrophe
it's often seemed to me that the stage is set for social upheavals of
a destructive nature. It's not at all unlikely that the situation in European history, as described in numerous illustrations by Norman Cohn

in his book The Pursuit of the Millennium, may be repeated in India
in the near future. He describes episodes where there were sudden
natural disasters or very rapid periods of social change (sometimes
accelerated by natural catastrophes like famines, floods, or outbreaks
of plague) in which whole groups of people found themselves deprived
of their customary support and security. At such times one found
bands of hungry landless laborers roaming in northern Europe. This
was the social context in which millennial movements arose; prophets
emerged, preaching a magical solution to all woes, the dawn of a millennium in which every individual would share the boundless riches
of the earth.

Cohn was prompted to survey the history of millennial movements by his experience of Hitler, and by Hitler's proclamation of the
thousand-year Reich, his promises of plenty for the elect, for those
of his race. But when one studies the relevance of that historical review to contemporary events in India, he is compelled to realize that
one can have a millennial movement and a millennial expectation only
in the context of particular cultural and religious beliefs—such as the
Jewish, the Christian, and especially I suppose, the Muslim beliefs—
in a heaven, a heaven that is often expressed in terms of a terrestrial
life, but one embodying the realization of wish-fulfillment. There is
no similar expectation in Hinduism. Hindus believe in the continuity
of life, certainly, but not in a revival of the individual personality,
not in the simple rewards of ministering angels and material plenty.

So perhaps a Hindu culture does not provide a fertile soil for
the prophet who preaches that the millennium is about to dawn, promising his followers immediate entry into a heavenly existence. Nor
is it likely that Hindus will be quite so ready to enlist in a jihad, a
holy war in which you are justified in taking risks with your life because you are instantly rewarded with the fruits of the hereafter.
Speaking as a nonreligious person, it often seems to me that religion's
function is to allay the human cognizance of meaninglessness—meaninglessness in one's individual existence, meaninglessness in the existence of the human race or even of the universe. A great many religions have offered this antidote to the threat of meaninglessness in an
optimistic consoling way, and that's why Marx referred to them as the
opiate of the people. But Hinduism, among all religions, is singularly
all-encompassing. Its pantheon embraces horrors and demons as
well as benevolent goddesses and gods. It's perfectly capably of
thriving in a cataclysm, in a catastrophe, because this too is part of
Hinduism.

The drawback, of course, lies in its stress on the puny power-
lessness of the individual, and of the human community. The only
context in which a human acquires power is in stepping away from
worldly things in tapas, in withdrawal into the spiritual. That doesn't

help very much the practical politician who's grappling with a materially difficult situation.

What can we expect when this cataclysm is actually upon us? (And I don't think many years are going to go before it will actually be upon us.) On the one hand, we can expect some desperate anarchic local upheavals among the starving, looting of the warehouses, and attacks on the merchants where they have any foodstuffs left in store. But where will constructive leadership emerge? I suggest—and I'm looking forward to correction from other points of view—that the only place it's likely to emerge will be from among those who have got something to lose, from among the wealthy landowners and the middle classes. It's not at all dissimilar to the desperate state of Germany in the 1920s in the aftermath of that wild inflation, with everyone suffering from a desperate insecurity about their own security and the future of their families. They were ripe for radical remedies.

The remedy they turned to, of course, was Adolf Hitler. It wouldn't be too surprising if India had a phase in the immediate future of becoming a police state or a military dictatorship—the two usually go hand in hand. I would like to say, however, that even if this does come about it's likely to be a temporary phenomenon, although "temporary" may prove to be as long as the regime of a Salazar or a Franco. But I still say, even if it lasts for a generation, it will be a temporary phenomenon; and I say this for two principal reasons. This police state would inherit a legacy of Indian society to which David Mandelbaum has referred, the legacy of factions; it would also inherit the tendency to tolerate corruption because corruption on the positive side means protecting your own. It's not just individual selfishness; it's protecting your kith and kin. That's why corruption is looked upon somewhat differently in Indian eyes than it is in Western eyes. Both corruption and mutual distrust due to factionalism are likely to be there in a police state in India, and both tend to undermine a police state. Eventually social inequality and private peculation lead to social upheaval and rejection, as we've seen during the last year in Portugal and in Greece.

The other reason that I think this police state, if it occurs, will be a transient phenomenon is the spirit of criticism that the educated classes in India have known and cherished, both during the last decades of the British Raj, when there was such vigorous criticism and challenge to the regime, and also in the period since Independence. You will agree that one thing that is always refreshing to the visitor is the straight and lively—indeed, cheeky—comment of the Indian press, which is still fortunately able to express itself freely and independently. Even if that were suppressed by a police state I believe that its memory would be retained for a generation and would eventually lead to the demise of the police state.

In summary, therefore, my perusal of David Mandelbaum's paper, and of the other papers circulated, has only increased my belief that inevitable population increase is going to lead to food shortages of catastrophic proportions within the next 10 years. I think it only too probable that we shall witness famines and local breakdowns of law and order, which will give rise to the emergence of a dictatorial regime, perhaps for a generation. At the same time, I share the faith, expressed by several contributors, in the Indian people's extraordinary capacity to endure privations and to survive.

Milton Singer: It's hard to follow the moving and sobering point of view that Morris Carstairs has presented. Morris Carstairs may be right. I really don't know. I would like to return to a somewhat more pedestrian level.

Professor Mandelbaum's paper makes a case for the role of the anthropologist and the microscopic, if not myopic, point of view—that is, the intensive observation of small numbers of people in the village or the family or an urban neighborhood, as a way of seeing the problems of population change in the context of social and cultural factors. The family, the kith and kin, the jati, the village itself, class, these, and other factors operate at the local level. I think this is a point of view that can contribute some very important insights into these problems, not ordinarily included in the statistical surveys and the analyses of the statisticians, economists, political scientists, or macro-sociologists.

In 1954 on my first trip to India I attended a conference in Poona, at which some very distinguished people, including some of Gadgil's economists and statisticians, were present. One of the economists, a very able young man, teased the anthropologists by saying, "Why do you spend your time studying these village superstitions and all this unimportant activity, instead of coming to grips with the important problems that have to be solved?" This challenge is constantly put to anthropologists. But those who study at the local level, as David Mandelbaum's book shows, can make important contributions. These studies give understanding of the nature of a person's motivations for having children or not having children, the importance of sons, as that motivation is mediated for individuals, for families, for groups, by the prevailing social and cultural values in which those individuals live. These motivations are not easily identified or understood through purely statistical studies or other kinds of macro-studies.

One problem often raised in India is why villagers in need of funds will go to the money-lender to get such funds when he charges them exorbitant rates of interest, instead of going to a cooperative or some government credit source. I think R. K. Narayan's novel The

Financial Expert answers that question. It comes out so clearly in Narayan's novel that the farmer has a personal source of contact; the money-lender sitting under the banyan tree knows his relatives, and he knows his immediate needs and can talk in a way that the more formal and organized channels cannot. While I know Narayan would not claim to be an anthropologist, I think he does achieve, on the basis of his knowledge of Malgudi, the sort of insight many anthropologists strive for in their microscopic studies.

These are the kinds of problems that Mandelbaum has raised in his book and in his paper. I don't mean in any way to suggest that the statistician and the survey are not important. They certainly are. If a government or a country is to deal with these massive problems, it certainly must know how to add and multiply and divide, and get the aggregate figures. What I am suggesting is that it is very difficult to evaluate and understand what those aggregate figures mean in human terms—that is, in terms of interpersonal motivations and the relationships of motivations to behavior—unless one has some of the intensive microscopic studies that provide just that context in which we can see individual human beings trying to cope with such massive problems.

David Mandelbaum does concentrate on the village scene, as he should, since about 80 percent of India's population lives there. He makes one or two references to the urban scene and to my own studies in Madras, to the adaptations of the Madras businessmen and industrialists whom I interviewed. Perhaps I could expand that reference a bit, focusing especially on the population question. That is foremost in this conference. This material is in my book, When a Great Tradition Modernizes, to which David referred.

When I wrote that book, I was not concentrating on the population problem; I was concentrating on how modernization leads people to adapt their religious and cultural values. I would like, by way of a dramatic contrast, to compare the attitude of an indigenous doctor who operated a free dispensary in one of the Madras suburbs in 1954, with the attitudes of some of the industrialists and businessmen whom I interviewed on my third trip in 1964. In 1954, on my first trip to Madras, I had an opportunity to meet and observe this indigenous doctor, who had been trained in the College of Indigenous Medicine in Madras, which at that time provided an education of about 40 percent modern medicine and 60 percent indigenous medicine. He was an able, well-trained, and public-spirited man who had organized health and education services, distributed pamphlets, and devoted a great deal of his time to the free dispensary. He also had organized a pharmaceutical company to manufacture indigenous drugs. He was, of course, very sympathetic to Ayurvedic medicine and to other forms of indigenous medicine.

When I talked to this man about family planning, population, and birth control, he was obviously convinced of a necessity for some form of family planning and some form of birth control, and he himself had only one child. So far as his patients were concerned, he said they had too many children. When asked whether he gave them any birth control information, he said he didn't and he seemed embarrassed by the conversation. I asked why not, and he said, they do not know about such things. And then he went on to say that many believe birth control is a sin because Manu says it is necessary to propagate.

The doctor's reply seemed in such contrast to all of his other commitments and activities in the fields of modern health care, until I realized that he was a very religious man. He was a Brahman and frequently passed out to his patients books of prayers he had obtained from one of the most influential religious leaders of South India, Shankara Acharya. I was puzzled by this dual existence of an apparently well-trained, educated doctor, committed to improving the health of the poor, yet doing it with a whole body of beliefs and restraints that limited his directions and activities, especially when it came to birth control information.

I found later that this was a general problem and that this kind of coexistence of modern and traditional factors in Madras clearly needed further research. Much of my further research and reflection on this general problem continued, at least over a 10-year period. I went back to Madras in 1960–61 and again in 1964. In 1964 I intensively interviewed 19 different industrialists and found that there was quite a striking contrast to the ayurvedic doctor in their willingness to talk about family planning and population problems. One of these industrialists, for example, had had himself sterilized and had been responsible for persuading the male members of his family to sterilize themselves, as well as about 3,000 of his employees. I couldn't get him to describe to me exactly what methods of persuasion he used.

Another striking thing was that these industrialists as a group averaged one to three children; at least this was true for 17 out of 18 for whom I had information. Only one out of 18 had more children than his father had had; he was an only child, and he had eight children. In the other cases, 17 out of 18, their fathers had had on the average five to eight children. Practically speaking, the number of children in these families was halved in one generation. Almost all of the industrial leaders believed in some form of birth control and family planning.

You might say, yes, but these were educated urban people, and a far cry from the villages that Mandelbaum is talking about. This example holds a very important set of lessons for us because, when you look at the families, they are not so different from the villagers. In fact, practically all the industrialists to whom I talked were born and brought up in a village or in a small town and had moved to Madras within one generation. So they are not far removed from the village environment we have been talking about. They represent in a way the trend of the future, the pace-setters; by looking at them we may find some reason for hope and perhaps a less cataclysmic future than that perceived by Morris Carstairs.

I want also to mention that these people were not secularized. Sixteen were Hindus; two were Muslims; and one was a Syrian Christian. They did not abandon their religious and ethical beliefs and practices. They changed these in important ways; they were much less ritualistic and much less given to Sanskrit and scriptural studies. They tended to be much more devotional, much more in favor of bhakti. They also tended toward a religion of faith and revival. But they generally drew upon either orthodox religious sources, such as Sankara Acharya, or a kind of Gandhian ethic and philosophy.

One of the industrialists said, "Poverty anywhere is a danger everywhere." When I talked to him about this, since it struck me as a very unusual statement, particularly coming from a wealthy and successful industrialist, he indicated that he had been influenced by Gandhi and that he tried to help the poor. He gives 25 percent of his income to charities for the poor, and if he can't help the poor at least he tries not to do them any harm, which I think is a good Hindu interpretation of Gandhi's version of nonviolence and ahimsa. I also think it's a much better rule than any that came out of the Rome Food Conference.

This Gandhian attitude, while somewhat exceptional in formulation in the case of this one industrialist, was not at all exceptional in terms of the general tendency of these industrialists sincerely to try and formulate an ethical code for their own conduct and their behavior toward other people. They were interested in assuring some sort of quality control, more jobs, and better living standards for people. The one conclusion I came away with was that this kind of coexistence of traditional attitudes and modern features, such as had puzzled me so much on my first trip, was more or less a standard condition, not a temporary condition—a standard persisting tradition among these and other groups in Madras. They were succeeding in reinterpreting, in the case of Hinduism, the traditional ideas of Dharma (religious duty), Samsara (rebirth), even Moksha (release) in terms of what they were doing as industrialists and businessmen. They believed they could fulfill their ethical and religious duties by being better industrialists, providing more jobs, more goods, and higher standards of living for people, and they did not feel any schizophrenic conflict in the process.

I asked several of them, "Don't you believe in yuga cycles? Don't you believe this is the kali yuga—a degenerate, immoral age?"

They said, "Yes, we know about the yugas, of course, but that's at a different level of reality; there can be no doubt about it, since 1947 India has made tremendous progress in all fields, and it's unthinkable that these trends are going to be reversed." I emphasize this because we tend to forget that there are people with ancient cultures who are adapting and coping with tremendous modern problems. From the humane anthropological point of view we must not forget these people, and if you don't have time to read anthropologists by all means read R. K. Narayan's novels on Malgudi.

Beba Varadachar: This is a very provocative paper that Professor Mandelbaum has written. Two broad things came to my mind when I read through it. The first is the question of what has been called moral or value stretch, and the second has to do with the role of God in village societies.

I will give you an example of what I mean by value stretch. When I was collecting data in the slums of Madras about six months ago, I spent some time with a Brahman—a Brahman who ate no meat, who was a proper vegetarian, who followed all of the caste rituals, who was not even close to the kind of person that Professor Singer was talking about. This man was a certified Brahman in every respect: He had a caste mark, wore a dhoti, and so on. I saw him about four months ago, taking his motorcycle all the way to a village about 40 miles from Madras. He came back around four o'clock in the evening and his entire motorcycle was covered with blood. I asked him what in heaven's name had happened? Who did you hit? He told me that he was going to enter into a new kind of business, having to do with exporting incense sticks to the United States and the United Kingdom, and he didn't want to have any failures of any kind. Someone told him that he should go to a village where there was a shaman who was going to butcher a buffalo, and that, if the blood fell on the front fender or the right side of the front wheel of his motorcycle his business would prosper, so long as it happened on a Tuesday. So he had gone to the village of the shaman. Thisman, who had a buffalo sacrifice performed to his motorcycle in 1974, is an example of someone engaged in a process that can be called value stretch.

My second concern has to do with God and morality. When you go to people in India's slums and ask, "How did this child come to be?" they are likely to say simply, "It was born: God gave me this child." If you ask an unwed mother, "Well, you do not have a husband; was it a mistake?" she is likely to say, "The first child, if it is born out of wedlock, is a mistake; but the second time such a thing occurs it is a bigger sin. If it occurs a third time, again out of wedlock, it is simply stupid." Here you have a series of differentiated responses, which contrast with the likely responses of the middle class. If you

go to middle-class respondents and ask, "Why did you have a child
out of wedlock?" the middle-class person will usually answer, "It
was wrong; it was bad." This is public morality among the middle
class—straightforward bad and straightforward good. If you go to
the villages and collect data, and you keep questionnaires, it is very
important to bear in mind that the inner logic, the world view of the
villager, is not simple and sharp. There are many series of grada-
tions.

On this score, there are three generalizations that I got out of
Professor Mandelbaum's paper: One is that part of the villagers'
world view is that land is power; land governs a great many things.
A second is that the villager is not concerned about national policies
and programs because his primary loyalty, his immediate concern,
is with his family and perhaps his jati. For a villager to think of a
nation, about a five-year plan, and so forth, is asking too much.
One has to be highly conscious of cognitive factors. A third thing is,
perhaps a small point, we do not pay enough attention to the fact that
the brain cells of the villager probably fire off very differently from
ours. We have to understand the language of the villager, the urban-
dweller, the slum-dweller. Just because I am an Indian does not
give me any special entree. In fact I have a feeling that some of you
who have had a long, long love affair with India would be much better
equipped to deal with these questions. I have a feeling that the first
thing I must do is to unlearn much of what I have learned in the past,
if not most of what I have learned in the past.

The village, from a cognitive point of view, has not been mapped.
All we have are a series of opinions, answers to questionnaires, information from records, and some notations about what villagers
have said. This is not to say that the data that anthropologists have
collected are totally useless, but on themes like morality, or attitudes
toward fertility and sex, or attitudes toward various rituals, I do not
think that we have decoded what villagers are trying to say. In fact,
I am sure that some of the villagers do not have anything to say on
these things; at least many do not say anything.

In order to decode the cognitive map of the villager I would like
to introduce here a person who has been ignored in much of the literature. The person that is missing from much of the literature, and
especially literature on family planning and population control, is God.
During all sorts of crises, during really critical moments when a man
is hit financially, spiritually, or morally, the one person with whom
he has a series of soliloquies of sorts is a god. Any of you who have
spent any time in or near or anywhere around a temple know that all
sorts of propitiations occur there; God is constantly being approached
for relief, and usually for immediate relief.

The kind of dialogue that goes on between a peasant and God is fascinating. That to me is another language, another world view, another domain, another cognitive dimension, which I think, again, will tell us more about the kinds of problems that Professor Mandelbaum has surveyed. In other words, I would like to see God brought into this conference, as an informant, as a villager, and as a respondent. For God is a villager in his own right. Professor Srinivas is trying to struggle with this in his latest book, <u>The Remembered Village</u>, where he devotes a chapter to what he calls "Man God."

There is one further comment that I would like to make at this point. In most of our discussions, even if we are inclined to say that we are not going to look at population as a problem, I still feel an enormous pull in that direction. We have been almost brainwashed into thinking about population as a problem in terms of fertility. In order to change our way of thinking we must ask the question "Can we look at society from the bottom up rather than from the top down?" as policy planners do. The trickle down now is from the policy planners, from the social scientists, from the government, to the village, and, at least in a numerical sense, to the individual peasant. What we must map is a different kind of journey.

I may be wrong, but when Professor Mandelbaum says that the people of Wangala have maintained more of a moral community than the people of Dalena, he is referring to the fact that rituals are being abandoned in Dalena. Is it possible that villagers in Dalena are not abandoning anything but are simply evolving a different set of moral norms? Is it possible to describe what is happening without using the word "abandoned"? It seems to me that an alternative here is that villagers have not abandoned any moral norms and that there are not two distinct moral communities. Could it be that there has simply been value stretch, to a different kind of moral parameter? If I can take the extreme view—just to provoke discussion—is it possible that the population explosion, or whatever word you want to use for it, is not a problem but is instead a solution to a problem, if you look at it from the bottom up.

In my village it is a solution to a problem, whereas you keep coming and telling me that it is a problem itself. It may be a problem to you because you are a policy-maker who wants to sell me some birth control pills or you want to change the face of the village. Could it be possible that what you are looking at as a problem is not indeed a problem but a solution to a problem?

Anrudh Jain: What then is the problem?

Varadachar: The problem is existence, survival; it is gathering wood or making cow dung cakes or trying to beat the next man in the litiga-

tion cycle, or whatever. Is it possible that some of the things we define as a problem are solutions to a problem when you look at it from
the point of view of the villager?

If this is the case, then, in terms of that perception there may
be no "abandonment" of roles, parameters, values, and so on. These
things are simply being stretched, these things are being shifted,
these things are being reinterpreted, to fit in with basic daily crises
as well as long-range crises.

I do believe the peasant is not a stupid fool. He has his own
ideas, his own language, his own inner logic, his own cognitive maps,
and if you decode that language and that world view, you will see that
he is not doing badly. If you can find a way to talk to him, you might
tell him that you have this population problem and this five-year plan.
He will understand. He knows this. He has dealt with this. In fact,
as Professor Mandelbaum points out in his paper, villagers are in the
habit of dealing with spacing and controlling families. They are also
familiar with foregoing things when they have many children. The
villager also is capable of looking at things from an economic point
of view, both in short-range and long-range terms. He is familiar
with doubling changes and with wealth and status changes. The villager may not be as much of a peasant as we think he is.

P. M. Belliappa: Do you assume that, in light of your remarks here,
the government's programs have not had any impact on the slums?

Varadachar: No. I would not say that. It is clear that these things
must go on, and, as Professor Mandelbaum has pointed out, there is
recognition of some success. I am just attaching a rider. These
things should go on, and probably they will pay off later. In fact,
they are probably paying off in certain areas right now. But, we
should simultaneously strive to listen to the villager. We should not
take the attitude that from me only flows knowledge. We should say,
let us have some knowledge from you too.

John Mellor: My intent is to keep the discussion going along the lines
that were set out for us this morning. I would like to give what with
all modesty I would call an economist's perception of the problem. A
quick reading of Professor Mandelbaum's paper suggests a number of
contradictions. A more careful reading might resolve these. In particular, one gets the view, especially in the early pages, that in all
social groupings, there is a rationality operating for large family
size. On the one hand this is discouraging, but interesting. On the
other hand, one sees later that there is a great deal of variation in
family-spacing practice among various groupings and perhaps that
raises some hope. It becomes a question of what it takes to get the

practice of lower fertility. A lot of people now hold the view, which
I tend to hold, that in some very complex way participation in what I
would call modernization, or a process of rising incomes, gives a
family a greater feeling that it can control its own destiny. That set
of processes is not seen in general to be associated with high fertility. It's also my view that the most efficient strategy for growth, providing a high proportion of the population with some sense of control
of its own destiny, is a strategy that has a very major emphasis on
increasing agricultural production and development of the rural sector, and, associated with that, a complementary strategy focusing on
medium and small industries.

I take it Professor Singer was talking about these kinds of things
in Madras. I think that there is some logic for this: This is a pattern
of economic development that is not very much different from the
strategy followed by Japan and Taiwan and a number of other countries.
If one buys the argument for that strategy, then one would like to raise
the question within that context, which may be generally favorable for
declining fertility, what can we do to accelerate changes in—I hesitate to call them values—what can be done to accelerate change in
"values" of the various socioeconomic groups that are participating
in this process?

In this connection, I want to emphasize one point. At least
from the readings in the literature in the West, we have had a view
of demographic change in the context of rapid economic development,
with an emphasis on large-scale urbanization but without a great deal
of emphasis on what might be happening in the rural areas. What I
am suggesting is the possibility that an efficient strategy for the
groups that we're talking about may need relatively more emphasis
on the rural sector and small- and medium-scale industry than we
have generally been aware of. I suspect there has been more of that
in practice than the literature has reflected. Perhaps we need even
less emphasis on the process of large-scale megalopolis-type urbanization and much more again on the small industrial side.

But what happens to labor forces in that kind of a strategy?
What happens to the peasant? I see the answers to such questions as
a complex set of different responses for separate classes with separate sets of problems; there are things to be learned about each of
them. Most important, however, and I'm sorry if this offends some
of you, analysis and study of such questions become relevant only when
the economic strategy is such that the mass of people are beginning
to participate in a process that does give them some sense of control
of their destiny. Until that happens, it seems to me that this subject
is not going to be very helpful to us.

Robert Cassen: One of the things that seems to me relevant this morning is that most people who have conducted resurveys always find that things have got worse. Someone undertakes a survey in Madras in the 1920s and comes back in the 1940s and finds that everything has got worse or that very few things have got better. The same is true of Scarlett Epstein's study, and the same is true of many of these resurveys of Indian villages. It always reminds me of the story that I was told, and many Englishmen are told when they go out to India for the first time, of the young clergyman who in Victorian days had been sent to a village in Bihar, and his saying that "this village has been subject to centuries of corruption and decay; I have arrived in the nick of time." When I hear people talk of impending crises, I always try to put it in this sort of perspective.

The most difficult thing to do is to perceive where there is some critical threshold beyond which you cannot go. Gilbert Etienne in his book came to the conclusion that the farmers in his village had about 10 years to go and the surplus they managed to generate was just enough to reinvest to cope with the increase in numbers. He was honest enough to put down just before this book was printed, "I had an opportunity to re-visit these villages and found agricultural productivity increasing considerably." In other words, he did not find that things had deteriorated nearly as much as he thought they would.

Now in some sense you know that population cannot go on expanding forever. In a 100 years at the present rate India would have five times the population of the world, and we know that this is not going to happen. The question is, "How is it not going to happen?" By what process is this not going to come about? There are an enormous number of ways in which the situation is adjusting at present. Improvements in technology give an additional ability to sustain growing numbers. Then there are rather obnoxious things, like an increase in mortality, which is going on at the present moment. Mortality has stopped falling, and it has now reached a sort of plateau, around which it fluctuates. There are many things that can happen. It is possible to create employment for people. There are many positive forces, but there are also many negative ones. It seems to me that although we feel that some crisis is impending, we cannot see, and nothing that anybody has written can identify, where it is going to run into some culminating upheaval. It is just not visible.

We can see all kinds of stresses and strains and all sorts of responses to these positive and negative forces. But it does seem to me that the most important fact is that it is very unlikely, in situations where family formation is governed to a considerable extent traditionally, that birthrates will begin to come down until the community itself feels responsible for its own numbers. And this is really the question of the entire village in relation to the whole society.

We have frequently heard that parents think that it is in their
interest to have large numbers of children. Yet, we know that, for
many families, possibilities of employment for their children is very
limited. In Scarlett Epstein's study, for example, there were very
few possibilities of additional employment except outside the village.
The prospect inside the village is dreadful. Why, then, are they having such large numbers of children? I think this is where the contradictions may be looked at with some benefit.

The villages are what is growing. The urban areas in India are
not expanding all that rapidly, so that the increase in the population
is being carried in the villages. One of the speakers has said that
parents say that a large number of children is their solution. Is it?
If they have a large number of sons, and if their sons become employed, then they may prosper as a result of their large number of
children. But, half of their children are not sons, they are daughters,
and a high proportion of the sons are not going to be employed. So,
what is the family really thinking about when it wants a large number
of children? What are the parents thinking about? Are they really
thinking about the welfare of the children or of themselves or the
family as a whole?

We know what the result is. Nutrition studies show that a dis-
proportionate number of female children show symptoms of malnutrition; female death rates are higher than male death rates. So it may
well be the case that ex ante, that is before the decision to have children, parents may feel that they will be better off, but ex post they
may not feel so unless they have males. Of course, females can be
employed in certain circumstances. Females also contribute within
the family, of course. In fact, then, considering their children's
welfare, parents would probably have relatively few children. There
would be fewer children among whom to divide up the family land, if
there is any land. They could feed and educate a smaller number of
children better. So I find this one of the deepest sources of confusion.

This contradiction is evident from a great deal of experience.
Mamdani, in The Myth of Population Control, said that parents wanted
large families. But who are these hundreds of thousands of Punjabi
women who have taken IUDs, who are having abortions? Who are the
men entering the family planning programs for vasectomies? These
are very difficult questions. It's one of my disappointments that, in
Professor Mandelbaum's paper, he points to all the factors but leaves
us with this mass of contradictions and with the question, "What do
they all add up to?" Some things are pushing in a positive direction,
some in a negative direction. There are encouraging and discouraging patterns. Some people are having more, and some people are
having fewer, children. But what is the sum?

The sum, at the moment, is about six children per marriage. The sum is also declining. But the family planning experience has not yet shown much in the way of conclusions. It has shown what a badly organized family planning program, with unsatisfactory contraceptive techniques, can do in circumstances of mass poverty. I think the situation one of immense complexity, and I think our job here is to try and see where these things finally are pointing, not to throw up our hands and say, "There are catastrophes and horrors."

Mandelbaum: We are not now in a position to give certain of these critical answers. What we can do is to stimulate research on these problems. However, there are some questions for which we have some clues. For example, why do the Harijans, on the average, have more children than do their higher-ranking and wealthier neighbors? There is much higher infant mortality among Harijans, and this has both psychological and physiological effects. If a woman loses her child in the first week of its life, she begins to ovulate sooner than if she were nursing an infant. Hence she doesn't have as long a spacing period between pregnancies. A poor woman tends to bear children later in her life than the wealthier women do, partly because of the higher infant mortality she experiences. We should also note again that in such villages as Wangala and Dalena, everything hasn't got worse. Indeed, half of the people are better off than they ever were before.

Joseph Elder: The assumption that children are wanted simply because there are many children in the family gives me an uneasy feeling, on the basis of my own two years' experience in a village. I think that the patent fact that so many children born were not wanted, or were not planned—perhaps explained after the fact by reference to fate—should in no way lead us to believe that this was seen in anticipation as something deemed by fate. It may, after the fact, be seen as God's gift, or as fate, or it may be explained in that way. But it is also seen as a bad break, and people are, very often, unhappy that they have had another child.

   In this context, I was struck by the fact that the village in which I lived was well aware of the dramatic cases where there were too many children and where this had broken a family. Villagers could point to people right there and say that a generation ago that was a big and powerful family, and now look what's happened. They've had too many children, and their inheritance was divided. So, I would just like to raise the question that has been raised, What really is the extent to which there is planning? What is the result of a lack of information, a lack of utilization? What is the extent of the gap between the information and the utilization of contraceptive techniques? There

are a whole series of questions that we don't really have the answers
for.

To assume that people in India are planning to have six or seven
children on the average seems to me an error, and I want to speak as
a villager against that. In the United States, for example, we have
discovered that something like one out of three children were not
planned. Now that abortion is possible, we discover a sharp drop-off
in certain areas, which reflects a new possibility to terminate a pregnancy in the case of an unwanted child.

There is another point I want to raise that may take us a bit
afield. This deals with the question of pilgrimage and the effect of
population growth on pilgrimage. We just finished a documentary film,
on a pilgrimage center in Rajasthan that has blossomed in the last 15
years. This was the pilgrimage center of a small cult that had gone
on from 1520 until the 1900s with very little growth. Suddenly, over
the last two decades, it has become a very large operation, with buses
and trains bringing people in daily, and so on. I wonder if this is occurring elsewhere in India. The people who are coming are middle
and lower class, urban and rural people who, perhaps, feel out of
place in Rishikesh or Hardwar or some of the classic centers of pilgrimage, but they still come to this Ram Deva shrine. Muslims can
go, Harijans can go, and I was curious if this was a wider phenomenon.
It occurred to me that, as there were more people, a small center
may begin to attract those who, in a sense, are not intended to go to
larger centers. This means we may have something between the so-
called little tradition and the great tradition, something that has to do
with the state or the linguistic area.

Singer: I would like to support what Joe Elder and others have said.
We do hear it often said that villagers have a desire for sons. Among
the businessmen and industrialists I interviewed in Madras, many of
them did point to the great value of having five or six sons. They said
that with several sons they could raise one son to be an engineer, another to be a finance pundit, another to be a good business administra-
tor, and then could build a tightly knit, tightly controlled family industry. In some cases they complained that they did not have enough
sons and had to take in nephews, if they were available, and, in extreme cases, with great reluctance, they might take a son-in-law or
two into the business. To have sons, therefore, was for these modern
industrialists a strong motivational factor. And yet only one out of 18
of these had as many as eight children. The others, in spite of a
strong economic motivation for having more sons, did not go beyond
two or three children in each family. So, obviously, there are many
other factors that influence these decisions and influence fertility as
well, and probably most of them are still unknown to us.

Perhaps it is a mistake to try and isolate single variables involved in people's decisions about family size. I am reminded of the famous Hawthorne experiment at the Western Electric plant in Cicero, Illinois, done under Elton Mayo's direction, of the Harvard Business School, where they tried to find the factors influencing fatigue and productivity by trying to control one variable at a time, while holding all others constant. They varied degrees of illumination, coffee breaks, bonuses, salaries, and many other factors. They came to the conclusion that none of these variables was really decisive, that it wasn't any one of these factors in isolation that was crucial; it was the interpersonal and social relations among workers in relation to employers, home life, neighborhood, and so on. Lloyd Warner took his cue from this conclusion and proposed a community study, but he found Cicero too disorganized, so he went off to Yankee City. As several speakers have suggested, we should consider a similar strategy here, instead of trying to be ultrascientific. One cannot really point to a desire for sons or to some other factor as the decisive variable. We should look at the problem more in the framework of people's relationships to one another and within the community in which they live.

A. M. Shah: One of the major attractions of this conference for me was that there would be less talk of family planning and other programs of population control than one usually encounters at population conferences these days. Although I recognize the need for population control, there are a number of other problems that need to be considered and studied. In India, scholars and others have so far given considerable attention to the impact of society on population but very little to the effects of population changes on society. I am glad that this conference is devoted to this problem. It is noteworthy that this problem was considered long ago by one of the founders of my discipline, Emile Durkheim. He asked, What happens to a society and to its basic processes, structures, and institutions when you vary its size? It seems to me that we should consider this general problem with regard to all the various structures and institutions in the society. This may or may not have consequences for the solution of the problem of population control, although I am an optimist and believe that continuing growth of knowledge will help us in solving problems.

Let us see how the religious groups in India are affected by population growth. Are the Hindus, Muslims, Christians, and other religious groups growing at different rates or at the same rate? The figures released by the Census of India recently show that all the religious groups are not growing at the same rate. It is even more important that the various religious groups reached to these figures. The point is that the religious groups have become conscious of the population problem. Just as there is a national consciousness of a population problem, we should expect this consciousness to percolate down the line to religious, linguistic, caste, and all the other important groups in society. We should ask, how do they react to the problem? Hopefully, we are going to have a discussion on this.

We should discuss the relationship between caste and population size. Castes differ in size. At one end of the spectrum, there are tiny endogamous groups. I know of some endogamous caste groups in Gujarat with only 100 to 150 families. In the case of one caste group, I could put almost all the members on one genealogical chart. At the other extreme, there are huge caste complexes. One cannot call them just castes; they are caste complexes. Take the Rajputs, for example. They are found all the way from Himachal Pradesh in the north to Gujarat in the south and from Rajasthan in the west to Bihar and even Bengal in the east. The Jats and Gujars in north India, the Kolis and Patidars in Gujarat, the Marathas in Maharashtra, the Kammas and Reddis in Andhra Pradesh, and the Vokkaligas and Lingayats in Karnataka are other examples of caste complexes. We must ask, what is the relationship between the size of a caste or caste complex and the nature of its internal structure and external relations? What happens to a tiny caste group when it is faced with growing numbers? What are its implications for the various social institutions, particularly for kinship and marriage? Along with the growth of population, a number of other things happen as well. For example, there has to be the growth of communications. How does a large caste complex consolidate itself?

Another problem we have to consider is, How conscious are the various caste groups of population growth? Have they become conscious of it? If they have, what is their reaction? At the present moment, we are aware of such consciousness at least among one category of castes, namely the Harijans. Only a few months ago, a Harijan minister in Tamil Nadu made a series of statements about the population problem in the country. She said that the Harijans should not take part in the family planning programs. She argued that, with growing numbers, the Harijans would become politically powerful. This way the Harijans would get more votes, more members in the legislative assembly, and more ministers, and so on and so forth. So, we must consider, when castes become conscious of population growth, and particularly of their numerical strength, what happens?

Let us now look at the village community. There are two major settlement patterns in the villages: The nuclear type where houses tend to be clustered together, and the dispersed type, where houses are strewn all over the countryside. In areas with nuclear settlements, what happens when population growth takes place? I will report from my own study. In the village I have studied in Gujarat, the population from 1825 until the present has more than doubled. This has had important implications with regard to housing and settlement pattern. The village nucleus cannot accommodate the entire population now. Then, where do the people build houses? If they do not find sufficient house sites on the village nucleus, where else do they go for building houses? We must remember that usually the land nearest the village nucleus is most fertile. It is like gold. In certain states, attempts are being made by the government to extend the area of the village nucleus by taking over the adjoining fields for house sites, but this has met with enormous resistance from villagers owning these fields. As an alternative, in many parts of north India now, there is a tendency for dispersal of house sites. The usual pattern is that when a farmer is unable to find a house site on the village nucleus, he moves to his own field—A moves to his field, B to his field, C to his field, and so on. As a result we find houses strewn over the fields where formerly there were only uncleared settlements. It is noteworthy that generally it is the poorer people who have to leave their house sites, not the rich. Since there is considerable competition for house sites, the rich are able to buy up houses and house sites from the poor, and the latter are then driven to build houses on their small farms. In some parts of the country, such as central Gujarat, there is also vertical movement. The rich people are building three- and four-story buildings. They keep their cattle on the ground floor, and give one floor to each son. The vertical movement of buildings thus helps make an adjustment to population expansion.

I am glad that Professor Mandelbaum commented on the jajmani system. This is an area where I think there is scope for doing research on the effects of population growth. I would like to ask, How can a village support more than a few barbers, blacksmiths, or washermen? There has to be an optimum limit. If a barber has three or four sons, and if there are not enough customers in that village, what will happen to the barber family? Also, what happens to landlord-tenant relationships and landlord-laborer relationships when the tenant and laborer families grow?

There is another question: What happens to the lineage when growth takes place? What happens to it when there are more sons than daughters, or more daughters than sons? I find an interesting development in many parts of the country. In the past, there used to be many deaths; often sons used to die and lineage segments used to go out of existence. But now, since there is a steady growth of population, this does not happen as often. With the genealogist around to keep the record of births and deaths, and to keep the lineage ties alive, we find more and more lineage groups growing. There has been a spurt in the number of ancestor shrines as a result.

So, in this manner, it is necessary to see the implications of population growth for the various groups and institutions in society and not talk only about the numbers in the country as a whole.

Abraham Weisblat: I think there are two kinds of themes that have been running through the discussion so far this morning. First, one of the principal effects of population on religion, ritual, and societal interaction is that economic pressures come along, and they begin to change the social and religious milieu. Numbers do have an effect on survival. Religion, ritual, and societal interaction represent, more or less, the rules or working procedures that give a society its continuity and its basic security. They also, it seems to me, represent the kind of rules and procedures by which a society survives. As economic pressures come on, these are the things that are beginning to effect the most fundamental changes in India. Institutions and processes have broken down, or in some cases they have failed to come up with adequate answers.

But one of the other things that has been emphasized is that there have also been some very positive factors associated with the development of new working rules in India. There is obviously a gap in terms of research, in terms of what we know, but if you accept and recognize that culture is terribly important—and here I mean culture with both a big C and little c—then it is clear that Indian culture has responded in significant ways to cope with and adapt to massive problems. We want to know the ways in which this change has been positive, in order that we can find ways in which we can help.

NOTES

1. I thank T. Scarlett Epstein and M. S. A. Rao for helpful comments. Secretarial and bibliographic aid was provided by funds from the Committee on Research, University of California, Berkeley.

2. Alan R. Beals, Village Life in South India (Chicago: Aldine Publishing Company, 1974), pp. 97-98.

3. David G. Mandelbaum, Human Fertility in India (Berkeley: University of California Press, 1974), pp. 16-23.

4. Malini Karkal, "Cultural Factors Affecting Fertility," Man in India (1971), pp. 15-26.

5. Mandelbaum, op. cit., pp. 23-37.

6. Ibid., pp. 23-41.

7. S. K. Satia and C. Rangarajan, "Optimal Targets for the Family Planning Programme," Economic and Political Weekly 9 (1974): 595-606.

8. Clarence Maloney, Peoples of South Asia (New York: Holt, Rinehart and Winston, 1974), p. 535.

9. Gilbert Etienne, "110 Years of an Uttar Pradesh Village," in Changing India: Studies in Honor of Professor G. S. Ghurye, ed. S. D. Pillai (Bombay: Popular Prakashan, forthcoming 1975).

Etienne's earlier work is summarized in <u>Studies in Indian Agricul-</u><u>ture: The Art of the Possible</u> (Berkeley: University of California Press, 1968).

10. See, for example, David E. Pocock, "Bases of Faction in Gujerat," <u>British Journal of Sociology</u> 8 (1957): 295-317. See also William and Charlotte Wiser, <u>Behind Mud Walls</u> (Berkeley: University of California Press, 1972).

11. Cited in Maloney, op. cit., pp. 535-537.

12. Cf. Caplan on the Limbus of Nepal and Furer-Haimendorf on the Raj Gonds of Andhra Pradesh in <u>South Asia: Seven Community</u> <u>Profiles</u>, ed. Clarence Maloney (New York: Holt, Rinehart and Winston, 1974), pp. 198, 255.

13. Joan Mencher, "Conflicts and Contradictions in the 'Green Revolution': The Case of Tamil Nadu," <u>Economic and Political</u> <u>Weekly</u> 9 (1974): 309-323.

14. Wolf Ladejinsky, "How Green Is the Indian Green Revolution?" <u>Economic and Political Weekly</u> 8 (1973): A-137.

15. V. M. Dandekar and Nilakantha Rath, "Poverty in India," <u>Economic and Political Weekly</u> 6 (1971): 25-48, 106-146.

16. In a village in Uttar Pradesh studied by Elder, the jajmani relations with the Brahmin priests, the barbers, and the sweepers were still maintained by most landowners, but those with carpenters, blacksmiths, and leatherworkers, had largely lapsed; many of these artisans had become landless laborers. Compare Maloney, op. cit., pp. 461-462.

17. Compare Ladejinsky, op. cit., pp. A-135, A-143. See also Mencher, op. cit., pp. 311, 313.

18. Mencher, op. cit., p. 313.

19. John Wyon and John E. Gordon, <u>The Khanna Study: Popula-</u><u>tion Problems in the Rural Punjab</u> (Cambridge, Mass.: Harvard University Press, 1971), p. 251. See also Mahmood Mamdani, <u>The</u> <u>Myth of Population Control: Family Caste and Class in an Indian Vil-</u><u>lage</u> (New York: Monthly Review Press, 1972), pp. 143-148.

20. T. Scarlett Epstein, <u>Economic Development and Social</u> <u>Change in South India</u> (Manchester: Manchester University Press, 1973).

21. T. Scarlett Epstein, <u>South India: Yesterday, Today, Tomor-</u><u>row</u> (New York: Holmes and Meier, 1973), pp. 57-58, 83.

22. Ibid., pp. 54, 88-90.
23. Ibid., p. 107.
24. Ibid., p. 238.
25. Ibid., p. 243.
26. Ibid., p. 165.
27. Ibid., p. 127.
28. Ibid., pp. 234, 238.

29. Ibid., p. 160.

30. Ibid., p. 260. An all-India survey of wage rates for agricultural laborers shows a very much smaller decrease in real wages in Karnataka State, of about 9 percent, between 1956-57 and 1971-72. But this survey is from official, aggregate statistics and does not, as its author points out, deal with the average number of days worked. It concludes that wage rates improved significantly in real terms in five states during the period studied and that "these states account for less than 30 percent of the agricultural labor force in the country." See A. V. Jose, "Real Wages of Agricultural Labourers," Economic and Political Weekly 9 (1974): A-25-A-30.

31. Epstein, South India, op. cit., p. 99.

32. Ibid., pp. 54-55.

33. Ibid., p. 161.

34. Ibid., p. 146.

35. Ibid., p. 156.

36. Ibid., pp. 45, 135, 207, 248, 251.

37. Ibid., p. 172.

38. Ibid., p. 91.

39. Ibid., p. 39.

40. Ibid., pp. 207-208.

41. Ibid., p. 130.

42. Ibid., p. 154.

43. Ibid., p. 182.

44. American Association for the Advancement of Science, Office of International Science, Culture and Population Change (Washington, D.C.: American Association for the Advancement of Science, 1974), pp. 43-44.

45. Ibid., pp. 222-223.

46. Ibid., p. 241.

47. Ibid., p. 226.

48. Ibid., pp. 194-196.

49. Ibid., pp. 179-181.

50. Ibid., pp. 127-130.

51. Ladejinsky, op. cit., p. A-141.

52. Gananath Obeyesekere, Land Tenure in Village Ceylon (Cambridge: Cambridge University Press, 1967); and Gananath Obeyesekere, "A Village in Sri Lanka: Madagama," in South Asia: Seven Community Profiles, op. cit., pp. 42-80.

53. Obeyesekere, "Village in Sri Lanka," op. cit., p. 74.

54. Ibid., p. 75.

55. Ibid., p. 77.

56. McKim Marriott, "New Farmers in an Old Village," in Entrepreneurship and Modernization of Occupational Cultures in South Asia, ed. Milton Singer (Durham, N.C.: Monograph 12, Duke University Program in Comparative Studies on Southern Asia, 1973), p. 212.

57. Ibid., pp. 208, 213.

58. David G. Mandelbaum, Society in India, vol. 1 (Berkeley: University of California Press, 1970), p. 256.

59. D. Banerji, "Health Behavior of Rural Populations: Impact of Rural Health Services," Economic and Political Weekly 8 (1973), pp. 2261-2268.

60. Ibid., p. 2264.

61. Ibid., p. 2267.

62. Mandelbaum, Human Fertility in India, op. cit., pp. 108-109.

63. One of the few anthropological studies of an Indian village that focuses on demography and family planning, by John F. Marshall, makes similar criticisms of the work of the Family Planning Programme in a village near Meerut. The planners and workers connected with the Programme seemed to Marshall to know very little about the villagers whose intimate acts and precious values they were trying to change. He notes that it is impossible to change effectively the people's image of a fertility-regulating method without a thorough knowledge of the culture. "I share the incredulity voiced by many others that so little of relevance is known about the people at whom family planning messages are aimed." John F. Marshall, "Culture and Contraception: Response Determinants to a Family Planning Program in a North Indian Village," unpublished Ph.D. dissertation, Department of Anthropology, University of Hawaii, 1972, p. 129.

64. Banerji, op. cit., p. 2264.

65. Ibid., p. 2265.

66. Ibid., p. 2268.

67. P. R. Gopinath Nair, "Decline in Birth Rate in Kerala," Economic and Political Weekly 9 (1974): 323-336.

68. Mandelbaum, Human Fertility in India, op. cit., pp. 42-59.

69. Kumudini Dandekar, "Age at Marriage of Women," Economic and Political Weekly 9 (1974): 872.

70. Cora DuBois, "Schooling, Youth and Modernization in India," in Population, Politics, and the Future of Southern Asia, eds. W. Howard Wriggins and J. F. Guyot (New York: Columbia University Press, 1973), p. 297.

71. Ibid., p. 315.

72. Mandelbaum, Human Fertility in India, op. cit., pp. 51-57.

73. Epstein, South India, op. cit., pp. 227-229.

74. Warren Ilchman, Population Knowledge and Population Change (Cambridge, Mass.: Harvard University Center for Population Studies, 1974), pp. 24-25.

75. Bharat Jhunjhunwala, "Population and Poverty," Economic and Political Weekly 9 (1974): 1059.

76. Myron Weiner, "Socio-Political Consequences of Interstate Migration in India," in Population, Politics and the Future of Southern Asia, op. cit., p. 228.

77. Maloney, Peoples of South Asia, op. cit., p. 529.

78. Harold A. Gould, "Cities in the North Indian Plain: Contrasting Lucknow and Kanpur," in South Asia: Seven Community Profiles, op. cit., pp. 258-293.

79. Sylvia Vatuk, Kinship and Urbanization: White Collar Migrants in North India (Berkeley: University of California Press, 1972).

80. Milton Singer, When a Great Tradition Modernizes (New York: Praeger Publishers, 1972).

81. K. Ranga Rao and M. S. A. Rao, "Slums," unpublished paper to appear in Report on a Socio-Economic Survey of Vijayawada City, eds. V. L. S. Prakasa Rao and R. Ramachandran (New Delhi: Vikas Publishers, 1975), pp. 87-90.

5

WHITE-COLLAR AND
BLUE-COLLAR FAMILY
RESPONSES TO POPULATION
GROWTH IN INDIA
Rama Mehta

Despite the fact that the government of India was the first government in the world to adopt a comprehensive family planning policy as an integral part of its development plans and despite considerable nongovernmental efforts, it is generally accepted that India's family planning campaigns have met with limited success. The birthrate has come down only marginally, leading to despondency in many quarters. Researchers have tried to assess the causes of failure, and government committees have engaged in a number of evaluations and reevaluations of various programs. The usual reasons given for the limited success of India's family planning effort have to do with the familiar syndrome of illiteracy, poverty, and a lack of motivation for restraint, due primarily to the belief that children are an economic asset. Since a simultaneous attack on all economic fronts is not feasible for India at this time, action designed to break through the illiteracy-poverty-population syndrome mentioned above and to change qualitatively its component units would seem to demand an attack in sectors where there is some promise of a demonstration and multiplier effect.

This chapter assumes the need for a demonstration or multiplier effect, and it perceives the opportunity to grasp such an effect through an understanding of the motivation for family planning among people with different family structures and values. The observations that have prompted this chapter can be stated as follows, in the form of a seeming paradox. Among a small sector of India's white-collar, urban-based middle class, there is clear evidence of motivation for family planning and an actual decline in the size of the average family over the past few decades. At the same time, among blue-collar workers, also urban-based and in the same income brackets, there has been no corresponding change. While fertility trends among blue-collar workers have been fairly representative of national fertility trends, middle-class status groups have demonstrated an increasingly conscious effort to limit the size of their families.

Moreover, while there was no family planning campaign as such in the pre-Independence period, the idea that family size should be limited had reached a number of married couples of middle-class status before 1947. In this case, the idea to limit the size of the family came indirectly from contact with the British Indian administration and the general Western style of life that was adopted by some segments of India's middle-class population. By comparing middle-class families exposed to Western ideas in the pre-Independence period with middle-class families of the post-Independence period, all the while bearing in mind the differences between white-collar and blue-collar life situations, it may be possible to gain some insights into a variety of factors that have led to a conscious motivation toward family planning among a significant portion of Indian families.

This chapter summarizes data gathered on 100 middle-class women who functioned in Indian families in the pre- and post-Independence periods. This is not a statistical study but is instead based on depth interviews with these 100 women, half of the sample having been educated and brought up in pre-Independence India and the other half in the conditions of post-Independence. I have not conducted depth interviews in the blue-collar section of the population, but, on the basis of research studies conducted by others, and through personal observation, I have attempted to make comparisons between my sample of interviewees and similarly placed women in blue-collar families. The attitudes I have attempted to understand are those concerned with family structure, orientations toward tradition and modernity, and aspirations for children. While my sample does not purport to be representative, and my comparison is not systematically designed, this procedure does make it possible at least to hypothesize about the reasons for striking differences in attitudes toward family size among families with similar incomes.

It should be pointed out that my interviews were not originally conducted for the purposes of this study but were instead designed to inform a study concerned with the changing roles of women in modern India.[1] While this earlier study was being conducted, data were gathered to elicit attitudes toward family size, and a series of hypotheses emerged that seemed worthy of further research. This chapter, therefore, is simply an extension of a previous more systematic study and is intended to be exploratory.

RESPONDENTS FROM THE PRE-
INDEPENDENCE ERA

The parents of the 50 respondents of the pre-Independence period belonged to the middle class white-collar professions and were
urban-based. They came from the family income range of 450 rupees
to 1,500 rupees. The respondents themselves were deliberately chosen from the age group that was between 20 to 24 years in 1947.
Thus, during their formative years they were exposed, either directly or indirectly, to Indo-British culture. For some period of
their school-going age, they attended missionary schools, where English was the medium of instruction and where they learned Western
values, either directly from the curriculum or indirectly by exposure.
All of them were graduates, and a few held postgraduate degrees.
All of the parents of these respondents were in the British administrative system and were, therefore, most likely to be influenced by
the alien culture. The sample did not include women who belonged to
the Indian traditional middle class, which had largely remained outside the British social environment and had little compulsion to acquire or imitate Western values.

Before proceeding with the analysis, it should be mentioned
that in this chapter, the definition of the joint family is one of a com-
mensual unit composed of two or more related married couples and
their unmarried children. The nuclear family is defined as consist-
ing of husband, wife, and their unmarried children. The nuclear-
linked joint family is defined as having separate residence from the
ancestral home, but being under the overall discipline of the joint
family while maintaining ritualistic obligations to it.

Taking the above definitions, 36 percent of the respondents
from the pre-Independence period sample came from joint families,
44 percent from nuclear households linked to the joint family, and 20
percent from nuclear families.

Respondents from joint families during the pre-Independence
period lived in households in which the head of the family was the
eldest male member. The respondents' father, if he were not the
eldest male member in the family, usually submitted to the patriarch's
authority. The respondents' lives were, for the most part, conducted
within the kin group and the local caste community. The discipline of
the household was determined by the norms laid down by the caste
community. The respondents, therefore, could be said to have been
brought up within the traditional joint family atmosphere. They were

sent to missionary schools, but as day scholars, and primarily in order that they acquire status within the emerging Westernized elite,
to which their fathers belonged through their occupation. However,
Western education and influence was not allowed to eclipse traditional
discipline and patterns within the household. Most respondents, in
fact, reported that they were sent to missionary schools to learn English and not really to imbibe Western ideas.

The parents of those respondents who belonged to nuclear households linked to the joint family were generally unwilling to make any
major decisions without prior approval of the head of the family. A
certain degree of independence, however, was possible, due largely
to the fact that the nuclear family was geographically isolated from
the ancestral household. Because of this, some of the respondents
were sent to missionary boarding schools, even though the caste community considered such a step contrary to the traditional norms of
bringing up girls. These respondents, however, reported that they
were subject to traditional discipline during their vacations and a
minimum of freedom of choice in their use of leisure. Parents were
aware that intense exposure to a Western system of education through
a boarding school life could alienate their children from Indian values
and life-styles. Therefore, conscious efforts were made by parents
to describe and emphasize differences between Indian and Western
ways of looking at things in general, and at men-and-women relationships in particular. Generally speaking too, Western attitudes were
considered by parents to be less respectable, less ethical, and less
moral.

In this milieu, the woman's duty was not to regard herself as
the equal of the male, but subordinate to him. Women were not to
see themselves as equal partners, even in the married relationship.
The ideal that was considered most moral was that of pativrata (that
is, the one who follows her husband's will and authority in all respects). Thus, while enjoying greater freedom than most Indian women, respondents in nuclear-linked families were restricted both in
their choice of friendships and their leisure activities. The respondents were so inculcated with the traditional idea of submission to
parental authority that, in spite of the greater freedom to which they
were accustomed in the school atmosphere, they usually did not object to such restrictions in the home. The attitude of unquestioned
deference to parental authority continued to remain a part of their
psychological makeup, even after they had completed their higher education. There was no question of children being regarded as individuals and having the right to be treated as such.

The upbringing of children in the joint and nuclear-linked joint
family households was, therefore, similar. In both groups, the value
system projected was Hindu and traditional in character. Education

was not intended, in either group, to be career-oriented or to make women self-reliant and look upon themselves as equal to men. Higher education was given to the respondents only as it was looked upon as a social asset in the emerging Westernized society.

However, among those respondents belonging to nuclear families, parents generally made a more deliberate effort to dissociate themselves from their caste communities and traditional orthodox values. This was usually part of an effort to seek greater acceptance in British-oriented circles. Among this group would be found, rather frequently, families that had rejected orthodox practices relating to food habits and other rituals they considered irrational. Parents of these respondents generally considered their peer group to be others who were in the orbit of Westernized society. This does not mean that they totally rejected their caste communities, but, due to socioeconomic differences, there was a clear alienation from caste-oriented culture in their daily lives. Within this group, higher education for women was taken more seriously. For example, parents did not necessarily terminate the education of female children simply because there were no women's colleges offering postgraduate degrees.

Respondents from nuclear families were not unfamiliar with traditional values, but since these were not woven into their daily lives, their influence was considerably less than was the case in joint or nuclear-linked families. The parents of respondents in nuclear families had usually given up the practice of segregating men and women; the respondents' mothers frequently accompanied the fathers to mixed social gatherings. In fact, married women in nuclear families during this period were often encouraged to imitate and adopt, as far as possible, Western etiquette and Western life-styles. Because of this mix of traditional and Western attitudes operating in the family at the same time, respondents from nuclear families felt that they gained a greater measure of freedom for themselves, and were thus able to ignore some traditional norms of bahavior. Even after adolescence, these respondents were allowed to go out to mixed social gatherings, if properly chaperoned. But, even in these nuclear homes, parental authority remained paramount and defiance of Indian norms of behavior was confined to a limited range of activity.

Notwithstanding the differences in the atmosphere in the homes, what emerged from the answers of the respondents was that, in an overall appraisal, there was a general similarity in the social life-styles of the three different structures of family life. The greater latitude that respondents from nuclear households enjoyed did not depart greatly from the inherent conservatism in attitudes toward women characteristic of joint and nuclear-linked families. In general, despite efforts to adopt and imitate Western ways for acquiring social standing, Indian society remained essentially traditional. Western liberal ideas could not drastically alter traditional opposition to female freedom. Even that segment of society closest to a Western style of life disapproved of Indian women closely imitating Western ways of behavior. For a woman to receive societal approval, she had to be modest, reticent, and timid in her relationships with men. Even when girls were sent to graduate colleges, the implications and consequences of such higher education were rejected. The emancipated and traditional society were both restrictive and nonpermissive with regard to women. The pre-Independence era did not accept the proposition that women should work in gainful employment alongside of men.

Among all three groups, therefore, the great majority of the respondents' marriages were arranged in the traditional manner. The average age at marriage was 19.3 years. Of the total of 50 respondents, 70 percent were married on subcaste lines; 20 percent were married, not within the subcaste group but within the major caste group of the respondents; and only 10 percent had intercaste marriages based on class rather than caste. Thirty-six percent of the respondents were married into joint families, 30 percent into nuclear-linked joint families, and 34 percent into nuclear households.

Those women that were married into joint families remained, by and large, within the traditional fold, generally accepting family obligations. They also found in their kin group their closest and most trusted relationships. It was to relatives that they turned in time of need, and it was with relatives that they shared their joys. In general too, they found life within the joint family both morally and emotionally satisfying.

Those respondents that were married into nuclear-linked joint families did not accept their roles as traditional daughters-in-law in the same manner as those married in joint families. Since they lived in separate households they were able to enjoy a certain amount of independence by virtue of their residential separation. This, however, did not basically change the life of the respondents, since all major decisions were still subject to the wishes of the head of the family. As daughters-in-law, regardless of personal considerations, these respondents were required to subordinate their interests to the demands placed on them by the extended family. They frequently reported, for example, that for periods ranging from six months to three years, not only their uncles' children (that is, first cousins) but even second and third cousins came to stay with them. In fact, it was expected that they would keep their homes open for all patrikin and caste community members. This was one of the main reasons given by the respondents for not being able to develop their own interests or to use their education in some useful manner.

When there was economic need, their husbands' salaries were, without exception, placed at the disposal of the patriarchs. Even when there was no such need, financial control and supervision of major family expenditures rested with the head of the family. The respondents usually resented this hypothecation of their husbands' earnings but were unable to assert themselves beyond urging their husbands to become more independent.

The women married in the nuclear-linked joint families also resented a stated lack of independence to run their own homes; they wanted to have greater freedom to lead their own lives without being obligated to observe the wishes of the elders in the family. But this was not possible, primarily because their husbands were not prepared to break with the traditional norm of filial duty. However, once the family lost its head due to death, respondents did assume greater control in the affairs of their immediate family. While the obligation to keep the house open to relatives remained, contacts with the kin group were also generally reduced.

However, when one or both of the parents-in-law died, the surviving elder, and possibly the younger brothers and sisters-in-law, came to live in the respondents' household, or the respondents' household had to assume responsibility for looking after such kin and establishing them in life. This shows, as Orenstein and Micklin have pointed out, that "nuclear households with changing cycles of marriage and birth grow into joint households and decline with separation and death into nuclear households again."[2] Most respondents, in these instances, would have preferred to retain their separate residential unit rather than have it turned into a joint household, but they also felt that they could not repudiate their joint family responsibilities. This was usually a result of the husband's unwillingness to reject what he considered his filial duty. In those cases where the husband happened to be the new head of the family, the women of the family were sometimes able to ignore traditional joint family etiquette toward in-laws who had become part of their household.

Many of the respondents in nuclear-linked families, though unable to change the basic attitude of their husbands toward parental responsbilities, were able to change their own style of living to suit their convenience. Many of the rites connected with feminine ritual purity, for example, were discarded by them. They also did not abide by the conventions of being segregated from their husband's social life. There was greater participation by them in outside activities. Such changes also correlated quite closely with a loss of preference for kin-group associations. Multicaste society seemed to have more challenges in it, and be more interesting, for women in nuclear-linked family situations. Part of the explanation for this, obviously, is that

educated women can relate better to other educated women than they
can to kin women who are not educated.

Those respondents who were married into nuclear establishments often faced demands that their homes be turned into joint households, either for economic reasons or because of the death of one of
the in-laws. But in these cases, there was a reluctance to take on the
responsibilities of joint family life. The vast majority of the respondents concerned were determined to remain separate from joint family life-styles and discipline. These women stated that they were prepared to accept financial responsibility for the support of parents-in-
law and brothers and sisters-in-law but were not prepared to have them
live permanently in their homes as they feared it would infringe on
their privacy and their leisure. The respondents indicated that, because of this attitude on their part, many of the parents-in-law and
other dependents preferred to live with other sons whose wives were
more understanding and accommodating to traditional values in regard
to family ties. The respondents in this subgroup had a greater sense
of their own identity and were not prepared to play the role of a subservient daughter-in-law.

One of the reasons that some of these women were able to assert themselves in this manner was that they came from families
with higher social status than that of their husbands' family. They
were, therefore, able to make greater demands for themselves without fear of being disapproved of by the joint family. It was also clear
that they were not dependent, emotionally or financially, on the joint
family unit. Kolenda calls this the "bargaining power of women."[3]
This self-confidence, born of economic independence, was reinforced
by Western-style education. Emotionally, such women could more
easily submerge feelings for kin group associates and caste community members. They generally found their own meaningful relationships in their multicaste society based on common interests and pursuits.

Regardless of the family background of pre-Independence respondents, however, there was a remarkable unanimity in the aspirations they had for their children. All of them wanted to inculcate in
their children goals that were professional and status-oriented. While
caste and patri-kin associations were generally considered valuable,
in the vast majority of cases these were to be kept subordinate to ambitions for upward social mobility. There was a full realization by
the great majority of the respondents that children, in order to take
advantage of new professional opportunities, had to be given the best
possible education of that status group. Even though, during this period, there was little economic stress and a relative lack of fear of unemployment for the second generation, there was still an awareness
in this middle-class group that too many children could be an economic

liability. Therefore, this group of 50 women had a family size of
3.5, which was considerably smaller than the size of families in the
rest of the middle class during this same period.

RESPONDENTS FROM THE POST-INDEPENDENCE ERA

Respondents belonging to the post-Independence era were drawn,
so far as possible, from the same social strata as those from the
pre-Independence period. They also came from white-collar, urban-
based professional families that had been accustomed to higher education. These respondents were between the ages of 25 to 40, the majority being at the time of the interviews (1973) between 30 to 35.
Among these 50 respondents, 30 percent came from joint, 26 percent
from nuclear-linked, and 44 percent from nuclear families. Since
there was little difference found between nuclear-linked joint households and nuclear households, the respondents belonging to these two
groups will not be dealt with separately. The respondents' parents'
incomes ranged from 450 to 1,500 rupees: 68 percent came from the
income range of 450 to 600 rupees, 20 percent from 650 to 1,000
rupees, and 12 percent from 1,000 to 1,500 rupees.

These respondents were married at an average age of 21.9
years, and their educational attainments were as follows: 18 graduates, 12 M.A.s, 10 trained teachers after their School Leaving Cer-
tificate (SLC) examination, 4 medical doctors, and 6 trained secre-
taries.

Respondents who were brought up in post-Independence India
had significantly different attitudes toward life, family obligations,
education, and their own roles as women than did the first group of
50 women who were brought up in the pre-Independence period. In
spite of British influence and higher education, the pre-Independence
group was largely deferential to, if not conformist with, the traditional value system. Before marriage, and even as married women,
they maintained, by and large, traditional orientations toward family
relationships. In general, their natal family discipline and environment had neutralized the impact of modern ways of looking at themselves.

In the post-Independence group, those respondents belonging to
joint families indicated that the atmosphere in their home had become
more liberal, less rigid, and less conformist to caste community
ethics. Whereas the group of women belonging to the pre-Independence
era were brought up to consider paid employment as not respectable,
this group of women had been encouraged to see in education a definite economic return. K. M. Kapadia has substantiated this as a
more general phenomenon in India:

> Another factor of great importance affecting the family is the employment of women which has become possible through education and present economic strains. Before the Second World War it was considered derogatory for women to take gainful employment. Today even members of the older generation desire that their educated daughters-in-law must help in supplementing the income.[4]

However, the responses of the post-Independence group indicated that, while women have accepted the modern attitude toward work, in a number of other respects they remain traditional. This is consistent with the findings of a number of other scholars that have attempted to assess the interplay between modernity and tradition. Milton Singer, for example, found in his surveys that being modern in one aspect of life does not necessarily mean being modern in all other aspects of life.[5] In Singer's words, "Traditional and modern attitudes are not mutually exclusive and are often found to be running parallel."[6]

Perhaps the greatest change that can be elucidated when comparing the pre- and post-Independence periods is that having to do with education. For the 50 respondents from the post-Independence period, education had become a necessity and normal, irrespective of family structure, an attitude that contrasts sharply with pre-Independence orientations. Needless to say, the older prejudice against higher education for women had all but disappeared.

Fortunately, the attitude of the caste community itself, while remaining conservative in many respects, had also changed radically with regard to female education. For example, girls were encouraged to go on to college and to take professional training. In addition, women who were between the ages of 25 and 35 had more education than those in the age bracket 35 to 40, indicating a liberalizing trend over time. Then, too, the majority of the younger respondents had obtained professional training and qualifications, in contrast to the older group.

Despite these changes in employment orientations, the great majority of the respondents' parents still regarded the arranged marriage of their daughters as a moral obligation. The parents did not consider that an educated child could, or even had the liberty to, look for her own spouse. Indeed, higher education was seen as a necessary qualification for marriage, not as an embellishment. While emerging middle-class men now definitely wanted an educated wife, the majority still looked for them from within their own caste community. A girl's eligibility for marriage in these middle-class, urban-based families was enhanced by the measure of her potential earning capacity.

In this atmosphere, education has in effect become a commodity to be included with other items in the bride's dowry and is often looked on as an equally oppressive burden. It was not always easy for the respondents' parents, who belonged to the middle-income group, to educate daughters and sons alike. But good education for girls has become an obligation, if the prospects of finding a well-placed boy are not to be compromised. For, even though education is looked upon as an asset in a bride, it has not reduced the demand for a dowry; on the contrary, the size of the expected dowry has, if anything, increased.

Where higher education of the respondents had been terminated prematurely, this was usually because marriage took precedence over education. While education itself was generally pursued in order to improve and broaden the chances of a good matrimonial match, parents were also careful never to reduce the prospects of their girls' marriage within the caste community. If some nonconventional considerations had crept in, it was in the knowledge that the caste community had accepted them as part of the socioeconomic changes taking place in India. For example, 25 percent of the respondents had been allowed to work before marriage, as there was no longer a stigma attached to an unmarried working girl, particularly if she was in an approved profession such as teaching.

Among pre-Independence respondents, it will be recalled, there was a very definite distinction between the degree of discipline in the joint family and the nuclear household. By way of comparison, respondents of the post-Independence period suggested that the gap between joint family and nuclear household disciplines had narrowed considerably. The respondents from either post-Independence structure, joint or nuclear, felt freer and less inhibited in giving expression to their views. In the recent period, the joint family was no longer a unit in which the elder women insisted on adherence to traditional codes in all respects. In some cases, the joint-family patriarchs allowed daughters-in-law to take up paid employment, since this was recognized for its obvious economic advantages.

In cases where married respondents were working out, their contributions to the joint family were both in cash and in services. Earnings helped the family budget, but daughters-in-law also shared in household work. However, this new role for women, even in conservative families, had to a great extent weakened the impact of traditional values on respondents. Respondents pointed out that they were exposed as unmarried girls to women in the family who were not completely family centered. There were also greater perceived differences between the generations, the older women generally abiding by traditional roles while allowing their daughters-in-law in part to change their roles.

Most respondents still stated that in their parental homes they had been conditioned to regard themselves as subordinate to male authority and to consider maintaining family ties as a moral duty. The traditional ideal of pativrata was still held up before them as the most moral and ethical, and their expected behavior was to be self-effacing and modest in relation to men. The husband was still to be viewed with special respect and regard, and the woman's duty lay in serving him and his family. It was hoped that education and its influence would not teach the girl to regard herself as an equal with males, even in the marriage relationship. Respondents' families usually discouraged them from having friends on the basis of shared interest and encouraged them to regard relationships within the kin-group as most fulfilling and ethical. Notwithstanding these injunctions, the influence of education in inculcating some elements of modern attitudes could not be completely neutralized.

Those respondents that came from nuclear households and were geographically separated from the kin group were usually able to make more meaningful multicaste relationships. They were also much more exposed to outside influences, emanating primarily from the mass media, Western magazines, English films, and contacts with people who were secular in outlook and achievement-motivated. When compared with respondents from joint families, those from nuclear families described a home atmosphere that was more diffuse and had greater links with modern trends in society.

However, all of the women from nuclear families described some concessions to the old etiquette regarding male-female friendships. In spite of their working with men, they still observed the feminine ethic of not forming independent friendships with the opposite sex. Respondents from nuclear families were still most at home with relatives, male and female, and it was the husband in these instances who determined the kind of people who were to be received in the home. Despite the decision to allow their women to work, husbands still seemed quite conservative. They did not approve of the Western concept of equality between the sexes, except in a very restricted sense. Women were expected to maintain symbols of respect, such as covering their heads in front of elders, touching their feet on arrival, and not talking in the presence of husbands in front of strangers.

All of the respondents in nuclear families reported that it was almost impossible for them to accept the traditional role of daughter-in-law. In fact, the position of overriding authority of the parents-in-law, whether in a nuclear home or in the joint family, was to a varying extent resented by the majority of the respondents. It would seem, then, that these women have only reluctantly accepted restrictions placed on their social life, or potential hindrances to a continuance of their careers. For example, even though the majority of the respondents were prepared to attend birth, death, and marriage ceremonies and also to fulfill religious obligations, such actions did not necessarily flow from conviction but indicated instead acquiescence with the wishes of parents-in-law.

Within this entire post-Independence group again, there was a growing awareness of means for gaining social recognition outside the family. Respondents, for example, were not completely within the status-building matrix of the caste community. They saw that money spent in other than ritualistic obligations could bring greater return to them and to their immediate family. The respondents who, after marriage, had nuclear homes or nuclear-linked joint-family households generally felt favorably placed to reduce their contributions to socioreligious functions, and most of them did so. They also felt that they had excuses for avoiding participation in such functions and did so. By way of comparison, respondents who lived in joint households generally felt that they could not afford to displease members of the family and were obliged to participate in and contribute toward such functions and obligations. But in both groups there was increasing realization that money spent in reaffirming caste community obligations could seriously affect the future education and well-being of their own children.

Even when wanting greater freedom for themselves, however, respondents did not completely reject a sense of traditional obligations as daughters-in-law. The majority of the respondents regarded the care of aged parents-in-law as an imperative moral duty. When no alternative arrangements were feasible, they were even prepared to share their limited accommodation and provide food for close relatives. But the respondents of nuclear households were generally not prepared to go and live in the place of residence of their parents-in-law. The old concept that a daughter-in-law must put aside her convenience for the sake of serving the husband's parents was less unquestioningly accepted. Similarly, the responsibility of sharing expenses for educating brothers-in-law and marrying sisters-in-law was tactfully shirked. Under economic stress this was due more to financial reasons than to a rejection of such obligations in principle. On the other hand, there was a much greater desire to use money to satisfy feminine vanities. The very fact that women now either worked or saw themselves capable of independent earning made them less willing to submit to male authority. The fact that the role of men and women overlapped and became less differentiated has given Indian women a new self-confidence.

I. P. Desai points out that "the real advance which has been made during this period is actually a revolution that is being brought about in the outlook with regard to the concept of the status of women and their role in society. Now a woman is no longer looked upon as a

child-bearing machine and a harlot in the home. She has acquired a
new status and social stature."[7] D. C. Dubey and A. K. Devgan also
argue,

> There are unmistakable signs that the traditional
> concepts regarding the place and role of women
> are slowly changing in contemporary Indian socie-
> ty. The process has been generated and aided by
> a variety of factors which are operating almost si-
> multaneously. Increasing opportunities for modern
> education, a greater geographical and occupational
> mobility and the emergence of new economic pat-
> terns are in the main responsible for this trend.[8]

The respondents confirmed the point made by Dubey and Devgan,
that, due not only to education but also because of the socioeconomic
culture around them, the position of women within the family has
changed radically. Even those who were part of an effective joint
family were no longer completely subdued or willing to accept the
dominant position of the mother-in-law.

The kind of family that the respondents were married into made
a crucial difference in the measure of the respondents' capacity to assert themselves as individuals. Those respondents who were married
into a joint family or a nuclear-linked joint household were less capable of establishing their rights as individuals, but even they were
aware of these rights and did not think it unethical to demand respect,
consideration, and accommodation from others. The economic circumstances and the financial contribution of respondents to the family
budget were also an important factor in reducing the respondents'
sense of obligation to the extended family. For the majority of the
respondents, the motivation to work was, in the first instance, to improve the standard of living for their immediate family. In most
cases, employment was accepted for reasons other than intellectual
self-fulfillment, usually as a means to afford greater material amenities or to gain status in a multicaste professional group.

Of the post-Independence respondents, 36 percent continued
with their professions or took up work immediately after marriage
and were earning between 350 and 750 rupees per month, while 30
percent took up jobs for the first time on an average of four years
and eight months after their marriage. Only 20 percent of the women
from this group were not working. Most of them wanted to work,
and the only reason they did not do so was because they were unable
to find employment. Notwithstanding their education and self-confidence, they were still not prepared to go against their husband's
wishes. Of the respondents who were working, the great majority had

done so with the approval of their husbands. But, even with their independent earnings, they did not go so far as to consider themselves
their husbands' equals in the marriage partnership. The husband was
still viewed in the light of the ideal of pativrata, even if the relationship was not characterized by the same kind of submission and commitment. The wives still left major decisions in the hands of their
husbands. Marriage was still viewed by the great majority as an in-
dissoluble sacrament.

This continuing deference to the traditional ideal has meant that
adjustments have had to be made in a variety of ways to changed social
conditions. The fact that these women were earning a separate income altered their attitude toward both their husbands and their in-
laws. Increasingly the women were unwilling to have their income
considered as part of the joint family income or even joint with their
husbands. Whereas the respondents were able to see their earnings
in a new light, as far as their ancestral rights were concerned, they
accepted the customary privilege of parents to distribute or dispose
of it according to their wishes. The majority were not prepared to
claim the right of equal inheritance with their brothers. The respondents stated that they would have liked equal treatment but were not
prepared to enter into a legal dispute to assert their rights. They
recognized that their parents were not completely just in how they
viewed the claims of daughters, but, at the same time, they understood the logic behind their parents' action. The respondents, in their
turn, stated that they would view their own male and female children
as "almost" equal. Even with the respondents, the sentiment per-
sisted that it was only with sons that they could share a home and only
to them that they would turn in time of need.

The great majority of the respondents were not prepared to
alienate themselves totally from their kin group. Any action on their
part to convert their parents to change their ways of thinking would
have brought with it severe criticism from the kin group. The respondents, therefore, exercised real control over their own families
but were not able to make a real change in the attitudes of their parents. Modern attitudes and a different pattern of spending was strictly
limited to the personal domain of the respondents' home. It was clear
from the respondents that, whereas they were prepared to go against
the caste-community ethics in many ways, they were not really prepared to break away from the kin group. Even those respondents who
were part of the multicaste secular society argued that kin group support was not to be discarded completely, primarily because it was the
most reliable source from which they could expect help in such things
as finding employment for themselves and their children. It became
clear from the responses that only those respondents who were highly
affluent and had upper-class status could afford to alienate themselves
from kin group support.

EVALUATION OF THE CHANGE BETWEEN
PRE- AND POST-INDEPENDENCE

This analysis of two groups of women, one belonging to the pre-Independence period and the other to post-Independent India, shows that their attitudes and goals were part of the social climate of two differing eras. The earlier generation of women were more willing to abide by traditional norms and more accepting of the conventional attitudes regarding the role of women. This was partly due to traditional upbringing and partly a result of the fact that the earlier generation of women entered families at a time when there was greater social and professional immobility, less threat to the maintenance of inherited social standing, and more faith in the continuance of the joint family in the future. Women then could afford to consider their education as an instrument that widened their horizon, giving them a greater interest in activities around them. There was really no compulsion to break with the existing prejudices regarding the society's attitude to keeping them mainly family-centered and their roles distinct from those of men. In that period, working was clearly not associated with economic necessity.

The women of the pre-Independence had really no reason to take up professional life or work as there was no economic compulsion to do so. Having come from families that already enjoyed status, they were also fairly certain that their children, by virtue of the parental position, would continue in the same economic and class strata of society. There was reason for them to believe that status was self-generating, and, therefore, there was no real anxiety for their children's future. In such a social climate, it was easier for the group of women belonging to the earlier generation to maintain joint family ties and remain within caste community ethics as far as possible. In spite of their own conditioning, and their links with the caste community, they were not willing to influence their children in the same direction. Being ambition-oriented, they wanted their children to profit from the new avenues that opened up, even if it meant violating certain traditional injunctions and norms. Though there was no pressing economic need, they realized that in order to give children the best possible education, they could not afford to have large families. This awareness was brought about, not through a family-planning campaign but because of widening horizons of interests. Even though women were still family-centered, they became more interested in activities outside the home. Children had already ceased to be the only source of satisfaction.

Women in this transition had also become more aware of the health hazards of having too many children. This group of women from the pre-Independence period, having a number of contacts with

Western patterns of education and values, but without economic
stress, show the first beginnings in the realization of the advantages
of fewer children. The average number of children in this group of
50 women was 3.5, which was far lower than the national average.
A more definitive positive interest in smaller families developed,
however, as the middle class faced economic difficulties. As has
been pointed out above, it is factors associated with economic stress
that have led to the most dramatic changes in the structure of the
family in recent years. Respondents of the post-Independence period
came to realize that if they had to maintain their standards of living
and improve on them, they could not remain inactive or continue their
roles as wives and mothers only. They were brought up to see in education an economic return. As parents, this need was reinforced.
They realized that if they were to provide for their children adequate
amenities, so that they could face the challenge of the future, then not
only had they to earn but they also had to reallocate their earnings, so
that children's education could get a greater priority in the family budget. This modern generation was also helped by the more liberal attitudes prevailing in society in redefining the role of women; society
became more accepting of their aspirations as individuals.

New constitutional and legislative enactments in India, combined
with social leadership and education, have transformed the rights and
status of women and given them a number of opportunities to enhance
their own positions. The government's policy of equal opportunities
for all, irrespective of caste, class, creed, or sex, has given women
an added incentive to enlarge their goals. Equality of opportunity has
also been accompanied by an urge for competitive merit as the basis
for mobility, and this has enabled women to overcome traditional disabilities and prejudices. At the same time, since merit, rather than
status, plays a larger role in determining entrance into government
schools, colleges, and jobs, the middle class has seen new threats to
its social status. Middle-class people have realized that the preservation of their social standing in the new situation is under a double
threat: the continuing advantage of the upper-class, higher-income
group relative to their own, on the one side, and the upsurge of new
competition from what was the lower-income group, on the other.

The middle class has therefore become aware that if they are
to face the challenge of egalitarian government policies, they must
make a new effort to preserve their own middle-class standing for the
next generation. It must be noted that, while the objectives of a more
socially just policy were proclaimed in millennial fashion, the expansion of facilities to provide equal opportunities, which in turn would
permit upward social mobility, was necessarily more gradual. For
example, primary education spread quickly, but there were limited
numbers of vacancies in schools or colleges or in employment. Pres-

sure against these limited opportunities increased fast. The middle class was quicker and more able to adjust to the new situation than those belonging to a lower income strata, and they generally set higher goals for their children in education when compared to those set by their parents. Altogether, my group of post-Independence respondents were vigilant against these threats, and this too accounts for changes in their social priorities and value systems.

In many ways, then, the greatest change between the pre- and post-Independence eras can be described in terms of a transformation in the status of women and their values regarding extended family responsibilities. While the former group viewed itself as subordinate to men and did not have the confidence or courage to defy conventional prejudices or their husband's authority over them, the modern educated Indian woman is more assured in her status as a separate identity. She has become more of an individual in her own right. The interviews clearly showed this difference between the two groups of women. This added confidence of modern educated Indian women is due to many factors, but one of the more important is the new rights conferred by post-Independence legislation.

The Hindu Code Bill of 1954-55 made Hindu marriage monogamous and established marriages as a contract that could be terminated by either party. Women no longer have to remain within the marriage fold because they have no legal way of getting out of it. The economic subservience of women to men's authority was also in the past due to the fact that women had no right to property. But the Hindu Succession Act of 1956 conferred on the widow, the daughter, and the mother the right to inherit equally with the sons. It is too early to state to what extent this legislation has, in fact, led to the transfer of ancestral property in equal share between the male and the female members of a family, but among respondents in this study it was found that the parents of the respondents were still inclined to regard daughters as unequal with their brothers with regard to the diffusion of property. Boys were still seen as the rightful heirs to family wealth.

As has been pointed out on a number of occasions, parents look to sons for support in old age and, in keeping with tradition, maintain that it is only with sons that parents can share a home. They still do not consider living with daughters as ethical or right. This being the case, parents naturally regard boys as more integral to the family psychologically and in terms of economic well being. Parents do assume full responsibility for unmarried girls and consider it their prime duty to see daughters well settled, but they also feel that parental responsibility ends with the marriage of a daughter. The parents accept responsibility for expenses on education and a dowry, but that is the limit to which they see the rights of the daughter over the family or its wealth. Respondents in this study who had not received equal shares of property from their parents had accepted this as part of their parents' orthodox orientation.

However, even though respondents did not legally challenge the rights of their brothers as the major inheritors of family property, they were, at the same time, not convinced of the justice of this way of looking at things. This was a great change from the pre-Independence era, when women accepted their role of economic dependence more passively. Even though the respondents did not protest against discrimination, the fact of new rights under the law of the land does give the middle-class women today a greater sense of security, psychologically, against possible contingencies of economic distress.

Next to change in the legal status of women, the biggest difference in post-Independence India has been the spread of education, both primary and higher, among women in all strata of society. Among respondents in this study, education was looked upon as both an economic necessity and an essential embellishment for a good marriage. According to the 1951 census, only 8 percent of the women of India were literate, and they were confined to the urban middle- and higher-income groups. According to the census of 1971, while 13 percent of the women in rural areas are literate, the proportion in the urban areas has gone up to 42 percent. As compared to the situation in the pre-Independence period, in the present generation education is being more systematically planned and directed toward future employment. The role of women in this generation has changed, strikingly, from one of being only wives and mothers to one of being coearners with the husband. As is clear from the interviews, middle-class women now are highly motivated to get employment, if only because it is through their own earnings that they can maintain their middle-class standard of living. This change in economic conditions in India over the last 25 years is especially relevant to the change in the attitude of women toward gainful employment. The rise in the cost of living and, simultaneously, the heightening of demands and aspirations for better standards have been important factors in moving middle-class women away from traditional roles.

The respondents' answers clearly showed that in the middle-class-status group, the moving away from traditional roles has in turn affected the life-style and structure of the family. Though studies by A. M. Shah, I. P. Desai, and K. T. Merchant show that there are more joint households in urban areas than in rural areas, in-depth interviews with these 100 women showed that, irrespective of the influences in the natal family, 88 percent preferred the nuclear household to the joint family. [9] In the pre-Independence group, in spite of education and social status, only a small number of women were able to establish nuclear households, but in the post-Independence group a much higher number was able to do so. The reason for

the latter group's becoming more independent of joint family authority
had to do with changes in status.

Because they are earning, working women have a greater say
in what kind of home and style of living they want to establish for themselves. Living in a joint household and yet earning independently
means that they have to play two roles, in one being subordinate to
the patriarch and in the other being equal to men. Family permission
to work is given, in modification of traditional joint family etiquette,
because additional earnings contribute to the maintenance of the family's middle-class status. However, there are other needs, such as
privacy, freedom to choose friends, and the desire to have greater
companionship with the husband, that make joint family living less
attractive. This new sense of a separate identity for women, born
out of education and earning capacity, has unquestionably disturbed
the harmony of the joint family. As M. S. Gore has pointed out in
his book Urbanization and Family Change, "maintenance of the joint
family as a system requires the effective subordination of the conjugal
tie and of the nuclear family as a distinct unit."[10] This was fully
corroborated by the responses of the 50 post-Independence respondents
in this study. When the wife became a working partner with her husband, the conjugal relationship was one of greater companionship and
mutual respect. Both husband and wife were now more concerned
with the well being of their immediate family than with that of the
joint family.

The cohesion of joint-family living has also been eroded because
the patterns of occupation are more divorced from kinship or caste
community culture. The members of families in white-collar professions cannot usually work as a family unit, or in similar occupations,
or remain in geographical proximity. The influence of caste in determining status has decreased with urbanized diffusion; it is now determined much more by education and occupation. The post-Independence
respondents in this study, whether they were nuclear-based or not,
were evaluating their status in new terms. Their peer groups had
changed; status equations were now within the secular and professional
hierarchy. The standards of living they emulated and the aspirations
they cherished were from the multicaste urban society; they were
much less interested in socioreligious practices that strengthened
their caste-community bonds. This does not mean that they had become less religious or less Hindu in their beliefs. It only means that
they had recast their religious obligations to suit their economic standards and needs. Milton Singer found in his study in Madras the same
reorganizing of religious rituals and practices to suit urban living.[11]

The first priority of post-Independence respondents was to try
and profit from the new professional opportunities and material amenities that came up before them in modern India. As stated earlier,

this priority of concern, both economic and social, centered around
the upbringing of children. Moreover, with rising costs, this priority posed a problem. Respondents recognized that, for their children
either to maintain middle-class status or to rise above it, considerable emphasis had to be placed on education. Most respondents,
therefore, sought to allocate the major share of the family budget to
send children to better schools, requiring high tuition fees, rather
than send them to the poorer free schools available in the government-
financed system. Most respondents also found that this kind of priority to education and allied expenses could be better given in a nuclear
home than in a joint family. Parents could give both greater attention
to children and also spend more on them without having to take into
account the children of brother and in-law.

Overriding aspirations, combined with economic stress and a
rationalization of priorities in the family budget, led respondents to
recognize the appeal of family planning, and the logic of restricting
the number of children. Almost all of them saw a direct correlation
between the future social advancement of their children and the size
of their family. Thus, the family size of the 50 respondents in the
post-Independence era has gone down from 3.5 (for the pre-Independence group) to 2.4. The post-Independence respondents clearly did
not see children as an economic asset; they were aware of the cost
of bringing up children and that a large family was not only a debili-
tating financial strain but also a threat to their own standard of living
in the multicaste urban society. Thus, in the middle-class status
group, women were generally not prepared to try for a male issue
after the third child. Since both boys and girls were regarded as an
economic liability, a male issue, however desirable, was not considered worth the risk of descending in the social hierarchy.

Besides this, servants in the post-Independence era were more
difficult to get and were increasingly beyond the economic range of
the middle-class family. This generation could not count on family
retainers, especially when they moved to urban areas. The upbringing of children, therefore, became largely the responsibility of the
wife. It was obviously difficult for a working woman to rear too many
children and at the same time have a job in which she sought to improve her prosperity. Women became increasingly aware that every
addition of a child increases the complexity of combining family responsibilities with occupational obligations, all the while reducing
future educational prospects for all family children. Being success-
motivated for the next generation, mothers did not want to lessen
their chances by having to spread their earnings on too many children.

In most families in the post-Independence sample, there were
no grandparents and dependent relations in the home to help look af-

ter children. Incidentally, it is interesting to note that the need for
help to look after the house and children sometimes modified the working woman's attitude toward having relatives living with her. In spite
of the preference for nuclear households, some women were more prepared to accommodate in-laws, if they could be useful and free the
respondents from domestic work and the caring of children. But, in
this kind of joint living, the woman still held her authority and independence.

We have seen that, from the pre-Independence period, there
has been a definite shift in the structure of the family from joint to
nuclear. We have also seen that this, combined with other factors,
has led the middle-class status group in India to become highly motivated in restricting the size of the family.

It may now be useful to compare, in a general way, these findings with attitudes in urban-based blue-collar families from the same
income levels.

WHITE- AND BLUE-COLLAR VALUES

In the cities, there are sizable numbers of blue-collar workers—
truck drivers, mechanics, masons, factory workers—whose family
income is in the same range as the respondents in the sample analyzed above (450 to 1,500 rupees). Such blue-collar workers have usually migrated fairly recently to the urban areas in search of better
employment opportunities. Among blue-collar workers, however,
fathers and sons are often both earning, and the usual practice is for
them to pool their incomes and live in the same household. These
families, though separate in residence from the joint family, are very
closely linked to it.

While differences between blue- and white-collar workers, in
terms of their gross earnings, has narrowed, the values and attitudes
of the blue-collar family have, comparatively speaking, remained un-
changed. While kin group and caste and community-centered family
obligations in the middle-class status group have increasingly been
viewed as economic burdens, the blue-collar worker has maintained
close links with the caste community when outlining aspirations for
himself and for his children. Because of this, blue-collar workers
tend to regard male children as economic assets. The investment in
a child's education is only for a limited period of time before he can
become a full-fledged earning member contributing to the family income.

The KAP Surveys have shown that, among urban blue-collar
workers, there is often knowledge of family planning but no consistent
practice of it.[12] It is, therefore, not ignorance of the methods or

means of family planning that come in the way of restricting the size of the family among blue-collar workers but rather the preference for male children because they are seen in terms of economic advantage. There is also, of course, some continuance of a fatalistic attitude about life and death and a belief in predestination. What is decreed by fate, including the number of children, is often accepted as inevitable, with man being able to affect his future only in marginal ways. Among people who believe this way, children are often viewed as a gift of God, for whom the Almighty will provide once they are born.

Unlike the middle-class status group, the peer group of the blue-collar workers is his own occupational class, and not the multi-caste ambition-oriented class. The urban blue-collar worker is still concerned with the maintenance of his caste community ties and the improvement of his status in it. He is, therefore, looking to enhance his prestige among his kin around him and among the caste community group in the place of his origin. This is often achieved by continuing to observe ritualistic practices connected with marriage, birth, and death, all the while making them more elaborate in order to gain status. Kin groups that cannot afford the same kind of lavishness are impressed, and, therefore, they confer greater prestige on those who spend more on ceremonies.

With the motivation to achieve standing in the eyes of the caste community, blue-collar workers with enhanced earnings usually give more dowry and include in them nontraditional items like transistor radios, watches, and so forth, which are not normally within the range of others in a lower-income bracket in this community. While the middle-class group, which attaches a high priority to private and higher education, has been cutting down on ritualistic practices and even on nonutilitarian consumption expenditure, the consumption patterns of the blue-collar worker are all moving in the opposite direction.

The family structure of the blue-collar worker contributes to a reinforcement of the spending habits of this class. In this group the position of the woman is still subordinate to joint-family discipline and, therefore, blue-collar women have very little say in family decision-making processes. Even if a woman has ambitions for her children, she cannot insist that a larger share of the family budget go toward their schooling because this would be considered a violation of joint family harmony. Nor can she afford to disengage herself from her body of relatives, since she has no other means to establish herself; indeed, it is only through the approval of the joint family members that she gains in her own self-esteem. It is the joint family that also makes her marriage secure. Moreover, her home has to be open to all kin group members, irrespective of the

family's convenience or economic possibility. The woman's contribution in such a household is not in monetary terms but in kind. Her
sociocultural environment prevents her from becoming an individual;
she remains completely subject to her husband's authority and decision-making. The status consciousness here seems to work in reverse; bearing in mind that the point of reference for blue-collar women is the rural situation, from which they have come—and where
women ordinarily do manual work in the fields—status considerations
are enhanced if a woman can stay at home without having the need to
work.

The blue-collar worker would also like to see his son become an
officer or a doctor, but he does not see the causal reasons pointing to
a decision to invest in higher education now for such a fulfillment for
the next generation. The conclusion emerges that the blue-collar
worker, while much better off in monetary terms, is much less liber-
ated from traditional values to profit from this improvement, and his
aspirations for his children are not radically different from his own.
Nor does the standard of living of the blue-collar worker rise in proportion to his enhanced family earnings. The reasons for the striking
difference between the blue- and the white-collar groups in this respect seems to stem not from their incomes but rather from their attitudes and value systems.

What is evident is that both the white-collar and the blue-collar
worker are motivated by status-building considerations. Indeed,
status-building plays a role in every stratum in every society. In the
analysis being undertaken here, the aspirations and directions of
status-building between the white-collar and the blue-collar groups,
though in the same income bracket, are becoming increasingly diver-
gent. In the case of the middle-class group, the combination of various factors and economic pressures converge to a conscious effort at
smaller families with significant investment in preserving and improving status-building in the present and for the future. On the other
hand, with the blue-collar middle-income group (also in the urban
areas), the quest for status-building is traditional in character, with
the result that children are looked upon as economic assets, and earnings still go primarily into consumption in ritualistic outlays.

What conclusions, if any, can we draw from this micro-study to
accelerate the acceptance of the logic of smaller families and to bring
about the necessary motivation and voluntary participation as a contribution to family planning programs? It is conceded that the middle-
class status group is small and statistically atypical. Therefore, ex-
trapolating on conclusions drawn from observing them can at best be
applied in a limited sphere. But this middle-class group, along with
the upper-income group in the urban areas, does show a definite motivation toward family planning. How can this motivation factor perco-

late to other groups, notably the blue-collar workers whose numbers
and earnings have significantly increased in the post-Independence
period? Could one make them see that freedom from economic anxiety could be channeled into new priorities and a different form of
status-building, not in the traditional manner, but into one that would
ensure upward mobility for themselves and for their children? In
order to achieve this, their spending patterns would have to change.
They would have to learn to see the results of a consistent investment
in the education and upbringing of their children.

If by some mechanism one could inculcate in this group of blue-
collar workers a desire of deferred status-building, and therefore
make them see, if not in their own generation at least through the
coming generation a possibility of rising in the social order and of becoming a part of the middle-class social status group, then perhaps
one could achieve some impact on them with regard to the number of
children they perceived to be economically desirable. Perhaps the
mass media, and particularly television, could focus on the differences between middle-class status groups and middle-income blue-
collar groups, showing that income alone has not brought about differences in standards of living and conditions of children. This kind of
comparison would also show that it is how one spends one's income
and what hopes and aspirations are behind the spending that make a
difference. It would show too, that middle-class status groups often
make enormous sacrifices when scaling down on nonessential material requirements (like expensive clothes) for greater prosperity in
the generation ahead.

At any rate, blue-collar families must be convinced that it is
possible within their income range to give their children a better
education and thus make it possible for them to change their social
status. Such mobility cannot be achieved if there is continued spending on ritualistic practices or changing status symbols, such as sil-
ver-wearing or gold-wearing. The quest for immediate prestige
through jewelry or extravagant marriage festivities may gain for blue-
collar families immediate admiration from their caste community,
but it is a short-sighted investment, and in it there is no hope for
lasting social standing. By showing them that the use of the same
earnings by another group of the same bracket did result in improved
living conditions and did make possible the dream of a child becoming,
for example, a doctor, it would make them realize that they are not
less privileged in society. They must be made aware that spending
on expensive clothing and indulging in drinking, smoking, and even
frequenting restaurants is not in itself prestige-building. This kind
of expenditure should be shown as detrimental to the well being of
children. If the blue-collar worker could be persuaded to recognize
that he commands the means for better living and social mobility if

his spending habits can be altered, then his dreams too could come
true.

Blue-collar workers are of vital importance, since decisions
by them to limit the size of the family could become the demonstration model whose influence could percolate back to the caste community, which is often rural-based. If entire caste communities could
be influenced by new spending habits and new aspirations, for elders
and for children, this could well lead to deliberate control in the size
of families. Indeed, family planners might well adopt blue-collar
middle-income families as a special target of communications.
Since the blue-collar class is growing rather quickly, it is in a unique
position to derive benefits from the facilities provided in urban India,
such as better schools, better accommodations, and greater exposure
to new ideas and opportunities. The blue-collar worker cannot be inspired by the life-style of the rich, which is beyond him, but he can
be motivated if he sees higher social status being achieved by people
earning no more than he does.

IMPLICATIONS FOR FAMILY PLANNING:
CONCLUSIONS

This is a micro-study of a small unrepresentative group. The
demographic problem implicit in population trends and the need for
controlling the growth rate are now fully recognized, and so are the
disastrous consequences to the entire developmental effort if population trends cannot be arrested and reversed. Some radical methods
for tackling this problem, such as compulsory sterilization through
vasectomy or tubectomy, are not open to democracies or to states
that have regard for human freedom. In a government that rules by
consent or one that depends on voluntary cooperation, the demographic
problem can only be tackled through persuasion. Individuals must see
the advantages of smaller families for their own future well being if
they are going to restrict the size of their families.

It is generally accepted, and these depth interviews provide con-
firmation, that the factors most relevant to successful family planning
are the following: (1) wider and higher education, especially for women; (2) equality of rights and property for the different sexes; (3)
higher earnings, leading to greater interest in higher standards of living; and (4) the knowledge and ready availability of cheap and effective
means of contraception.

But the crucial element of individual motivation to restrict families is not necessarily higher earnings, the availability of the means
of contraception, or even a stimulus for greater propensity in consump-
l of these factors may be necessary, but they would appear to

be most effective when geared to a value system that sees in fewer
children a greater fulfillment for the family and better prospects for
the second generation.

The single most important factor in changing family values is
the spread of education among women, which in turn brings about
greater respect for women in the family. The legal emancipation following the Hindu Marriage Act has spurred aspirations for equal
rights, higher education, and independent fulfillment, particularly
within the middle class. The stigma of middle-class women taking to
paid employment has already been diluted in the last two decades, especially in urban areas. This becomes a powerful factor in women taking up jobs along with men and then continuing with these jobs even after marriage. Where a woman is working, or where both husband
and wife work, there is evidence of smaller families and changing
motivations. Despite economic compulsions, it is not easy for women
in joint families to work, whereas it is becoming normal for women
in nuclear families to do so. Members of nuclear families can now
freely aspire to a better standard of living and, above all, to different
priorities in social motivations.

If the conclusions from this micro-study are valid, it may have
implications in determining the thrust of national family planning policies. In bringing about participatory motivations for smaller families, massive investment in raising living standards may not be
enough. Social policy might well address itself to the promotion of
the white-collar worker's psychology and its use as a demonstration
model for wider imitation. Along with other aspects of the population puzzle, the crucial importance of education and the employment
of women in bringing about a change in the motivation for smaller
families must be recognized.

In a paper on women in rural areas, Mehra Masani gives these
details:

> Of the 50 million (adult women in rural areas), just
> over 3 million are classified as workers, while 47
> million are non-workers. Most of these are house-
> wives who render very useful service to society,
> but they perform unpaid household duties and are
> thus not treated as workers. The total urban work
> force is 32 million and women constitute less than
> 10 per cent, which is very low. Of the 29 million
> who are illiterate, only 2 million, or 6 per cent,
> work. Of those who have studied up to the matricu-
> lation level, 5 per cent are workers; of those with
> graduate degrees, 20 per cent work, and of those
> with specialist qualifications, over 60 per cent work.[13]

The majority of teachers, especially at the secondary and college levels are men. In 1965-66, women constituted only 24 percent and 37 percent of the teachers in the lower primary and upper primary schools, respectively. In this same year, only 17 percent of the teachers in schools for vocational education and institutions of higher education (arts and sciences) were women. Women teachers in colleges for professional education comprised only 11 percent. This shows that the number of women teachers in comparison to that of men teachers is still very low; this is the case even in teaching, which is a favorite profession for women.

According to the 1971 census figures, of the total of 170,000 unemployed women degree-holders, 90,000 (53 percent) were not seeking jobs. The situation is not so bad with women with technological degrees or vocational training. Only 9 percent of unemployed women with vocational training and 18 percent of women with some professional education choose to remain unemployed.

The point is that there is a great national waste in trained and educated women not seeking employment. Every effort must be made to encourage and provide work opportunities for educated and career-minded girls. Women in India can take up white-collar jobs, such as teachers, nurses, typists, and so forth. The old notion that a woman at work deprives a man of someone to look after his household has to be balanced against the advantageous spill-off of female employment and its impact in family planning motivation. Since there is a higher proportion of vocationally trained women seeking employment and continuing with it, a more deliberate policy to include women on the vocational side must be encouraged as part of the family planning strategy. More and more facilities for part-time working women should be created. This, in turn, means more day-care centers, kindergartens, and other facilities in the urban areas. Adult literacy must be made attractive for women, and that too especially for vocational training.

If better education for fewer children as a means to status-building plays such a telling part in family planning motivation, then the status-building associated with better schools, requiring some payment of fees to cater to the middle-income group, must be encouraged and receive government's indirect support. This may appear as a compromise with the goals of egalitarianism and social justice, but sociological data point to a program not just large in outlay but effective in its results.

By and large, notwithstanding the hold of old values, Hindu society has shown a much greater capacity to adjust to modernity than many sociologists had considered likely. With a corrective thrust in national plans, and programs of persuasion toward the imperative of family planning, the necessary motivation for voluntary participation can spread more quickly, holding out the promise of success, at least in sections of society where poverty has been lifted and where the opportunities for education, health, and better accommodation are now within the reach of sizable numbers.

DISCUSSION

<u>Joseph Elder</u>: I would like to begin with a number of appreciative statements about this paper. First of all, the sheer quality of the interview material from the 100 middle-class women is something that is still much sought after and not easily attainable. For those of us who have tried as males to interview females in India, and who have discovered the incredible cultural barriers, it's fine to have data gathered from women by a woman researcher. I have a feeling of reality and factualness from the interviews that she reports.

A second note of appreciation has to do with the clarity with which she presents her findings. I was able to cull three rather nice, tidy propositions out of the paper. The first of these is the proposition that pre-Independence college-graduate daughters of British administrative personnel have smaller families than other pre-Independence middle-class daughters. There were two types of middle-class people in the pre-Independence sample. One came out with a few more daughters than the other. The second significant finding that she presents seems to me to be the finding that present-day urban white-collar families are smaller than the pre-Independence white-collar families. Questions can be raised as to how one interprets this, but the finding is there in front of us and the data seem quite convincing. The post-Independence families had 2.4 children on the average, the pre-Independence families 3.5 on the average. The third significant finding is her observation that the urban white-collar families today, in a given income bracket, are smaller than the urban blue-collar families in the same income bracket. I'll raise some questions about this later on, but the proposition is there, and it's tidy.

A third point of appreciation that I'd like to state has to do with the clear articulation of her suggested explanation for these propositions. Again, I think it's fairly rare for one to come across a statement that spells out, or makes an effort to spell out, a relationship between cause and effect. Moreover, it is a great credit to a paper when you can take the same data and present them sufficiently clearly so that you can come out with an alternative explanation of cause and effect, which I will try to do. It is Mehta's data and her clarity of expression that have stimulated an effort to come up with some kind of counterthesis.

Finally, a fourth note of appreciation deals with this strategy proposal, the policy, the target possibility, the message. Again, this is rare to encounter, and it is set up there very nicely for everyone to explore. In terms of another perspective on the same contribution, the balance of the depth of interviews with the middle-class families, I thought, was reflected in the absence of interviews with the blue-collar families, and blue-collar women especially. Mehta acknowledged that this was something that was missing. I had a feeling that, in a sense, the richness of the one was counterbalanced by what seemed to be, at some point, speculation as to why the blue-collar people were behaving as reported. One would hope for such systematic interviews with blue-collar families as well.

In terms of the findings, do they stand up under scrutiny? I felt that two of them fairly well did, while the third I have some questions about. The two that seem to me supported, at least by the evidence presented, are the ones about the pre-Independence British administrative families and the other middle-class families. There's one cell missing in the figure, if one were to draw cells, but I won't take time with these kinds of details. Also, the observation that urban blue-collar families today are larger than middle-class families today, in the same income bracket, seems accurate. Again, there is a cell missing, but I won't take time with that.

The finding that I have some question about—not that it may not still be true, but I just felt that there was some additional data that I would like—had to do with the comparison between the post-Independence white-collar families and the pre-Independence white-collar families. The pre-Independence families averaged 3.5 children and the post-Independence families 2.4. These figures I am quite willing to accept. But there were other variables besides simply the pre- and post-Independence variables that seemed to be worth looking at. For example, the post-Independence marriages began later. Perhaps family size in this case is more attributable to later marriages than it is to the values that Mehta suggests.

The second question I have about this is that the interviews with the post-Independence women were largely with women between the ages of 30 and 35, while those with the pre-Independence women were between 46 and 50. It seems to me there is a chance that the women who are now between 30 and 35 may still have another child. We won't know until we can say definitively that this is as many as they are going to have. So, it may be an artifact of the ages at which we're interviewing, and to confirm the observation is would be necessary to continue the study further.

But those, in a sense, are minor points. On the blue-collar/white-collar comparisons, I have a question about whether these really were from similar income groups. The income was stated as com-

bined family income for both the blue-collar and white-collar groups.
A range of 450 rupees per month to 1,500 rupees per month was given.
However, it should be pointed out that in the groups we're speaking
of—in the critical groups, the educated women—that many of them were
working; and they were drawing salaries between 350 rupees per
month and 750 rupees per month. If one combines that with what
their husbands were getting, presuming the husbands were earning
more, one ends up with what would seem to me a substantially richer
group of people. You mentioned that the blue-collar families often
had a son and a father working to produce a combined family income,
but I'm not sure if that makes incomes completely parallel. If we're
speaking of parents' income and combining it with that of the children,
then it would seem to me that one would have to take the mother's and
father's income among blue-collar and white-collar families as the
resources available to the family. If we have to take the children's
income and combine it with the parents' income, it seems to me there
is a measuring problem here.

     This does not raise any fundamental questions about the major
findings. I am willing to accept the presumable observation that blue-
collar families, with roughly the same income, have many more children than white-collar families. The question I raise is with regard
to the exactness of the parallel.

     Turning to the explanatory model, here is where I come up with
a somewhat different conclusion, and this is based on the same data
that Mehta presents. She makes a thoroughly strong case that family
structure and an ideology of autonomy on the part of women are the
critical variables. To the extent that nuclear families are accepted,
and to the extent that one can accept women appreciating not having a
joint family around them, to this extent one has pressure for smaller
families. This is, in a sense, a key link. For the pre-Independence
period, there seems to have been a definite shift in the family from
joint to nuclear. This, combined with other factors, has brought the
middle-class status group in India to become highly motivated to restrict the size of the family. Going back to the internal figures, I was
struck by the relative continuity in the proportion of women in both
pre- and post-Independence periods with joint families. The pre-Independence figure was 36 percent, the post-Independence figure was
30 percent. I was more startled that there was not a greater degree
of difference than this. Also, the various studies that have been done
that ask, "When is a family nuclear, when is a family joint, and when
is it something in between?" raises questions, and some of Mehta's
data also indicated that. So, I am not sure that the evidence is that
clear-cut. I am not sure that it is family structure that is linked most
highly to the number of children one has.

In fact, it is clear that at certain points, when wives are working for example, that they would like to have relatives with them to watch after the children. This raises the possibility that contemporary values may be such as to reactivate the joint family, in part for the purposes of the mother, so that she has a mother-in-law and some sisters-in-law there to take care of the children. Among the blue-collar workers, since we do not have the richness of data, we do not know whether they have joint families, nuclear families, or something in between. So it is impossible to make a comparison there.

The second variable Mehta raises, in addition to the structure of the family as a critical joining variable, was the point about legal rights—the marriage act, divorce acts, inheritance and tax legislation, and so forth. She implies that changes in legal rights make for changes across the board—among urban families, rural families, and blue-collar families. I'm not sure that the case is made one way or the other. It may be true, but I think some alternatives may be plausible.

A third variable that Mehta talks about, and I think here the evidence is quite impressive, is the spread of education. As a crucial variable, the linkage between the desire for smaller families and the spread of education did seem to me to be quite convincing. However, one could interpret this in such a way as to come up with a counterexplanation. It seems that a key figure here has to do with the fact that many of these educated women, in fact 80 percent if the figures are correct, were employed outside the home. I think a case can be made that, if not education alone then education plus a reasonably high-paying job outside the house, would be a strong stimulus for smaller families. This may be more important for the joint family than for the nuclear family. If a woman has an education and has a chance for a job outside the home that draws between 350 and 750 rupees per month, I can see her motivation for wanting to have as few children as possible, if only because this is a substantial increment for the family income. This I suggest as a counterexplanation for the phenomenon.

Finally, for the target group of blue-collar workers, Mehta suggests that the message is one of changing attitudes, trying to get people to want smaller families, and also changing consumption patterns from wanting finer clothes, transistor radios, dinner out at restaurants, and so on, using their money instead for schooling, since this seems to be a critical variable. The target is that blue-collar workers will imitate white-collar workers in reducing the size of their families. Eventually Mehta hopes for a percolator effect, with blue-collar workers imitating the model of the white-collar workers and blue-collar workers serving as a model for their relatives out in the countryside.

If one accepts the counterexplanation, then it seems that another variety of strategies would be called for. I am not certain how large a percentage within India's population would fit into the blue-collar category, but my guess is that it would be a relatively small group. If one is going to go at this thing, it seems to me that we may want a message that appeals directly to the larger bulk of the population. It seems to me that the target here should be rural wives and rural families, and a message might be called for that was directed particularly at them.

With regard to the message itself, I have mixed feelings. I question the assumption that blue-collar workers are deliberately not sending their children to better schools, that they'd rather spend their money on restaurants, expensive clothes, and so forth. From what I've been able to see in a number of research papers on the educational apparatus in Delhi, getting into a good school in Delhi is a very complicated process. This involves family contacts, prestige, and intellectual friends. It may be that the blue-collar workers would be very happy to have their children go into prestige schools, but, realistically, they are barred by the way in which the admission procedures screen out the people who do not have contacts, even if they do have income. So we may be blaming a particular group of people for not doing something prevented by social institutions.

On this question as to whether blue-collar workers really want their children in school, I have seen some information and data, in surveys that I gathered myself, to the effect that there is a high and often unrealistic aspiration among parents of all classes for their children, and particularly with regard to education. Very often in Indian society when the question is put, "What would you like your son to be if money were no problem?" there seems to be an overwhelming response similar to that contained in my data from south India, which indicated that there'd be such an overload of doctors and lawyers that it would positively skew the entire employment picture. So it may be that there is a pressure there that acts as a brake on aspirations; perhaps this explains the tendency of blue-collar workers to put money into clothes, dowries, and so on, because they cannot get their children into prestige schools.

It does seem to me that, ultimately, the hope is to convince people that it is to their own real advantage, whatever other sets of values they have, to want to limit their families. This brings me to my last point, which has to do with understanding the cognitive map of all groups in society. There has to be an appeal to rural workers, blue-collar workers, and white-collar workers. For each group, one has to ask, "What is in it for them if they limit the size of their families?" At present, there does not seem to be very much in it for limiting the size of the family in many sections of society.

There was a suggestion this morning that, in many sectors, there seems to be something in it to have as many children as possible, and this suggests that the whole system of institutional mechanisms, cultural mores, and so on, are involved. I will just clip off a series of suggestions here as to the kinds of things I would look at, although none of these are terribly well thought out. These are simply presented as topics for argument. If it is women's employment out of the home that is the crucial variable, then it would seem as though a useful strategy in the planning of jobs or in arranging public investment might be the creation of a new cadre of out-of-home jobs for women. If it were possible to, say, triple or quadruple the number of Public Health Centers and to train, say, high school equivalent paramedicals in these centers, this might provide, in a sense, a source of incentive for families to postpone having their daughters get married because there was a real obvious benefit to their daughters in getting jobs in these centers. Someone suggested that creation of rural industries might be a way to provide economic alternatives close to villages so that daughters could work for a few years at tasks for which they were qualified, to earn salaries that might, in the end, help with their dowry. Other things, like day-care centers, are obviously needed. Even persons at middle-trained levels could perform useful services here and make it useful and practical to defer one's marriage. In fact, the key to the success of such schemes may be the maintenance of an interest in having few children after marriage.

The second suggestion I would make is the possibility of adoption. This could be advertised, recommended, and made publicly acceptable, at least to the extent that family planning has been recently. A third suggestion, in a broad strategy, would be some kind of relatively secure provision for the elderly who for some reason or other end up with no children to support them. Relatively speaking, this would not be a costly program, but people should feel that, should everything else go wrong, should their son die, there is some place for dignity and a minimum of comfort where they could live out their years without facing starvation. This might add incentive for smaller families. Another sort of draconian measure that Kingsley Davis talks about is free urban housing for males. This might encourage factory workers to leave their wives back in the villages. If it costs something to bring the wife and children in to rent a place, and you can live for nothing alone in quarters that were just for men, this might reduce the chances for more children since the men would be in the cities and the wives in the villages.

Phillips Talbot: Excuse me, Joe. That has been the pattern in Bombay and the textile areas, and in other cities . . .

<u>Marcus F. Franda</u>: . . . without reducing family size.

<u>Talbot</u>: That's right; that was my point.

<u>Elder</u>: I realize this might not go very far, but it should be suggested. Other things that might be mentioned are plans for savings for couples when they're married, or programs where they receive benefits for delaying having second children and third children; details would have to be worked out, but it seems to be worth exploring. Finally, my last suggestion, which dips into new technology. It seems to me we still do not have the ideal technological device for family planning. Experimentation is going on with morning-after pills, one-year pills, five-year pills, and so on. I realize that the IUD was the great hope that failed, but it seems to me that we still need a technological breakthrough that will enable people who want to limit their families to prevent the kinds of mistakes that have gone on.

<u>A. M. Shah</u>: First of all, I do find a category of people, in certain employment sectors, who have more or less accepted the idea of limiting family size. I would be in broad agreement with Mehta's findings in this respect, not on the basis of any systematic study but on the basis of personal observation. My major difficulty is that, while one can discuss a number of variables that might account for this, Mehta has put them under the broad general labels "joint family" and "nuclear family," and I have some reservations about that. I don't think this is an important problem so long as we are discussing the various variables that are there, without putting them under these broad labels.

   Mehta's paper suggests two things. The first is the importance of the husband-and-wife relationship. Unfortunately, despite all of the attention given to the family in India, we hardly have any good piece of work on husband-wife relationships in any sector, whether it be rural, urban, or any of the classes or groups. But it is very clear that the husband-and-wife relationship has changed during the last 25-30 years. The most important change that has come about is that husband and wife consider themselves as some kind of equals, which was not the case before, and this clearly comes out in this paper. Arising out of this is the fact that husband and wife discuss a number of problems among themselves that were previously not discussed. One of the items of discussion between husband and wife is the question of family-size limitation and the way of going about it. Another very important change that has come about among middle-class people is in attitudes about the desirability of a son versus a daughter. I can cite a number of cases of people in this category who would consider a son and daughter as equal in terms of desirability.

Urban middle-class couples may want both a daughter and a son, but
if they do not have a son they do not make too much fuss about it.
A fuss is still made in the rural areas. Many things follow from
this: Brother-sister relationships are changed; brother-brother relationships are changed; and sister-sister relationships are changed.

Is it likely that the norms and attitudes of these people will
spread and be taken over by others? So far as the rural areas are
concerned, we do not have many studies to go by, but I think we can
make some general observations. First, I would say that, in the villages as well as in the urban areas, there has been an addition of at
least one idea to the cognitive map of the people over the last two
decades. That is that they should consider the question of limiting
the size of the family. In the villages that I am studying, I find many
villagers, when they gather together in the panchayat area, or when
they gather around at night, discuss this problem, and from many
different angles. Whenever they go to the town, they pick up whatever
cheap literature on the subject is available. One also finds that this
literature is being discussed. So, I think there has been considerable
spread among villagers of the idea that limiting the size of the family
should be considered.

I am not a demographer, and I do not know much about family
planning, but it seems to me that the villagers do discuss family
planning, particularly in two respects. First, I find, in the villages
that I have studied, many husbands worried very much about the health
of their wife because of the number of children and pregnancies.
There is some talk of sterilization or other methods of family planning in this connection. Another thing that I have found many villagers
talking about is the relationship between property and the composition
of the family. These things were not discussed in the past. This
awareness seems to me very significant.

To take up Elder's point, I have noted the emergence of more
and more homes for the aged. Some castes are building them. Generally, the homes for the aged are located in pilgrimage centers.
This way you can combine two things: You can enjoy your old age and
be taken care of in terms of your religious needs. You must not forget the function of the large pilgrimage centers, like the Great Brin-
daban complex and the Benares complex. There, traditionally, people have been going to spend their old age, particularly those old people who have no one to take care of them.

Mehta: Professor Elder's detailed criticism of my paper is very
valid. There are a lot of figures that are missing, and I did not do
interviews among the blue-collar workers. However, I think that one
cannot get away from the fact that the changing status of women is
important. Ultimately the nuclear traditions can only be taken advan-

tage of if the woman is independent to some extent from caste and family. If, as I have seen in my divorce studies, a woman is in any way
financially dependent or psychologically dependent on her caste and
her family, then for her to take any actions that run contrary to her
caste, or to her family sentiments, is extremely difficult. She may
win in the court, but she will be bereft otherwise. So that is one
level of using the corpus of law effectively.

Second, there is no question that the knowledge of the legal provisions is very, very difficult in India and is only shared, even in the
urban areas, by those who are highly educated. Again, through contact and proximity with others knowledgeable in these matters a woman may learn that (after 1954) she can divorce, but the process of
law remains a complicated and expensive process. It isn't really
capable of handling all problems by all means. So the fact of legal
provisions does not really apply equally in the urban and rural areas.

Of much greater importance is the fact that, for the first time
after 1956 and the Succession Act, the woman becomes a partner.
This is an enormous change since, for the first time, a woman can
inherit the property. In my own studies, very few women have inherited their legitimate share of the family property; and these are
not the ignorant. These were women who had education and knowledge.
One has to understand that these provisions, though necessary in any
society, can only be used as benefits where there is high degree of
sophistication in conceptualizing the position of man and woman. Few
in India today would disagree that it is right for a woman, when it
comes down to inheriting something, to get less than a son, because
of the continued dependence of the aged on the son. The idea still
persists that it is with the son that the parents make their home, not
with the daughter. In certain sections and under certain conditions,
it is possible for the parents to stay with the daughter, but, by and
large, the other pattern prevails. If that pattern continues, naturally
the parent is going to give a greater share of attention to the son.

Finally, the traditional continuance of certain factors, such as
the dowry, which are on the increase, makes both the parents and the
sons feel that if so much is spent on the girl, for dowry plus education,
then she really does not have a right to share the inheritance, particularly when she goes into another household at marriage. That, I
think, is the crucial set of factors.

Talbot: India has not yet had to face the same intensity of social adjustments to population density that some other societies have, and
there may be lessons in the variety of means other societies have
adopted in facing higher densities. Perhaps, as a "Second India"
comes, India will be faced with some of these same adjustments. We
can easily see the economic consequences of increased density in the

village, or in the city, or in the country generally. It's much more
difficult to get at the cultural and cultural-institutional sorts of consequences.

Our discussants so far this afternoon, and this morning as well,
have indicated that, at the family level, a variety of adjustments are
now being observed in response to increased density. Some of these
relate to a more independent view on the part of family members to
meeting their own needs, as compared to an earlier generation; others
tend in other directions. With respect to the larger social groups discussed above, could one hypothesize that increasing population density
is likely to reinforce the functions of such social groups as jatis and
lineages? On the ground that increasing population density develops
new pressures in the community—not just economic pressures, not
just pressures for land, but other kinds of pressures as well—and
that these are the sorts of pressures that can hardly be coped with by
the individual, can they not be dealt with more readily by the group?

Some Sinic societies seem to have discovered new mechanisms
and adjustments to help them live together in relative harmony despite increased population density. On the other hand, their pressures
could develop defensiveness, which would certainly find expression in
groups. Greater competition for available resources, for social and
cultural advantages, or for whatever, almost by definition would need
to be expressed through groups. We have seen that the democratic
political process has given a new function to subcaste and other groups
as the organizing instrument to bring out individual votes. Similarly,
might not this "Second India" mean the acquisition of various social and
cultural functions by individual subcastes? Such developments would
reinforce the individual members' loyalty to and participation in the
group and, therefore, increase their identification with the group in
ways other than traditional religious activities.

Marc Galanter: I want to go back to Mehta's response to Joe Elder
with regard to the possible effect, or causal significance, that one
attributes to the legal variable and to changes in family law. This
certainly cannot be generalized across the board because the law does
not apply across the board to all groups in society. I thought Mehta's
response was accurate and to the point, but I cannot resist restating
it in my own terms. I'm also tempted to try to connect it to the point
that has just been made about the impact of increasing population
pressures on institutions.

So let me try to restate what I think was her response in this
way: Legal rights are being distributed by governments. This is one
of the things that governments can give out rather cheaply, especially
if the rights are not used by many people. And so governments have
a great tendency to give out legal rights. It's like printing money.

For the recipient, it's a little like getting half of a dollar bill. It is very nice if you have the matching half. You then have something very useful and valuable. But if you do not have the matching half, it's a worthless piece of paper, perhaps decorative and valuable in that sense. What the government is giving people, giving women, when it gives them new rights under the Hindu Code Acts, are these halves of valuable currency that have to be matched by resources on the recipient side. By resources I mean knowledge, wealth, lawyers' skills, whatever it takes to provide the strategic ability to use those rights (for example, an alternative place to live while you're fighting your relatives).

Ability to use rights must be seen in light of the two-faced character of law. Rights are equal and universal in their application, but their usefulness to a person is directly proportionate to his capacity to use them. That capacity differs with financial and other resources; it is not a one-to-one economic matter. One of the faces of law is the face of equality and universality. The underside, the other face, is the face of benefits in proportion to what one already has, if you don't take me too literally. This duality itself is variable because we know that some legal arrangements and programs are very passive—that is, the burden is thrown very much on the would-be beneficiary to come up with the matching resources to combine with their potential benefit. In other cases of government programs or legal rights, the government takes a more active stance and supplies some of the sources to enable the potential beneficiary to utilize the law—legal help, free legal services. It might bring around the public address system to tell you what your legal rights are, or provide free legal services, or provide assistance in other ways. For example, workmen's compensation commissions in the United States sometimes functioned at the more active end of the scale. Civil courts, on the other hand, are at the more passive end of the scale.

What effect is increasing population going to have on legal rights? Government, as population increases, may be more inclined to give out more rights because they're very cheap to give out, and there are lots of demands generated in a growing society. But government will tend to be passive; it cannot give out rights equipped with resources to help you use the rights, so it gives out bare rights in this passive manner and, having done so, of course, then confers on groups of possible beneficiaries the option of using them. Some people will be in a much better position to utilize those rights than will others. One effect of population growth, I submit, will be to make government use more programs of the passive type, rather than the active distributive type and, as a result, to increase the difference in the ability of various groups in society to utilize their rights. One sees here, too, the closing of the circle: Population increase will have effects on law, making it more passive and thereby making it less able to come up with solutions to control the effects of population growth.

Milton Singer: Marc's comments remind me of the old adage that "Democracy is a Government where everybody is somebody, but nobody is anybody."

David G. Mandelbaum: It struck me, in listening to Marc Galanter's comment that one of the relevant matters we have not discussed as yet is the brother-sister relationship. It is a crucial relationship for a person over much of India. It is another reason why village women generally do not like to take advantage of the inheritance laws and the other legal rights they now have. If a village woman asserts her legal rights, she raises the possibility that her brothers will become her competitors rather than her chief allies and her main support outside her husband's family. That is just what village women don't want to happen. This consideration enters into another aspect of population growth as well, in that a village woman who has only daughters thinks, "How can this daughter get along well in later life if she has no brothers?"

John Cool: I have been thinking that, although we purport to be talking about the impact of population change, so many of the relationships that we are discussing really stem from more complex patterns of causality. I am not sure that we have the instruments and the methodology to be terribly rigorous in separating the effects of population growth from the numerous other variables. What we have talked about is modernity or development. Some of us at this table have been struggling all our active lives with ways to wrest the villager out of his "long-run fatalism" and apathy; to stimulate village development; to give him a sense of his own self-worth and his capacity to effect meaningful change without relying on the central government or its agencies. Some of this has begun to happen. In the process, some of these attitudinal changes, it seems to me, have borne fruit.

Now we see, for example, that, within the structure of the family the individual in many cases has become less dependent on the network of kinship obligations and the kind of reciprocal warmth and support that the family has traditionally provided, particularly as younger people move into cash employment, wage earning, and away from the farm homestead. One of the concomitants of this is that their fertility behavior is altered in some way, but whether one can say that that's due to population change, increased density, or psychic crowding is less clear. I have doubts about the usefulness of density as an indicator of very much except in geographical terms, because clearly human beings have developed civilizations in situations of great density by world standards, in all parts of the world. I often have had to call to mind for purposes of clarifying my own thought the hunters and gatherers looking down into a river valley from the hills some 10,000 years ago and seeing the first settled agricultural communities and saying, while shaking their heads, "Our way of life will never survive that kind of density." Clearly it didn't. But, it seems to me we have to be clear that we are not ascribing to population change the whole transition from subsistence agriculture to industrialization that has been abroad in this world during the past 450 years.

Population change is itself a product of many of those other ideological, technological, and psychological inputs. I'm not clear how precise one can be in narrowing down what it is we want to ascribe to population growth here as we look at the next 30 years, but we can look at the experience of these past 30 years, during which population has doubled.

The one thing that seems clear to me is the very hopeful and central thesis that the human family and small community have exhibited an enormous absorptive capacity. Although we have transferred many of these earlier functions of the family—for socialization and for providing education—to some larger community, the family continues to give meaning and purposefulness to individual life. Without family what would life be like, not only in Asia but in most civilized communities? What will be the pattern of family life 30 years from now? I have been looking to see if in any of this there is something that would be useful to guide us.

I know John Lewis is concerned about the implications for policy, and I too am wondering what is there in this that would give guidance to a person in a position of responsibility looking at the next 30 years. We need something concrete to grab on to. So far I have gotten an agenda for research and for problems that need to be carefully thought out. One of the first ones, I would argue, is to say with a little more precision what it is we can attribute to population growth and how we can rightfully ascribe the function of population in relationship with the other variables.

Singer: I have one small comment based partly on my own experience, which is quite limited. During my first trip to India in 1954 I had the good fortune to meet and see something of Douglas Ensminger, a rural sociologist who was in charge of the Ford Foundation office in India and was pushing community development—village development—very hard. He had around him several able economists and rural sociologists. During the 1950s hope was running high that economists and sociologists could go into a whole series of villages and stay for a few

days and draw policy conclusions on the basis of their observations.
When some anthropologists proposed more intensive village micro-
studies, where an anthropologist would go and live at least a year in
a village, the economists would throw up their hands and say, "That's
much too slow; why do you have to do that? That's wasting time;
there isn't that kind of time." Yet, one of the last papers Doug Ensminger wrote, just before he retired, was an evaluation of his work
in village development. In it, he said—and this stuck in my mind—
that to evaluate these changes properly one needs the perspective of
at least 30 years, or about one generation. This of course is the anthropologists' perspective.

        Within that kind of perspective, I cite one observation apropos
Mehta's point that the white-collar group seems to be much more
"modern" and progressive in accepting the new norms for family size
than the blue-collar group, which is much more traditional and far
more ritualistic and conservative. It seems to me that M. N. Srinivas' theory of Sanskritization and Westernization and some of the later
work based on it might apply here. This research tended to show that
as the upper castes in particular villages were won over to modern
ideas about family size and education, with women working out of the
home, the lower castes were tending to become more Sanskritized
and more traditional and ritualistic. Because of the fact of cultural
lag, the lower castes were moving into a life-style that they thought
was still prestigious at a time when the pace-setters were to some extent moving out of it. This has happened in the United States, too.
It's hard to pin down that lag in specific terms, but in Madras, specifically among the businessmen I have some information about, it
happened in one generation, during a move from a village or small
town setting to an urban setting. Particular cultural patterns that
may appear new or very modern do in fact filter down and get taken
over, and they become prestigious models for other sectors of society
to emulate.

John Newmann: I should mention that I have no specific experience in
India, and I am learning a great deal from the discussions. Much of
the conversation has been in the form of examples and has included
what you might call economically favored groups or groups that have
achieved some higher economic status—white-collar workers, businessmen, and so forth. The observation that blue-collar middle classes,
while attaining higher economic status and resources through their
incomes, have not necessarily limited their families at the same rate
as the white-collar workers, can perhaps be explained by a lack of the
type of education that might bring them up into a higher-status orientation. I was wondering if anyone around the table here could shed
some light on what is happening to the urban poor. Certainly there

are large sections of Indian cities that are neither white- nor blue-
collar. Is there any evidence that, perhaps because of the tremendous strain and difficulty in feeding and providing for their families,
the urban poor have begun to limit their family size, or have they
maintained much of the same orientation that has been described for
the rural areas, where sons are clearly an asset?

P. M. Beliappa: This same question has been bothering me. Newmann has referred to the slum-dwellers. What about the large sections of Indian society that are below the poverty line? There are
millions and millions of them. What sort of description and what
sort of responses do we have from them? Can anyone tell us, for
example, about the condition of landless laborers?

Mehta: It is clear that family planning has not touched that group.

Beliappa: That is where the crunch is. For the other groups we have
some access, and we have some information to deal with.

David Horlacher: I would like to restate John Cool's question and direct it as forcefully as I can at Mehta. Let us suppose that the population of India was stable, was not growing. Would these changes
that you describe have taken place in the structure of the Indian family then, and, if so, what is the relationship between population growth
and changes in the Indian family?

Mehta: Well, I think some of these changes have nothing whatsoever
to do with population growth. For instance, the fact that the status
of women has improved and women are wanting to do other things has
nothing to do with population growth as such. These result from the
desires of women to be free from domestic chores and not be bound
by so many children. This desire plays a part, whether there is
growth or not. On the other hand, certain changes are definitely due
to an increase in population, which in turn results in a rising cost of
living and shortages all along the way. There is greater competition
for education—for colleges, for example—in this growth process.
That has had a very important effect on limiting the size of the family
because the family knows that admission into colleges is next to impossible unless you are in the 1 percent status group of achievement.
Every aspect of Indian professional life is oversubscribed, and that
is directly due to population growth.

Anrudh Jain: I would like to raise the question whether even middle-
class white-collar people can send their children to those colleges
and schools referred to by Professor Elder. If one is talking in terms

of the public schools in Delhi, people who have four children often
cannot imagine how they can support their children through those
schools. This has nothing to do with white-collar or blue-collar.
It's simply that in the income bracket 400 to 1,000 rupees, many are
now having difficulty imagining how they can even survive the present
economic predicament.

Abraham Weisblat: On the question of the poor, I have difficulty determining whether it is population that you worry about with regard
to this group, except to say that maybe it is population pressure that
makes for their disadvantages, at the same time that it makes their
hopes of rising anywhere so futile. However, shouldn't we begin to
think of differentiating the poor in India in terms of both regions and
conditions, both culturally and in economic terms, to see what the
implications are for different groups of poor? For instance, one of
the poorer groups generally are tribal people. A second I would
describe as pockets of poverty in the midst of plenty—for example,
the poorer people in Punjab. The question is, what do you do to mold
them up? When you get to this question I'm not so sure that it's population pressure that's going to be the significant factor. There are
a variety of constraints, in addition to numbers, that will affect the
ability of these groups to rise, and the only thing that population may
do is clinch once and for all their inability to rise.

Cool: In response to questions about the poorest segments of Indian
society, one of the major problems here is with the data, particularly
in urban areas because it is not disaggregated, and there are a lot
of methodological problems in using it. One does not even try to generalize even within a single urban area like Bombay. But one thing
we do know is that gross acceptance of family planning programs is
higher in urban areas than it is in the rural areas. One reason for
distortion is the enormous number of single-member households; in
Calcutta at one time the number of single-member households was
more than half of the total households. This means that the wife and
the children, where they existed, lived in rural Bihar or Orissa, or
in the villages of West Bengal. So it's hard to measure the degree to
which our vital data have any impact or any generalizability in that
kind of a situation. There is also an established pattern of first-gen-
eration urban women, finding they are with child, going back to their
rural homes to deliver. This means birthrates in metropolitan Bombay are statistically lower than they are in some nearby rural districts, but it does not necessarily ensure that the conception didn't
take place in Bombay.
　　The other observation that I would make has to do with changes
in family structure. We have listed the status of women as an impor-

tant variable. I think this requires a much more thorough and careful analysis. The Hindu Code is social legislation. So with the age
of marriage legislation. They are indicative of what the legislators,
under pressure from progressive organizations and secular leaders
of great stature in the mid-1950s, thought was necessary or desirable.
But I would argue that there are other things that are much more significant in shaping family structure. Among them is increased access
to education by women and extended life expectancy for both men and
women, which have changed the whole character in India of marriage
as an institution and altered the pattern of demands after the fundamental procreation and child-rearing functions have been served. I
suspect (although we have not had enough time to measure this, and
I don't think anybody is looking at it very carefully) that the capacity
of women in India, both in the urban middle class and increasingly
in rural areas, to regulate unwanted conception, will result in an
enormous cumulative impact on their self-esteem and their attitudes
toward themselves and their bodily functions. This, I suspect, will
have an enormous impact on the family structure and the role that women are prepared and permitted to play in society 30 years hence.
These are terribly difficult things to measure, and they may, as I
was suggesting earlier, have little to do directly with population
change. They may be symptoms of the systemic process of modernity
that is already well advanced in India.

Singer: With regard to studies of the poor, I want to mention that
there are at least half a dozen relevant anthropological studies. Oscar Lewis, who became famous, or at least controversial, for intro-
ducing the concept of "the culture of poverty" on the basis of his
studies in Mexico, Puerto Rico, and New York, considered India
and several other countries as places where there were poor people
who did not have a culture of poverty. He had made observations in a
village near Delhi. Several other studies have been done by anthropologists and sociologists along these lines. These do tend to support
Oscar Lewis; these poor villagers and the poor people in the urban
slums do not get demoralized and alienated in the same way as the
people whom Oscar Lewis characterizes as having a culture of poverty. They do maintain communication with the larger society. They
do have some information about family planning and related programs,
but they are not very successful in improving their living standards,
not because they have a culture of poverty but because they are poor.[14]

NOTES

1. Findings from my earlier studies are to be found in my
books, The Western Educated Hindu Woman (Bombay: Asia Publish-

ing House, 1970) and The Hindu Divorced Woman (Delhi: Vikas Publishers, 1975).

2. Henry Orenstein and Michael Micklin, "The Hindu Joint Family: The Norms and Numbers," Pacific Affairs 39 (Winter 1966-67): 315.

3. Pauline M. Kolenda, "Region, Caste, and Family Structure: A Comparative Study of the Indian 'Joint' Family," in Structure and Change in Indian Society, ed. Milton Singer and Bernard S. Cohn (Chicago: Aldine Publishing Company, 1968), p. 358.

4. K. M. Kapadia, "The Family in Transition," Sociological Bulletin 8 (1959): 71.

5. Milton Singer, "The Indian Joint Family in Modern Industry," in Singer and Cohn, eds., op. cit., p. 444.

6. Ibid., p. 440.

7. I. P. Desai, Some Aspects of Family in Mahuva (Bombay: Asia Publishing House, 1964), pp. 231-232.

8. D. C. Dubey and A. K. Devgan, Family Planning Communications Studies in India (New Delhi: Central Family Planning Institute, 1969), p. 90.

9. See A. M. Shah, The Household Dimension of the Family in India (Berkeley: University of California Press, 1974); I. P. Desai, "The Joint Family in India: An Analysis," Sociological Bulletin 5 (1956): 146-156; and K. T. Merchant, Changing Views on Marriage and the Family: Hindu Youth (Madras: B. G. Paul, 1935).

10. M. S. Gore, Urbanization and Family Change (Bombay: Popular Prakashan, 1968), p. 77.

11. Singer, op. cit., p. 430.

12. The KAP Surveys, a series of questionnaire surveys of the existing knowledge, attitudes, and practices of family planning in India, have been conducted since the mid-1950s; for a summary of their results see K. G. Krishna Murthy, Research in Family Planning in India (Delhi: Sterling Publishers, 1968).

13. Mehra Masani, "The Status of Women in Rural Areas," unpublished paper prepared for a conference on Rural Women, organized by the Social Institute, New Delhi, April 1974, p. 21.

14. Some of the studies referred to by Singer include the following: G. Djurfeldt and S. Lindbert, Pills Against Poverty: A Study of the Introduction of Western Medicine in a Tamil Village (Lund: Department of Sociology, 1974); R. S. Khare, "A Study of Social Resistance to Sanitation Programmes in Rural India," Eastern Anthropologist (Lucknow) 17, 2 (1964): 86-94; G. Kurian, The Family in India: A Regional View (The Hague: Mouton, 1974); Madras School of Social Work, Social Welfare in the Slums of Madras (Madras: New India Printers, 1965); J. M. Mahar, The Untouchables in Contemporary India (Tucson: University of Arizona Press, 1972); J. F. Marshall,

"Culture and Contraception: Response Determinants to a Family Planning Program in a North Indian Village" (Chapel Hill: Carolina Population Center, University of North Carolina, 1973); Seminar (New Delhi Monthly) nos. 162 (February 1973); 163 (March 1973); and 167 (July 1973); Paul Wiebe, Annanagar: Social Life in a Madras Slum (Urbana: Department of Sociology, University of Illinois, 1970); and Gertrude M. Woodruff, "An Adidravida Settlement in Bangalore India: A Case Study of Urbanization" (Cambridge, Mass.: Microfilm HN 14, 1959).

CHAPTER

6

LAW AND
POPULATION CHANGE
Marc Galanter

From a quick scan of the literature, I am convinced that there is no study or even speculative discussion that takes law as the dependent variable and asks what is going to happen if population increases, which is the task set before me today.* Therefore, let me put in a few caveats before embarking on this speculative venture.

First, I would emphasize that this is a "comment," not a scholarly paper in the strict sense. It is intended to provoke discussion rather than to present empirical findings. Second, although we are talking about population change generally, I will talk only about effects I attribute to increase. I realize that these effects are not necessarily going to obtain at every point on the scale of population increase. What I have to say has to do with population increase only where that increase is accompanied by severe scarcity effects, which,

---

*The general approach to law in this comment reflects a point of view that is adumbrated in a recent paper "Why the "Haves" Come out Ahead: Speculations on the Limits of Legal Change," Law and Society Review (Fall 1974) and that draws inter alia on studies of the functioning of law in contemporary India, such as Robert Kidder's "Courts and Conflict in an Indian City: A Study of Legal Impact," Journal of Commonwealth Political Studies (1973) and my "The Abolition of Disabilities: Untouchability and the Law" in The Untouchables in Contemporary India, ed. J. M. Mahar (Tucson: University of Arizona Press, 1972). This critical perspective is directed to problems of law and development in the third world in a forthcoming article by David Trubek and me, "Scholars in Self-Estrangement: Reflections on the Crisis in Law and Development Studies," Wisconsin Law Review (February 1975).

I take it, is not always the case. Third, I will be uncompromisingly
macrosociological, in contrast to the more balanced discussion that
we have had so far, largely because there is so little data in the area
I will be discussing. Finally, I shall ignore the limitations that
would result were I to conceive of this as a discussion of customary
law. As I thought it over, I found puzzling the conference organizers'
invitation to discuss customary law, as if that were some separate
realm of experience or activity. I should point out that areas previously regulated by customary law, so-called, are now fairly entwined
with the government's law, and I know of nothing to suggest that what
happens to them as a result of population change is going to be terribly distinctive. So I really don't see why they should be treated separately. I would argue that they are likely in large measure to share
the future of law in general in India, and it is to that that I would like
to turn.

I'm going to try to do this with a schematic model, which is
subject to the usual problems imposed by a two-dimensional surface,
which happens to be rectangular (Figure 1). I've tried to start from
population increase and trace out some of the things we might expect
to happen to a legal system of the general kind that India's is. I
have drawn thin lines to represent asserted lines of influence or cau-
sation. I don't know if I would make a very strong claim for all of
them. Probably there should be more of these lines, and certainly
they should differ in their weights. The thin lines suggest expected
lines of influence; the heavier lines represent problems or dilemmas
that I think the other lines will lead to. Let me sketch this briefly
because a lot of this is abbreviated in a way that you may or may not
be able to decode. I start in the northwest corner with population increase and scarcity and conflict, which are taken, at least in this setting, as increasing along with population. Going eastward now, legal
institutions will be faced with many more claims as a result of more
conflict and just more people around. There will be more business
to be decided by the courts. But because of scarcity the social facilities for handling disputes are not likely to increase their capacity correspondingly. These institutions will then be overloaded; that overload
will lead—and we know this from studies in other settings—to delay
and then to devices for extraordinary bypasses around the delay.
Overload also means that institutions are more likely to be quite passive and to throw on those who come to use them the burden of going
forward and assembling their case, bringing in lawyers and other experts, and so forth.

Overload also means that the institutions are likely to ration
very carefully full-dress individuated attention and be more inclined
toward the kinds of things that can be handled in a more routine and
stereotyped manner. Overloaded institutions try to rid themselves of

FIGURE 1

Postulated Effects of Population Growth on Law

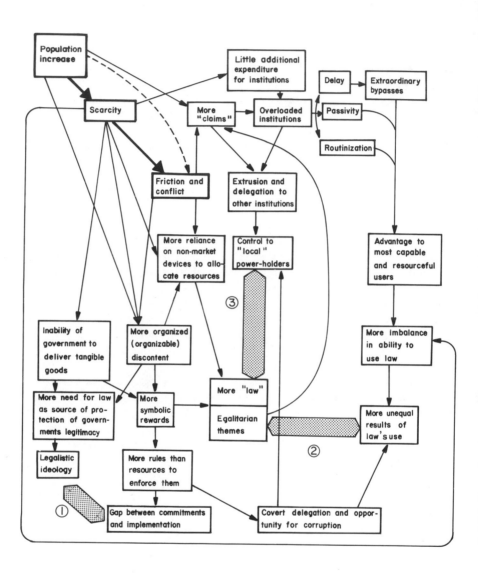

Source: Marc Galanter

business by restrictive rules as to who can come before them, so other institutions, other decision-makers, begin to get the overflow business. Real decisions, then, begin to be made elsewhere. At the same time, the situation of overload, with its consequent passivity and delay, confers advantages on those potential users who are most capable and resourceful, and corresponding disadvantages on the casual, inexperienced, not well-resourced potential user.

I want to emphasize while sketching this chain of consequences that I am not saying that these are things that are solely or even principally the results of population growth. These are basic structural problems of a modern liberal democratic legal system. These are the fault lines that are built into it. I am describing pressures that are not created but are amplified by population increase. I'd like to speculate a bit about what might happen as those pressures become more and more intense and about the kinds of conflicts that will be engendered.

A second link—moving now to the southeast in the figure—suggests that as you have more friction and conflict, a government cannot depend on the market to allocate scarce resources, so it makes more laws, that is, more rules to decide who gets what. In the Indian setting, given the country's present commitments, this law is going to be based on egalitarian themes. I suggest we will have more law of an egalitarian sort at the same time that there are intensified imbalances in the ability of potential users to utilize that law to their advantage. So we come to a major paradox. There is more law with an egalitarian tone to it and yet more unequal results from the law's use, because the law is not self-enforcing and the enforcement process is delegated in large measure to those affected. This discrepancy is amplified: Egalitarian laws turn out like land reform, for example, or the village house sites regulation that Professor Shah mentioned yesterday. Laws that on their face and in their intent are egalitarian turn out to have very different results.

Now let me trace out my third linkage—the one that comes straight down the page. As you get more scarcity, more friction, and more conflict, you have at the same time the government having less tangible rewards to distribute and at the same time more organized discontent clamoring for various things. This leads, on the one hand, to greater government reliance on law as a source of protection and legitimacy. Government has fewer instrumental means for getting people's loyalty. It depends more on the symbolic and the ceremonial with which to do it. As I mentioned yesterday, passing laws is one of the least expensive things that governments can do, in the short run at least.

There is a tendency to reward groups that are clamoring for something by passing a law. So you get more rules. In any legal system, the Indian or our own, there are many more rules around than there are resources to implement them. One result of this, of course, is that those who are in a better position to use their initiative prod the government and get the laws that favor them enforced. A second consequence is massive covert delegation. As soon as you have more laws than resources to enforce them, there is tacit delegation to officials all down the line to decide which of the things on the agenda to do and, of course, enormous opportunities for corruption as a result. This covert delegation is connected with the fact that overloaded legal institutions are pushing things out to other institutions. Both of those, It seems to me, lead to a massive delegation of control to various local power-holders who acquire vast decision-making power under these circumstances.

What I'm suggesting in the lower left hand corner of Figure 1 is that government becomes more dependent on the legitimizing power of law at the same time it is creating law that it cannot enforce, exacerbating the gap between its commitments and its power to implement them. One short-run solution is for the government to portray law as a constraint on its ability to perform effectively. But by eroding the law as a source of legitimacy, government invites judgment of its performance by tangible utilitarian payoffs, exposing itself to the risk of disappointing the high expectations it has cultivated.

This rather dismal scenario that I am drawing pictures the growth or intensification of three kinds of gaps or shortages: Number three is a shortage of control, number two is a shortage of equality, and number one, down in the corner, is a shortage of legitimacy. I am suggesting that in a system in which these fault lines are already there, population may produce severe shortages of these three kinds.

I want to emphasize that I am not necessarily drawing a picture of breakdown. These are the points of strain or fault lines in a modern democratic legal order of the sort that exists in India. There are devices for reconciling these strains, and the question is whether one sees this (in terms of Chapter 2) as necessarily a "doomsday scenario." One can imagine various solutions to these three types of shortages or dilemmas. One, for example, would be a major relinquishment of control by the central government—a decentralization and formal delegation scenario. Another would be to give up major equality commitments. Another, going further up the chain, would be to suppress conflict, or at least suppress the crucial ability to express discontent openly and to organize it—that is, the repression/police-state way of breaking the linkage.

Finally, and somewhat fancifully, one could imagine that as the legitimizing power of law wears thin, the government might seek some law with greater and fresh legitimacy. One might think, for example, of a government-sponsored Hindu law revival, something that the government has resisted and has joined the legal profession in deriding. This would, by the way, provide a graceful way to back away from equality commitments and central control commitments. One could imagine government seeking to revive customary law and in the course of that displacing a lot of critics from important positions and certainly distracting intellectuals for years.

This is mere speculation, but there are studies of other places that suggest at least some of the linkages depicted in Figure 1. These also suggest some research possibilities in this area. One might play this futurology game retrospectively. We might just run the film backward and ask if all of the effects we are attributing to population change or something like them took place during the last century and a half. Of course we know that whatever effect population had on law during the last century has been confounded by enormously powerful influences of other kinds—political, intellectual, and so forth. I wonder if any of you here know whether any research of this kind has been done, attempting to separate out population effects from others in this kind of retrospective study. If this were to be undertaken, one would want in the research design some way of investigating the effect of other factors, too, in addition to population. Such a project might well be possible in India, where the record-keeping in the legal area has been pretty good for the last hundred years.

Let me mention some crude and preliminary explorations I made in another connection. In the 20th century, civil litigation in India on a per capita basis rose through the 1930s. But then it dropped, from 147 per 10,000 (in undivided India) in 1931 to something like 47 per 10,000 for the same area in 1961—that is, it dropped to something like a third of the former rate from 1931 to 1961. At the same time the use of criminal law has been climbing steadily through the century. Criminal cases were about 50 per 10,000 people in 1911 and 77 per 10,000 in 1961. So the per capita use of criminal law seems to have increased through this century by perhaps half, while civil litigation has declined precipitously. Their respective positions have undergone a curious reversal: Where there were three civil cases to one criminal case in 1931, there are now about three criminal to two civil cases. I mention this as suggestive of the possibility of creating some very interesting indicators of the effect of population and other variables in the legal field.

DISCUSSION

Bhupen Mukerjee: If we are going to use this topic as a platform from which Professor Galanter has jumped off, I should be lucky if I could simply crawl out of it. Congratulations to Galanter on his daring comment.

It was, I think, Professor Maitland who pointed out the traditional isolation of law from other studies; and Dean Pound went on to
explain that, from the 16th century right up to the 19th century, the
law had remained quite aloof and self-sufficient. But it was realized
at the beginning of the 20th century that it was the insufficiency of the
law—of the doctrinal approach to law—that failed to meet the functional
needs of society. In India the social aloofness of law is notorious;
"Justice," it is said, "is wrecked upon the rock of scholasticism."
It is time that we take the famous definition of the American sociologist E. A. Ross. He for the first time propounded the idea of law as
"social engineering." We lawyers do not know what law is; so we have
to depend on the sociologists to tell us what the law is!

This brings us straight to the scope of our subject, which I
gather is not population responses, but social and cultural responses
to population. We must stick to that. Being a lawyer, I believe in
what is called "jurisdiction." This is my jurisdiction; and you know
(my lawyer friends will bear me out) that even by agreement you cannot extend jurisdiction. Therefore I want to limit myself to this jurisdiction—"customary law and population change." First, it means the
effect of population change on customary law; second, in the Indian
context, it must necessarily mean population growth. I do not blame
Professor Galanter for bringing in law in general because that is necessary. If we try to talk about customary law without talking about
general law it would be something like writing a chapter on "snakes in
Iceland" in a book on Iceland. There would simply be one sentence in
the chapter, to the effect that there are no snakes in Iceland.

This concern for population is not new in India. When I was a
student in England, in 1937, the British House of Commons passed a
resolution expressing anxiety over the depletion of population, and I
remember hearing broadcast talks from people like T. H. Marshall,
Carr-Saunders, and others who were expressing deep concern about
depletion of population. Professor Gunnar Myrdal—before he wrote
Asian Drama, of course—in 1938 in his Godkin lectures at Harvard
was expressing great concern over the depletion of population. While
they were thus busy in considering the consequences of the depletion
of population, in India after World War I a neo-Malthusian league was
started in Madras. In 1925 the first private birth control clinic was
set up in Bombay by a Dr. Karve, for which he lost his job. In 1930
the Mysore government sponsored the first government family planning clinic, and, in 1935, as you all know, a national planning committee headed by Jawaharlal Nehru advocated family planning and family
size limitation. Now I do not mean to take undue credit for India.
This is nothing extraordinary if you remember that population and poverty have been India's chronic ailments. It's only natural. But here,
for the first time, we can say the response to population growth in so-

cial and cultural terms—both official and unofficial—is being observed.
By official I mean governmental response.

I may make a little diversion. It is interesting to note the difference between the situation in India and the situation in the United
States. In the United States, from the late 1930s to the late 1950s,
the federal government, under the Social Security Act, with the maternal and child health grant, allowed birth control under cover, not
openly. In the late 1950s President Dwight D. Eisenhower did not
show any federal concern about population. It was President John F.
Kennedy who, for the first time, I believe, expressed concern about
population, and it was not until 1967 that the amendment was made to
the Economic Opportunity Act of 1964 for the "forgotten poor at home"
where family planning and birth control formed an integral part of
health services. In 1970, of course, President Richard Nixon
appointed a population commission. Thus, in America what we see
is that people are pushing the government into population programs.
In India, the government is pulling the people into the population field.
These two are entirely different situations. Therefore, when we try
to do some research or try to understand the Indian situation we must
bear this constantly in mind.

Now the point is, where shall we begin to see the effect of population on law? As you all know, the decades up to 1921 were characterized by a decline in population growth in India, followed by a slow
rise and then by a fast increase in population growth. In those days
we believed in Nature, and natural control was responsible for such
situations. Since 1921 the growth has been steady, and after World
War II it has taken an explosive turn. But this period also coincides
with our independence, a period during which Indian leaders have
been trying to bring about three revolutions simultaneously: the political revolution, a social revolution, and an economic revolution.

The political revolution came in the end with Independence. The
social and economic revolutions are yet to come or to bring results.
In the late 1940s and early 1950s, the leaders had a choice as to how
to proceed to bring about changes. They had the examples of Russia
and China to choose from, but they have chosen the democratic model
of the Anglo-American type. I believe the idea behind this choice was
to preserve the traditional values in India, such as nonviolence, tolerance, accommodation, and also they didn't wish to give too violent a
jerk to the traditional social institutions like family, kinship, and village. Therefore, when we now try to understand the situation and find
out what sort of responses Indian society is making to population, we
must bear in mind this background. Otherwise we will become impatient. Some highly placed people are now getting impatient. They say
we must have compulsory sterilization. But we have this democracy,
and we have accepted voluntarism.

Now where do we look for the people's response? There have
been many studies of various cities, but this urban population forms
only 18 to 20 percent of the people. Our study must extend to the
rural sector, for two reasons. First of all, the vast majority of the
people live there; second, it is there that you find traditional customary law still operating. Therefore, I suggest that research is
needed to find out the spontaneous response of people to population
growth in India and that it must be carried out in rural settings. So
far as the urban setting is concerned, it is fairly easy in a sense because one can get around and visit the people and get a grasp of the
situation. Being a lawyer, I have not had any field experience at all,
so I must totally make a speculative venture. Coming from Calcutta,
I have seen what is meant by density. Living in Calcutta reminds one
of some experiments that were done with rats and mice, and it makes
you apprehensive whether ultimately you won't have ratlike behavior
among men. Man in India's cities has definitely been devalued.

As a result of the devaluation of man, crime in India has risen;
it is unbelievable that between 1960 and 1970, crime rates have risen
by 57 percent while the population rose by 37.4 percent only during
that period. By adding population we are increasing the criminal section of the society. Since man is devalued, the natural consequence
is a laxity of criminal law administration. I have some experience of
Indian courts, particularly the sessions courts. If there was a murder
case going on in the pre-Independence period people would flock around
these courts; but today nobody takes any notice of a murder because
people have gotten used to such things. This is a direct result of population increase—the devaluation of man in crowded conditions and
the laxity in criminal law administration.

As I say, I have nothing to offer you by way of responses—that
is, the spontaneous responses of the people as a result of population
increase. Work has to be done; and I do not know who will do this
work, where the funds will come from, and where the work will take
place. But this is a wonderful field for research.

A second aspect of the responses has to do with the governmental
effort. There is a general feeling that any change in India must be
initiated by the government. As I have told you before, it is not like
the United States, where the people are conscious of the rise in population and conscious of their freedom, and they are pushing the government. A case like Griswold v. Connecticut is unthinkable in India because in India there is no ban against contraception in any law; nevertheless the people do not act, and therefore the government has taken
the initiative to get the people to act in their own interests.

Unfortunately, I understand from the writings of social scientists that there is a cultivated misconception about Indian society; and
there are two common cliches: that the Hindu society in its overall

organization is detrimental to developmental growth and that Hindu society is constructed in such a way to cause people to be lazy and "no good." But this has been refuted by a number of scholars. The shocking thing about the situation is that many of the decision-makers, whom one of our Indian sociologists has called the "new elite," share these misconceptions. Their idea of the village is still what was established once by Sir Charles Metcalf, and their idea of the rigidity of caste is what Megesthanes, in 300 B.C., told us. But there has been and still is social mobility. As a result of these misconceptions the decision-makers are trying to break away from the past. There have been many attempts to change the village, the caste, and the joint family, the three main carriers of the Indian tradition. They have introduced egalitarianism against the caste hierarchy. They have insisted on individual freedoms in the Fundamental Rights, whereas the basis of Indian society is the concept of duty.

We lawyers have become sick and tired of our Fundamental Rights. Every individual right is a Fundamental Right; and, as Professor Galanter has pointed out, it is easy to give away rights in the negative form. When it is in the positive form, then you don't give a Fundamental Right, you reserve it under the Directive Principles of State Policy, which cannot be enforced in a court of law. As a human being, not as a lawyer, I would argue that I have a more fundamental right to eat than to have property; but this fundamental right to eat entails some responsibility on the part of the government, if the right is to have a corresponding duty. You cannot have rights in a vacuum. A right must be balanced by a corresponding duty. The duty happens to fall on the government. Therefore this right is not enforceable.

Under the modern situation, it is possible that our own institutions—like the joint family, the caste, and the village—may yet function. To take just one example—the village panchayat. The village or caste panchayats have now been challenged by new panchayats given by the government; but the government panchayats have not become very popular. Why? Because they are judicial, they are fundamentally different from the tradition we have inherited from the past.

For example, an old panchayat in India: When a case is placed before it, the panchayat is not necessarily required to give a decision. In fact the panchayat tries to avoid giving a decision in a given case. It takes time, it consults, it discusses, and then a sort of compromise is brought about between the two parties; thereby both the defendant and the plaintiff save face. They have to live in the same village; so there is no personal stigma attached to either of them, and neither of them is hurt. Second, in the case of a panchayat dispute, the parties are not treated equally because even in the case of a contract, the contract is based on status.

Take for instance the contract between a landlord and a tenant. The British law will treat the landlord and the tenant as entirely equal. This villagers do not understand; they see that the old panchayat can dish out better justice because their conception is not "What is equal is just," but rather "What is just is equal"; and there is nothing wrong with this new approach to law, which is our own approach. To quote Dean Pound again, he showed that the basis of common law is relationship, not will, as in Roman law. When there is conflict between a landlord and tenant, or where there is property—private property—the relationship is between myself and the rest of the people, who are not to disturb my property. The relationship prevalent in India, in the contract of tenancy, is not only a contract, it is also a status position.

There is nothing wrong about it. Instead of trying to break this village, caste, and joint family—which, by the way, cannot be done, it is impossible—it is better to find out the dynamic forces operating under these institutions, and channel them to the modern way of life. For this I think it is necessary for the decisional leaders and the "new elite" to have faith in our old social institutions, which can adapt themselves to new situations. If they couldn't, they would have died long ago. There have been many invasions and many encroachments on them, but they—the joint family, caste, and village—go on and on in India; and you would be surprised that caste is not an exclusively Hindu institution. It belongs to Muslims, Christians, Jews, Jains, Sikhs, and even Untouchables.

I am afraid I could not give you any better picture than this, but I will say that we should consider in this meeting the responses to population growth, and we should confine ourselves to it as much as possible.

P. M. Beliappa: In responding to Professor Galanter and Mukerjee, I can only say that I find it very difficult to be faithful to the topic and accept Professor Mukerjee's proposition that we should look at the effects of population change on customary law. We could quite easily juxtapose this and look at it from the point of view of customary law impinging on population change.

Perhaps the best way for me to respond is by discussing some of the dynamics that have resulted from legal changes in response to population growth. The most fundamental change has been the provision of equal rights to men and women to inherit from their father. It is quite obvious that this is resulting in fragmentation, and at this point I must confess that I'm fully convinced that this piece of economic legislation has been solely motivated by a concern for population growth. In terms of chronology there is a large measure of fear and concern in India that has led the government to introduce the abolition

of zamindari and the various land reform acts. The effect of this, in
the rural areas, has been fragmentation of small holdings, with consequent effects on agricultural productivity.

I should mention that in the pre-British period, land was not
salable, and custom had reached its limit with regard to the money-
lenders' ability to expropriate the peasant. This is very important.
If small holdings have to be developed, and if one has to invest to
get payoffs from modern agricultural technology, it is inevitable that
small holders will turn to the local financier for money. This money-
lender is not always motivated by the best interests of the loanee. So
you find a situation where today, as a result of land legislation, the
small farmer is being driven into the arms of the moneylender, and
that has its own vicious consequences.

Aside from this, there has been a diminution of absentee landlordism. In the old days, when there was the joint family structure,
it was quite possible for members of the family to be working at some
distance away from their land holdings; they could still expect the other
members of the community to give them a hand in developing their
property. But, today, with land legislation, the additional rights of
tenants, and this great change in landlord-labor relationships, this
business of absentee landlordism is becoming an impossible proposition. In some areas it is disappearing. I wouldn't say it's entirely
due to population growth. It may be in part a response to that, but
it's also due to the growing political trends in the rural areas and
various political compunctions.

If you look at the other forms of property, you'll find that, again,
property has been fragmented in response to the introduction of economic legislation. Each member of the family now has a right to the
property, which means there is less for each. Consequently, unviable
domestic units must now be supplemented in urban areas by men and
women going out to work. Because both men and women go out to
work, and more so because women do, people are now exposed to new
situations. Particularly in urban society this results in some cases
in the breakdown of social barriers, caste privileges, and social
prejudices. Because caste prejudices are broken down there is more
intercommunal marriage in urban areas and more consciousness of
the need to control population and limit family size. There is also a
growing tendency toward urbanization, which in turn has consequences
for the distribution of goods and services such as sanitation, lighting,
housing, water supply, and education.

So you find that in the rural areas there is a situation where
there's a lot of fragmentation of holdings, which impinges on both agricultural production and on political currents; in the urban areas
there is a breakdown of social barriers and all the evil consequences
of growing urbanization. I should, therefore, like to take issue with

Professor Galanter on this point about the government's dishing out
legislation. I have always thought that law responds to the needs of
society and if there is a need that has been generated by society, it
is sanctified by law, not the other way round. We certainly do not
adopt a piece of legislation and then expect society to respond to it.
Perhaps I can be enlightened further on that.

Galanter: I have to be the one to tear away the veil of illusion. The
government does indeed respond to the needs of society, but it does
so through a very complicated process that introduces a great deal of
noise. That government responds to some needs does not mean that
the laws reflect even approximately some hierarchy of needs in society. Of course, if you measure needs by the law, then you always
have a perfect balance. But law implies the presence of strategic
positions from which it is possible to make law, and laws can also
be made to serve the needs of those who occupy those positions. At
least in choosing among which of the many laws the various parts of
the public seek, incumbents the world round show an inclination to
enact as law those that not only serve the needs of some part of the
public but their own needs as occupants of these positions.
        Therefore, in any polity, it seems to me, the stock of laws at
any given time is going to correspond only imperfectly to the needs
of the population. The law is in some important measure going to
represent an attempt by ruling groups within that society to maintain
their status and positions. That is the way I see it.
        When I made the somewhat facetious prophecy that there would
be a revival of an indigenous law ideology, little did I know that Professor Mukerjee was going to come along and make a case for it. I
might point out that he is a man who has occupied many eminent positions in the Indian legal world, including principal of the University
Law College at Calcutta. Ten years ago, when I went around India
trying to trace why the indigenous law movement (movement is not the
right word for it) in the 1950s had fizzled out completely, I could find
only one person in the entire legal elite who was a sympathetic spokes-
man of such a position. So the population of such sympathizers known
to me has at least doubled in the last five minutes. I am very pleased
that Mukerjee has confirmed my prediction.

Mukerjee: I will respond to Galanter's last point in a later intervention. First let me say, in response to Beliappa, that the government
is supposed to supply social needs. Fine. But is that what it is trying
to do? Even the act that was passed that was called the MTPA (Medical Termination of Pregnancy Act)—you see how we have avoided the
word "abortion"?—this has been passed. Now what is it? Is it an
antiabortion act? From the government sources, they say it has noth-

ing to do with population at all. It is a piece of social legislation to emancipate the women of India. Is this women's lib? Is it intended to destroy the mother concept of women in India? Second, do we have enough clinics to cater to the needs of the village population with regard to abortion?

Beliappa: I want to take you up on that. What about this abortion law? Was it proabortion or antiabortion? It legalizes abortion. If the government were not serious, if they wanted only a gimmick, they could have passed this law much earlier. Why did they wait until 1970, when the mood in the country and the need for it was so obvious, to enact the law? Has the law followed the elite? No.

Galanter: You said the demand came along, and the government followed.

Beliappa: Yes.

Galanter: Yes, but the correspondence of law to that demand is not exact. That is the point here. From the point of view of those who make the law, factors other than demand enter.

A. M. Shah: I can do nothing but support Professor Galanter on this. I find that Beliappa suffers from a number of presumptions and suppositions about law in society. Who are the people who make these changes? It is the MPs and MLAs who make the changes. Do they really represent the country as a whole, its culture, and so forth? Let us take the Anti-Dowry Act. Who says that dowry is so prevalent in the country? It affects only a very small fraction of the society.

Beliappa: You mean dowry?

Shah: Yes. Among most Indians you find bride price but not dowry. It is only the upper castes who suffer from dowry. So when the Indian legislature is passing an antidowry act, they are doing it only for the upper castes, not for the rest of the society. In the rest of society there is exactly the opposite custom. So when demands are made, they are made by a certain fraction of the society. Usually they happen to be the dominant faction.

Beliappa: Well, according to this, then, it would be expedient for government just to formulate legislation without being serious about its consequences or implementation.

<u>Galanter</u>: That is clearly the case in the Anti-Dowry Act. There couldn't be a clearer case of symbolic legislation that the government had no intention of enforcing seriously. If later a wave of antidowry sentiment develops, they might bring a few prosecutions. But I can't imagine that there was ever any intention of proceeding to prosecute people. It was enacted to please a segment of the population who wanted a visible attack on this institution. In a much more important way, the Medical Termination of Pregnancy Act also makes Shah's point about being responsive to certain sections of the population. The MTPA was premised on the notion that something like one in seven of all pregnancies in India are terminated by abortion and that most of these are done by village midwives. What the act does is to say that abortions are all right when performed in hospitals by doctors, if the doctor fills out a little certificate. That changes exactly nothing because the doctors were already performing abortions in hospitals at the request of their middle-class clients. Maybe a few were not, and those few middle-class people who could not manage previously to get a doctor willing to perform an abortion now have the benefit of being able to do that. For the 15 million every year—or whatever the number—who get abortions from village midwives, the act did exactly nothing because it left this type of abortion still stigmatized as illegal and still unregulated. The government can now say we have legalized abortion and that's a major progressive step in population policy. Of course, the government has responded positively to the need of some urban-dwellers to get this service in a legitimate way, but the government has done nothing about the really massive problem of illegal abortions in the countryside.

<u>Asok Mitra</u>: I perhaps should not speak on law because whatever cases I have tried in my career have been immediately reversed in the courts! But even then I'll have a go at it. In 1803, the great pioneer Rammohan Roy said that one of the great accomplishments of British rule in India was the establishment of the rule of law over the rule of man. If by rule of law he meant deliberate, rational law, I think the government of India as successor to the British Raj took a very big first step by ushering in the Constitution.

    The power of the rule of law was demonstrated by Tilak in his fight against the British administration. Tilak accused the British government, in his cases over the <u>Keshari</u>, of trying to reverse the rule of law and reinstate the rule of man. He proved that the British Rah, in the Keshari cases, was trying, in Tennyson's words, "to mete out unequal laws unto a savage race" because the law laid down by the British was being applied unequally in his case. If the consequence of what follows from our Constitution strikes at the root of our customary laws, which are in the ultimate analysis mere laws of

privileges, I don't see why there should be such wailing and gnashing
of teeth.

After all, most customary laws in India are laws of privilege.
There is no question of modern contract in any of the customary law.
I notice that Mukerjee waxes cloquent over customary law. Even if
granting to him that some laws were no more than symbolic—like the
Anti-Dowry Act and so on—or even if the MTPA has not been able to
embrace the whole of the population in terms of implementation at
this point in time, yet they create a climate for the enforcement of
the rule of law and you can fight over it as Tilak fought in his time,
for the ground is already prepared by the Constitution and the various
laws that are enacted. To fight is what is important. If there are no
fighters, then that is another matter.

Then there are conflicts within the rule of law, too. There are
state laws and central government laws, and the state laws make a
great many compromises with customary law. But in any case let's
be a little wary of the glamor of customary law. Let us examine
around the table whether there is any customary law in India that is
not in favor of privilege. If you have a country of 600 million people,
with enormous problems of economic development, and if we are really
talking about equalities of income and various other kinds of equalities
—again not in a symbolic way but in a real way—then we must go hammer and tongs against many of the customary laws. What is the viability of the situation Beliappa is talking about? It is entirely privilege so far as I am concerned.

Milton Singer: I had the very strong impression when I was listening
to Marc Galanter that his comments sounded more like a picture of
the American than the Indian system. Certainly his three shortages
are all very characteristic of the American legal system. I wonder
whether in fact he wasn't considering what happened in the United
States as a result of population growth and other factors in construct-
ing his model.

I was also very much reminded of William James's definition of
democracy, when he spoke of it as a system of government in which
people holler and the government tries to do something to silence
them, and after it has acted another group hollers and as a result the
government tries to do something about that, and so on ad infinitum.
What I would like to ask Marc to do is to compare more explicitly the
American experience in this respect with India; and I would like to
ask him specifically whether he was not perhaps overly influenced by
the American case.

David G. Mandelbaum: This discussion showed us a variety of the
"two cultures" idea. One vicw of law is what we absorbed in our edu-

cation and another is what some of us learned when we studied the villagers' view of official law. Although constitutional and legislative law is egalitarian in theory and in purpose, the way it frequently works in the village is that it is law for the privileged. The powerful villagers can use it and do use it. When Beliappa said that social need is sanctified by law, Shah immediately asked <u>whose</u> social need; it is not the need of the poorer villagers in many cases. It is something imposed upon them from above. The villagers find this law is not in accord with their idea of justice, or with their interests, but it is something they have to cope with.

We share the widely held belief that government must take the initiative in dealing with all critical social problems. But the history of governmental efforts toward either curtailing fertility or raising fertility has been a spotty one. Official efforts may well be useful and have some effect, but they seem not to be decisive. Like their counterparts in other countries, many legislators in India want to do something about the problems of the great population increase, and one of the proposals is raising the legal age of girls at marriage. There is precedent for that in the Sarda Act of 1929 and the Hindu Code Bill of 1956, which raised the legal age of girls at marriage to 14 and then to 15. These acts had some effect but by no means the total effect that was intended.

There are still a great many prepuberty marriages arranged in India. I am not sure that is as bad a situation as has often been depicted, for reasons I do not have time to go into here. But it is quite clear that a further raising of the legal age of girls at marriage at the present time would not be beneficial so far as the problem of population is concerned; indeed, it might well be harmful. In the first place, the age of girls at marriage does not begin to have significant effect on their total fertility until that age is about 20. If a new law stipulated the minimum age of girls at marriage to be 20, there undoubtedly would be many evasions of such a law; it would be exceedingly difficult, perhaps impossible, to enforce. But it would also give the village enemies of a family another way of waging the power struggle by bringing a man to the courts on the grounds that he had arranged a marriage for his daughter at an illegally young age. Litigation and prosecution would increase the load on a legal system that is already overburdened and waste scarce resources in litigation.

Marc Galanter's observations about the decrease in civil litigation and the rise in criminal litigation may be related to the common use of the law as a weapon in villagers' status competition. Litigation has been an essential weapon for dominance within a village. It was viewed, in large part, as a means of justice for villages but was often a means of fighting your enemies of the other factions. Those who won in the courts were those who could hire better lawyers and get better witnesses. There are now some other arenas for that kind of struggle, principally the voting arena. That might explain the drop in civil litigation. The rise in criminal litigation may be indicative of the weakening of the village sense of community. Previously, when a crime was discovered in a village, the villagers' inclination was to keep the police out of the matter and to settle it among themselves. Nowadays that is not so easily done because of the weakening of village ties.

One of the customary laws that has been weakened among the "twice-born"* castes is the ban on widow remarriage. This is much less rigorously enforced than it used to be among many of the higher-ranking groups. A young woman who becomes a widow may now be married off again. No longer must she be celibate for the rest of her life, and she keeps on reproducing. Even more important is the change in the old customary rule of getting a girl married very soon after her menarche. The age of girls at their nuptial rites, the beginning of effective marriage, has been rising. This is, in part, due to economic reasons, especially in the Punjab. But it may also be due to a diminution of the fear of having an unwed postmenarche girl in the house. Why people are no longer so fearful of the rumors that inevitably float around in such cases is an interesting question. The rumors still are raised, but somehow parents are now strengthened against them. Such empirical factors are more effective than any legislation that could now be passed for raising the legal minimum age at marriage.

Robert Cassen: If I could follow in the wake of that last comment by David Mandelbaum and Asok Mitra's comment, the legal system in India is just another example of the way in which institutions left by the colonial power serve the privileged groups' interests after the colonial power has departed. Examples of this abound.

From all the experience of demographic history around the world, what we in fact observe is the failure of societies to respond to the implications of population increase. This goes all the way up from the problems of registration of tenancies to the treatment of taxation in the courts. Tax arrears cases pending in Indian courts now total over 6 billion rupees. As we all know, that is an awful lot of taxes, considering that the government never even manages to ask for them, at least from those who ought to be paying them. From the

---

*These are the castes that have two births: a physical birth and an intellectual birth. The second birth for the twice-born usually comes in the teenage years of an individual, when males are granted the right to wear a sacred thread around their bodies. Such a right is not granted to members of lower castes, who only have one birth.

point of view of maximizing government revenues, it would pay the
government to set up more courts to press on with these cases more
rapidly; but this does not happen either. So I think that this issue can
be related back to all of the difficulties we have discussed. Population change always ends up bearing on the balance of power in society.

Lawrence A. Veit: What has interested me in this discussion is the
subject that Mukerjee brought up and that came forward also with
David Mandelbaum—the growing incidence of crime in India—and I
wondered if we could pursue that just a bit further. I'm too ignorant
to give answers, but I do have many questions. I am not even sure
that we have the right ones, but has there been any substantial change
in the kinds of crime in India? Can we notice differences among regions in India in the incidence of increased crime, and can we draw
any connection between the population changes in those regions and
the changes in crime levels? And then again this problem that I
raised yesterday. It strikes me that it makes a great deal of difference what the density of a population is as to its social structure, but
the way in which you get there—that is, the rate of population growth—
may be as much a factor in determining the local law or administration as the actual density itself. If we could somehow make a distinction between the rate of change and the density, it might be useful.

Krishan Bhatia: I just want to add a few lines in defense of what have
been described as symbolic laws in India. There are plenty of them;
but they are not quite as useless as some of them would seem. They
are not always expressions of previous thinking on the part of law-
makers. They are often designed to buy time in the face of a social
problem when political leadership does not exactly know what else
to do. A law is frequently enacted and then forgotten.
    Especially with regard to social legislation, however, a law is
useful in the sense that it stimulates movements in a certain desirable
manner. Even if it does not immediately solve the problem, it encourages people to move in a desired direction. So it is a small step,
but an important one. An example of this is the legislation on untouchability. The fact that there is a legal code on untouchability does stimulate certain action, although not as fast as it should.
    Almost all social laws, so far as I can see, affect only a seg-
ment of the population. Hardly any social laws would affect the entire
population. In a large and diverse country like ours, one cannot have
such comprehensive complete organization of the laws. The fact that
the Anti-Dowry Act affects a small group—and that dowry is not
widely practiced—does not mean that there should not be an anti-dowry
law. There should be a law to ban the sale of brides, too, if that is a
desirable end.

John Cool: Two points. Once or twice it's been suggested that there is a positive correlation that we can accept as already being proven between crowding, urbanization, and criminality. I would like to know whether, in fact, there is a basis for this. Perhaps it is in statistical collection methods that one finds this rather than in reality. Certainly, as has been suggested by some of you who have had long experience in the villages, there is a great deal of insecurity and in some sense lawlessness in village life, which never gets recorded. One of the principal reasons why human groups have taken to the comfort and shelter of cities has been precisely because, at least until the recent past, cities have, relatively speaking, afforded a measure of security and protection for the individual that he did not or could not be assured of in a rural setting. We may be guilty of what I perceive to be a very widespread bias of intellectuals, both Western and Indian, against cities. This bias fails to recognize that most of the good things that have happened in this world, those that we label civilization, happened in cities, and have arisen from the vitality and intellectual interchange that cities make possible.

The second thing is that there seems to be a confusion regarding what we are talking about. Sometimes we are talking about the law and sometimes we are talking about the administration of the law. While I would agree that the administration of the law is far from equal in India, as it is far from equal in almost every other country, the laws themselves—the laws enacted under the Constitution of India —by and large were constructed to provide a framework in which, if not perfect equality, at least something more nearly approaching equality in the human condition could be achieved. They are, of course, subject to all of the problems of laws in every country. They have to be administered by mere mortals, and mortals are often, very often, in error.

One of the things we haven't touched on is how an India that will be rapidly increasing in scale and complexity in the next 30 years can begin now to think of restructuring, if you will, the system of administration of the law and of the courts, so as to bring back a little more of the human involvement and interpersonal communication that made law a living thing in the days when the magistrate used to ride the circuit. Maybe that's too much to hope for in an India of a billion human beings. But I would think—certainly we see it in the West— there is an enormous penalty that is paid by poor people for whom justice is almost uniformly delayed.

One reason why criminal and even civil litigation may not be increasing is that it's just not a feasible proposition economically for people to "bring cases" any longer. They have to go to places far removed from their homes. They have to pay very large fees. They are involved in complex procedures. These kinds of bottlenecks are ones we see commonly in the United States among poor people. I wonder if there is any way that those who are concerned about leveling out some of the inequities can plan to restructure the administration of law in ways that would make it truly more accessible to poor and less educated people in India.

John Lewis: I found in Marc Galanter's comment quite a stimulating thesis—partly, I suppose, because in somewhat different terms it comes at something I have been thinking about. I too think there are rather strong pressures toward decentralization. I suppose in a sense they really are a result of population. I don't know that one needs to rest the case on the dynamic growth of population, but surely if one simply looks at the very large systems that are gathered under one sovereign tent there are pretty strong pressures toward decentralization generated in those systems. This tends to be the case in China, the Soviet Union (from what I know about it), and the United States.

What was interesting to me about Galanter's thesis was particularly the way he gets to his conclusion. He thinks about it in terms of the increasing volume of conflict resolution that has to be done. Too big a burden of this kind is created in the center of the system. I think you can also make the argument in terms of sheer administrative management. Also, I have been increasingly impressed in the Indian context by the very strong case for decentralization that can be made in terms of resource raising. That is, I don't think you can raise enough internal resources for various things that governments have to do unless more of the responsibility is passed down to the states and the localities. If the states and localities are going to have more of the fund-raising responsibilities, then they also are going to demand more of the action.

In terms of the dilemmas that Marc poses, if there were time, I would give what to me is a sufficiently satisfying answer to the control dilemma. I think that is a somewhat false issue; central planners have created a problem that in a sense does not exist.

As for the shortage of legitimacy, I will comment only briefly. I think Galanter's argument as to the way in which scarcities compounded by concerns about equity tend to make for additional controls, and therefore create gaps in the ability of the government to deliver, as well as to generate corruption through the mediation of the price system, is very interesting. I think that is a good descriptive analysis. But a normative case can be made, on the other hand, that, just as large numbers tend to cause systems to delegate downward within the official structure, they also should motivate a delegation sideways, to decision-making systems that lie outside the official structure—for example, to market mechanisms that in some measure produce answers without involving bureaucrats. The market becomes a labor-saving device for bureaucrats. Now, obviously the market cannot be a free-standing mechanism; it has to be conditioned and bounded. But if you can use such self-adjusting feedback systems, this is another logical response to the complexities posed by a large population. It also seems to me that there is some inclination in India to move in this direction.

But the thing I wanted mainly to emphasize is my agreement with Marc Galanter that there is a severe conflict between decentralization and equity. For, just as he says, passing decision-making to the localities tends to mean passing it into the hands of the least disturbed elites, who are likely to be least compassionate in their dealings with the poor. Here I think we are pretty much at the crux of the reform issue in India. The question is the extent to which a central regime is interested in and has the capacity to try to shore up the equity situation for the poor in a more decentralized context.

This could be one area that it would be most interesting for us to pursue. As we pursue it, I suspect, we get closer to one of the fundamental cultural differences among the people represented around this table. Some of us come at these things with reform lenses and make hopeful noises about how reformers can contrive this or that. People who are studying the traditional society are inclined to say— sure, there was and is great inequity; there was great privilege in traditional society; but, damn it, it worked, and before somebody from Delhi or Washington or one of the Cambridges starts moving in and changing things without even knowing what is there, think twice! We reformers, however, are impressed with the scale of the equities problem. If you're concerned about it as Cassen is and as I am—if you believe that if that equity problem in due course is not effectively attacked then something very substantial is going to happen—then you hope against hope that the leadership is sufficiently declassed and has sufficient persistence and shrewdness to strengthen the poor to bargain more effectively in the local arenas of more decentralized decision-making.

Finally I come to my additive point. It is that, rather than assume that less violence in the villages is desirable, we should be expecting and indeed hoping for more violence—more class violence really—in the villages. It would be part of the reformers' aim in various ways, by helping to organize politicoeconomic organizations of the poor and by trying to weaken the dependency mechanism through which the village elites keep the poor subservient, to generate greater capacity in the poor to compete for resources in the local arena. We could expect this to lead for some time to quite a lot more violence in the countryside, although hopefully contained within some kind of more or less orderly frame. I think that, if you see poverty at least in part as a joint product of population and population growth, then you can say that one effect would be, through this sequence, to increase violence and conflict in the countryside—in a way that I would regard as constructive.

Beba Varadachar: Law is a luxury, and yet the poor man is the one man who seems to use law the most in India. This is a social contradiction. I do not know how it happened.

Another contradiction: Why is there not more lawlessness in India? Why is there not a great upsurge of chaos? How is it that these people contain themselves? When new slums come up, especially after the first three months are over, each fellow is watching which of the others is going to pull out his bathroom or take his wife or his utensils away. But slum-dwellers do not let a policeman in. Mandelbaum is absolutely right. The one thing to do, the first thing to do—whether in a village or in a slum—is to keep the police and the officials away. These people govern themselves. They formulate laws. They enforce their own laws. In a country where enforcement is one of the biggest headaches, at the policy level, these people contain themselves. How is it that the slum gets to be a viable working society right smack in the larger city?

I am not sure that there is an increase in crime or a lessening of crime. With the introduction of modern weaponry, like guns and so on, there surely have been changes. But this is a small thing. It does not interest me very much. What interests me most is that there hasn't been that much violence as to attract the attention of anthropologists, sociologists, and others, and, more important, attitudes toward crime have changed. There is now a whole complex of new attitudes.

Cheating, lying, and the other things Gandhi spoke about—but dishonesty and violence were the two he kept emphasizing—these are the very two things that serve as the topics that concern most people. It is all all right now to cheat in some ways. There is a certain kind of tolerance. Here again there has been a moral or value stretch. These attitudinal changes are much more central than loading our heads with the number of times various crimes are committed. The fact that there were a certain number of crimes 50 years ago and a certain number last year doesn't tell me very much. Attitudes toward crime, as defined by the local man, can tell us a great deal. One of the things we are learning about now is oral aggression, which is slowly replacing litigation because litigation is very expensive. The agencies of litigation are also getting very sophisticated. Everywhere in India one finds that use of oral aggression is in the ascendance.

Rakesh Mohan: One source of information about villages for those of us who do not get to villages very often are many of the novels written in Hindi. One of the things that does come out of these novels is the emphasis in the village on the police and the administrators. They are really regarded as terrorists rather than anything else, and that's probably one of the reasons—as Varadachar suggested—that Marc Galanter's figures are very low.

Beliappa: I don't look at all like a terrorist, I hope.

Mohan: The response of the administration in general—perhaps not Beliappa in particular—seems to have escalated recently, especially in the use of the Maintenance of Internal Security Act and the use of firearms by the administration in curbing violence.

The last point that I want to make is one that has not been touched on in this discussion of law, and that concerns white-collar crime. White-collar crime, and corruption generally, at least from a superficial observation, is much more accepted now. You cannot do very much in the cities, for example, without using black money. When you go to buy a railway ticket and you have to pay five rupees extra for that, you don't resent it any more; you take it as in some sense an invisible tax that goes to supplement the salaries of the people who are administering these things. But that again is a point that Varadachar made. The idea of law has changed to the extent that there is tolerance to that kind of lawlessness. One assumes that the reason why there haven't been stronger laws and a stronger administration in these matters is precisely because the people who make the laws and who administer them would be affected most by the kind of laws that would curb these kinds of things.

David Horlacher: It seems to me that Beliappa's presentation gives many examples of changes in the law without very many clear linkages of those changes to the growth of population. It also seems that Galanter gave us very many very interesting and detailed sets of linkages without any examples of these linkages in the Indian context. I wonder if Beliappa could perhaps provide us with some examples, and how they are linked to population changes, in order to tie the two things together.

This is the first thing I wanted. Second, most economists feel that when a nation is faced with serious problems, this will trigger responses that not only are directed at meeting the immediate problem but also sometimes put into place new institutions, technical changes, and other kinds of advances that move ahead the whole developmental process of a society. Now all of the linkages that I see in Professor Galanter's presentation are detrimental. In what ways does population increase result in impacts that are perhaps favorable to the society? These are two questions that I have.

<u>John Newmann</u>: This may be risking the purpose of this meeting, but I would like to reflect upon Mukerjee's point that India began an interest in population control long before many other countries. It is interesting to note that one effect that his concern for population growth has not had on law in India is the enactment of legislation that might have some influence in curtailing population growth. Laws have not been passed favoring smaller families through tax incentives, savings programs, educational opportunities, and so forth. In recent years all of these have been suggested. Singapore is one of the few examples where governmental programs of this nature have been established.

The argument that suggests that laws often reflect the vested interests of the upper classes doesn't necessarily hold here. If there is an interest in conserving resources to enable the privileged to maintain a high standard of life, wouldn't there be a corresponding interest in limiting the numbers of people who compete for these resources? We don't find legislation suggesting this, as it would be very unpopular in a democratic society and would challenge the prospect of the growing middle classes to maintain and accumulate additional power.

<u>Anrudh Jain</u>: These social laws, or laws that are made for social reform and its acceptance by the population, lead to two other factors that have to be taken into account. The first of these is the time lag between the law and its implementation. If it requires a number of services like the MTPA, then such services cannot be provided overnight. But if the law is not there, then the services obviously cannot be provided. The second is the reward system. In making laws like increasing the age of marriage or the Anti-Dowry Act, or making registration of births and deaths compulsory, what is the reward system for the population that has to follow these laws? As for the gradual acceptance of the later age of marriage after the Sardah Acts, I would take another stand: These provide legitimacy, buttressing parents against social pressures to marry their girls during puberty.

<u>Mitra</u>: I do not know if we have moved away from the point that John Lewis made. His point reminded me of the period of the United Front government in West Bengal. The law then provided for the redistribution of surplus land. At this particular time, a minister of the United Front government was presented with a list from the Director of Land Records of about 300,000 acres of vestable land. The minister consulted his law department and other people and was told that to get those 300,000 acres of land for redistribution through the law courts would take something like 25 years, and he seemed to be in a hurry. So he organized what was near violence and a rough and ready redis-

tribution of this vested land to landless laborers living nearest to those vested or surplus lands and had them occupied and tilled. Of course this led to a considerable amount of unrest at both the state levels and the federal levels, and there was also a lot of violence.

I do not know the full history of who was responsible for what kind of violence, and the real story of the violence has not yet been written up. The picture is quite clouded. From many sides, it is quite biased and prejudiced. The result was that the United Front government had to go, but there were other consequences that followed. One was a considerable reduction in the administration and ownership of land by absentee landlords. Landlords were in a hurry to get back to their lands. The other was that Bengal has remained one of the few states where, and this is particularly important in light of the rising prices of grain, part of the wage for agricultural labor is still paid in kind and partly in cash. Part payment in kind compensates for the inflation. Another wide effect that occurred was a step-up in the production of rice, and I think in spite of its so-called bad record Bengal has shown considerable step-up in the production of rice in the last seven or eight years. What is more relevant is that more than 400,000 tons of wheat are now grown in Bengal, as a result of which employment for many agricultural laborers has gone up from something like 110 to 120 days a year to about 220 days. These are rather complex things.

Lewis: Yes. Bengal is one case. Another is Kerala. It seems to me that radical politics over the years really has broken the backs of the local elites much more than would be the case in other states. Therefore, redistributive programs have more effect in their intended direction in states where there have been radical political movements than they do in many other states.

Mitra: One of the other factors that must be taken into account in Kerala is the tremendous strides that have been made in literacy and education and a certain sort of freeing of the woman from the home.

Irene Tinker: I want to make a general comment here. We saw yesterday that customs, mores, religious rites, and religious rituals constantly do change and that they have responded to various changes in population growth. None of these things are fixed and immutable. They are in fact constantly subject to change. One of the major mechanisms governing change is the balance between available resources and population size. Societies develop customs and mores all the way from prohibited times of intercourse to the kinds of marriages and laws in order to institutionalize adaptations.

What we are seeing now, as a result of the rapid rate of increase in population and the disorientation of resources, seems to be a society somewhat out of kilter in almost every field; to some, this appears as a series of contradictions. In the field of law, because much of customary law has been written down in terms of legislative law, change may seem to be even slower than in other areas. To some, Indian law may even appear to be a kind of reaction to keep the society from adapting.

Generally speaking, however, there is usually less mobility when there is greater pressure on resources. I think it's interesting that we're getting a kind of call for the reestablishment of privilege, or the comment that in fact we have never gotten away from privilege, at a time when all indications would be that privilege would be reinforced. With population increase and resource scarcity, one would expect that people would sort of stay in their place and that, as a result of this, you would tend to protect the resources you have and increase the number of people on the margin, the number of people who are in fact in the poorer categories.

Beliappa: There is a whole range of questions that have been directed at me. Some of these I think I will leave to my colleagues. I should like to start with David Horlacher's point that I've not been able to link up examples to population change. I must admit that I am having difficulty isolating population growth as the only motivating factor in society.

As you will agree, there are obviously many factors responsible for social change, and if you look at the economic legislation that has been enacted relating to land, I think there is a strong set of egalitarian forces that have brought about change. To quote just one example on the possibility of linkage, I should like to refer to the village panchayat, which has been referred to while we were discussing crime. It was an institution of great usefulness at the local level, and it handled many problems that confronted village societies. When one talks of decentralization and the prospects of villagers running their own affairs, one would wish that the village panchayat were more active. That institution perhaps disappeared because of the impact of population growth, when people had to move away from villages and settle down and find employment and migrate from the village. I have not referred to it as a specific example, but this is one institution that has definitely suffered as a result of population change.

I was particularly interested in Professor Lewis' suggested that there should be more decentralization. This is a demand that has been gaining currency in India, but what worries me is the fact that this demand seems to stop at a certain level. There is a great hue and cry and a great demand for greater autonomy and greater decentralization from a higher level, but as long as that decentralization is talked about there is a reluctance to pass it down to a lower level, to a more local or a more micro-level. To be more specific, state governments would like to get more powers from the central government, but at the same time they are being a little chary of passing on all those powers to local governments or to panchayats or to institutions that are closer to the ground.

The reasons for this are numerous. They could result from an administrative lack, or from political expediency, or it could be that some states want to oversee the performance of many programs more effectively, with all good intentions. At any rate, they want to retain powers for themselves. There is a case for greater decentralization especially in relation to economic development. But this is a point that cannot be discussed in five mintues. There have been various commissions and various reports and various studies, all attempting to determine the extent to which decentralization is feasible.

Two more points. Mitra referred to customary law as being support for privilege. Perhaps I am wrong. I did not get the impression that I was defending customary law and privilege. I was only trying to explain the consequences of land legislation, and economic legislation related to land, and what has happened in the fields. I was holding no brief for the privileged or for customary law. In fact, I don't very much share Professor Mukerjee's nostalgic feelings.

I am aware of the facts that there are many pieces of legislation that have remained on paper, and that it is possible that governments will enact fanciful pieces of legislation. But I do not think we should generalize in the manner of Galanter. When we look at the whole context of legislation, and then at these isolated pieces of enactment that have not gotten off the ground, I think it is clear that they do not explain the whole story. Bhatia has covered the point. These laws point in the direction that we want to move, and they provide an opportunity for the weakest in society to have recourse to law when the necessity arises.

Of course, immediately you will say that the legislative process is too expensive for the poor chap to get at. All I would say is that measures that have not taken off the ground point in the direction we would like to move. I somehow did get the impression—when Professor Galanter referred to legislation being dished out—that governments might be irresponsible and may be trying to get away from the main task of development by taking to convenient pieces of legislation. I think the main area of activity is to concentrate on economic development, and, in the Indian context, to control population. The answer does not lie in escapist legislation.

Galanter: I just want to say a couple of things about the incidence of
crime. Part of the problem is clearly an increase in reporting,
which may reflect the point David Mandelbaum made about the break-up
of the integrity of the village, allowing outsiders to report about crime.
Also, there are more police to become aware of crime and more people in urban and heavily settled areas whose crimes might be observed by the police. There is another direct impact of population on
crime rates, if the American experience is any guide. The population has gotten younger, and we know that in the United States most
crime is commited by males between the ages of 15 and 25—that is,
the kinds of crime whose increase is visible, not white-collar crimes.
Presumably that is an age cadre that has increased enormously in India.

Many of you are aware of how inaccurate police statistics are
for measuring crime rates. There is a very interesting new development called "victimization studies" in which, instead of asking the
police how many crimes there were, you go to a sample of the population and ask, "Have you been victimized, has a crime been commited
against you? If so, tell us about the incident." Then you obtain detailed descriptions of incidents, and these are sifted by experts,
lawyers, and law enforcement people, who ask whether these are indeed instances of burglary that are being described, or robbery, or
whatever? Then you can derive victimization rates that turn out in
the American setting to be something like twice the level of crime reported by police.

Let me go on to the problem of paper or symbolic legislation.
I agree with Bhatia and with Beliappa that indeed there is something
to what they say. I did not mean to take a completely debunking stance
toward such legislation or to say that it is all just on paper. I agree,
it has an extremely important positive function as a pointer, a commitment, a kind of mortgage to the future. As Albert Hirschman says,
you create a facade but eventually the facade takes on a life of its own.
The point I would make is that some facades are better at taking on a
life of their own than are others. Some, like the Anti-Dowry Act,
have very slender possibilities. Others, like land reform legislation,
might, if some organized political muscle were put together with that
legislation, serve as an instrument to bring about change. I would
argue that the Untouchability Offences Act is unfortunately closer to
the Anti-Dowry Act in this respect than to more effective pieces of
legislation. And there's another side to this. The pointer may involve costs. One of the costs is that you relieve the itch of the intellectuals and reformers and thus defuse the issue.

This brings me to the distinction John Cool drew between the
law and the administration of the law. As a student of law I find it
a threatening and objectionable distinction. I feel as though I were a

student of religion and somebody had said, "You just study the scriptures; don't worry about the church or people's religious feelings or what they actually do." I find that very confining. My personal position—and it is one that is shared with a small but growing sect—is that we cannot be textual scholars. We want to see how law operates. So we will not buy the distinction between law and the way it is administered, except as indirectly pointing to a very important reality about law—that is, that law has two faces. It has the face of the way in which these norms are embodied in official and popular practice. It seems to me very important that we look at both faces.

Now let me come to Milton Singer's point about projecting U.S. experiences or reading Indian experiences through American lenses, which are in a very fundamental sense the only ones I have. I would only say that in many important respects the American and Indian legal systems are the same kind of animal and the same kind of analysis does apply. True, I'm bringing to the Indian political system a formulation that I developed in work on the American setting, but that in turn was a direct outgrowth of my experience in India—an experience that helped me to unlearn the identification of law only with its benign face.

Mukerjee: I want to say a few words, not in defense of myself at all but in defense of the rule of law. I am a firm believer in the rule of law. We cannot condemn anyone unheard. He must be given a chance to defend. So it must be my fault that in my hurry I may have given a very wrong impression that I have a nostalgic view for customary law. No, not at all. The rule of law is excellent. Nobody can quarrel with that. I would be the last person to have anything to say against it. But the point is, when the rule of law in actual practice becomes the rule of lawyers then what do you do? The entire purpose of a rule of law or of customary law is "social engineering" and if our rule of law is set from above and does not percolate into the villages then what happens?

You have to depend on the dynamic forces that already exist and study them. The point is, before we start to introduce new laws we must study the situation and see what is best. So far as I have been able to see, the legal structure that we have introduced after independence has not been popular. Take again the village panchayat. The old panchayat was not by elections. Mitra is perfectly right. It was a law of privilege. If you go deep into it, perhaps you will find people who were selected as panchayat leaders were selected by virtue of their character, by virtue of their honesty, by virtue of their experience; but the new panchayat that has been introduced is chosen by election.

<u>Beliappa</u>: By virtue of the community also.

<u>Mukerjee</u>: Of course, of course.

<u>Shah</u>: They are all from the dominant castes.

<u>Mukerjee</u>: Yes. If you examine and find them wrong, chuck them
out. The ultimate object in the established rule of law is justice;
the goal is justice, which I cannot compromise with. The structure
you may select from the dominant castes, or from whatever else
there is, but it belongs there. They have a sense of belonging to that
system; but when you introduce universal adult franchise in a country
where the people are illiterate, then instead of having popular democracy you have publicized democracy. You know what is happening to
these elected panchayats. Villagers themselves are moving away
from the elected panchayats and going back to the old panchayats. I
have not done any field work, but from the little here and there that
I have seen the villagers have greater confidence in their community
panchayats than they do in the new government-elected panchayats.
Before reforming further, then, I suggest you study this very carefully.

One last point about John Newmann's intervention. So far as
population-responsive laws are concerned, there are many, and government must pass such laws. With regard to population-restrictive
laws, I should point out it is not necessary in our country to adopt
any legislation authorizing contraception or authorizing sterilization.
It was necessary to pass a law authorizing abortion, so we have done
that. If I may draw an analogy, it is like supply and demand—there
are laws that create demands for control of reproduction and laws
that enable supplies of goods and services to meet those demands.

POPULATION, CHANGE,
AND THE MASS MEDIA
Promilla Kalhan

While the world has shrunk, effective communication of ideas remains one of its most difficult problems. Communication between cities that dot the globe has become easier. Ideas and phrases catch on speedily. In Moscow two months ago I saw crowds of people queuing up to see an American film. Outside the Kremlin palace auditorium, where I had gone to a ballet, female members of the audience wore jump suits and mini-skirts. At an exhibition, some teenagers had on American-style jeans. Scrawled across the jacket of one of the boys were these words: "I don't make love all the time. Sometimes I sleep!" My guide smiled and explained, "the influence of foreign films."

Ideas give rise to demands. Only a few years ago, perhaps, Russia's mother heroines never thought of keeping slim. Nor did they worry about the style of their dresses. Today one of Moscow's most sought-after figures is Zaitsev, a young man in his 30s, who is a designer of women's fashions. True, his creations are not daring or dramatic, but the fashion idea has caught on.

New York is nearer to New Delhi than New Delhi to some villages in the interior of eastern Uttar Pradesh or Bihar, at least insofar as the communication of ideas is concerned. The problem of effective communications in India, then, results not so much from the size of the country but from the fact that its massive population is spread over remote villages. While some might blame the communications media in India for failing to do a better job of communicating, much of the task of communications must be the responsibility of the nation at large.

Urbanizing villages, in the best sense of the term, is to my mind an important factor in the whole business of communications. Development, it has been said, is the best contraceptive. Development,

ense, means higher living standards, including more
nedical care, education, housing, gainful employment,
pirational levels.

media can obviously do much more for the literate than
ttered. Take the case of Kerala, which has a higher rate
than any other state in India. Over the past decade the
birthrate in Kerala has fallen from about 37 to 27 per 1,000 or less,
while the death rate has dropped from around 16 to 8.5 per 1,000.
While the decline in the death rate has leveled off, thus holding out
the prospect of the survival rate significantly narrowing, population
growth is still falling. The infant mortality rate in Kerala is now
57 per 1,000, the lowest in India. The national average mortality
rate is still around 140 per 1,000 births.

India was among the first countries to have adopted an official
family planning program, and the program has thus far had mixed
results. Nevertheless, its communication effort has not been as ineffective as some would make it out to be. This is clear from the
relatively high levels of awareness of the need for family planning
that exist in India now, as contrasted with a few years ago. It is also
clear from the fact that at least three or four modern methods of contraception are now widely known, among a vast population that previously had very little knowledge of even one such method. Posters
and billboards of small happy families, bearing slogans like "two, no
more," or "a small family is a happy family," or "we two and our
two," have become commonplace throughout India. They can be seen
not only on walls and billboards, but also on buses and scooter rick-
shaws, on match boxes, in movie theaters, and in a host of other
prominent places. A small-denomination postage stamp, used by
just about everybody, bears a similar message, effective enough in
communicating with the unlettered.

A recent survey conducted by the Indian Institute of Mass Communications has tried to evaluate the effectiveness of the poster idea,
and to contrast the effectiveness of posters with such things as talks
on the radio, films, newspapers, and other forms of communication.
The survey points out that wall writings, radio, films, and newspapers
have all been "quite successful" in making people aware of the family
planning idea. And awareness is essential, if only because it is the
first step on the way to adoption. Awareness means the shedding of
prejudice and the possibility of acceptance of an idea.

When continued awareness does not lead to motivation to put an
idea into practice, however, it becomes a matter of some concern.
In this sense, the gap between awareness and the practice of family
planning in India is a matter that must be explored fully in the years
ahead. But here it should be pointed out that the practice of family
planning differs greatly from region to region within India, and even

from district to district in the same state. It is significant that in
those states where the largest number of couples are protected against
fertility, through one method or another, per capita income is high.
Areas where family planning methods are being used with frequency
are also those that are educationally forward and enjoy facilities associated with urbanization. These areas include most districts in
Punjab, Haryana, Maharashtra, Kerala, Tamil Nadu, and the Union
territories of Delhi and Chandigarh.

Particularly in poorer countries, the connections between mass
media consumption and socioeconomic development are rather direct.
In a situation where educational facilities are limited, the mass media
act as educational instruments while being dependent on levels of education for their effectiveness. Since the educational level is higher
in urban than in rural areas in poor countries, the media have proved
more successful in motivating people to take to family planning in urban than in rural areas.

City people also have more opportunities than do rural people
to translate ideas into practice, if only because of the wider variety
of options available in urban centers. City people, therefore, do not
need as much active motivation toward creating alternative life situations. Moreover, the housing problems in the cities, as well as the
other general shortages and the desire for emulation of higher visible
living standards, all act as motivating forces encouraging people to
seek out family planning aids. Little wonder that hairpins, combs,
and condoms sell side by side in New Delhi's pavement shops and are
in demand.

It should be pointed out here that the integration of family planning centers with general health clinics has helped people to seek advice on family planning, and in this sense has served a communications function. Indians being a shy people with regard to matters of
sex, means must be found to preserve the privacy of family planning
activities. So long as family planning centers are part of health
clinics, the seeking out of family planning advice and assistance is
likely to attract little more attention than entering a snack bar or a
soda fountain.

Again, this is particularly so in the cities. Making a city audience aware of the population problem may be almost all that is required, since most urbanites can be expected to put ideas into practice
on their own. That, however, does not seem to be the case with rural
areas. There, some form of follow-up through personal communication has been found to be necessary once the mass media have done
their job. This perhaps has so far constituted the weakest link in
family planning communication in India.

Village doctors and midwives, plus other rural health personnel, have often been singled out as the most likely personal motivators

with regard to population matters. The survey mentioned above, however, points to the need to prepare village opinion leaders to motivate
rural people more effectively. If village opinion is to be prepared,
attention must be directed at socioeconomic factors in the rural areas.
The old image of India's village folk as people steeped in prejudice is
not wholly applicable today.

On this score, there has been a good deal of change. Take the
case of Punjab in the north of India. Success on the agricultural
front—the Green Revolution—has brought its rewards. A good deal of
the profits from the new agriculture, of course, go back into agriculture. But not all. The area has been swept by winds of change.
There is now almost a craze for education. Unlettered farmers in
Punjab frequently raise funds from among the community, as their
share toward a new college, with the result that the glut of first-gen-
eration urban students in Punjab is now buregoning. Then, too,
young men in Punjab are demanding educated girls as marriage partners, and the preference is for those educated enough to take on jobs.
Village girls are thronging not only to big-city colleges but also to
small-town colleges and educational institutions.

The result is that colleges for women are springing up in Punjab's rural areas. One might even argue that the gap between towns
and villages in Punjab has been largely bridged. Village opinion
leaders in Punjab today are no longer village elders, but rather young
and progressive farmers who have made good. They, and their wives,
sit on innumerable village councils. There are even examples of women being elected chairpersons of these councils.

In short, there is a visible race toward modernity in Punjab.
Nobody has made any noise about the need to liberate women there,
and yet studies made at Punjab Agricultural University in Ludhiana
have shown that the status of farm women has risen appreciably.
Rural Punjabi women increasingly make decisions regarding personal
and household matters on their own, or in some cases jointly with
their husbands. Husbands now consult their wives in matters of land
and property. In contrast to the past, Punjabi women are now more
than equal partners in the business of farming. Most of the poultry
farming is done exclusively by women, and where farms are small
and the men go out to work women often look after the fields as well.

In Punjab, tubectomy has been a popular method of family limitation, perhaps because women feel strongly about the need for limiting family size and do not wait for their husbands to do something
about it. There are villages where demands for abortion facilities
have been rather strenuously made. From the perspective of Punjab
as a whole, one might argue that tubectomy is still considered a drastic measure, generally resorted to only after a number of children
have been born, while adequate facilities for abortion are not yet
available. However, throughout Punjab, things are changing rapidly.

Even in the less progressive rural areas of Eastern Uttar Pradesh, which are considerably poorer and more backward than Punjab, the demand for family planning is coming from women rather than men. Woman after woman in villages there told me recently that they were keen to limit their families. "Give us something to put a stop to the yearly burden of childbirth, something we can use on the quiet without our mothers-in-law or even our husbands knowing," they said. Perhaps the antinatal vaccine that India has helped to produce could be the answer to such pleas.

If the motivation for family planning is present in both affluent and poor areas, this is so because such things as posters, postage stamps, and radio advertisements have done a fair job. In the backward areas, requiring more aggressive motivation, visual media (mainly films and popular activities like discourses and puppet shows) could perhaps be more effectively used. The survey referred to above suggests training of village leaders in knowledge about family planning methods and an emphasis on in-service training to family planning workers in extension education. The village midwife, the single most powerful factor in the lives of village mothers, could perhaps be used in some manner, although efforts to use midwives have thus far been relatively unsuccessful. Training for midwives has now been taken up on a large scale.

Various research projects have revealed that misconceptions regarding the IUCD and sterilization do exist in India here and there and that in some extreme cases people consider such family planning methods as harmful to health. Since one case gone wrong can scare an entire village population away from family planning clinics, it can undo the achievements of the mass media over a period of years. This points to the need for better clinical facilities and follow-up as part of the communications effort.

In the final analysis, the success of the mass media in any situation can only be temporary, if its efforts are not followed up by a proper delivery system. At present, a general demand for contraceptives has been created in India, despite the survival of some pockets of prejudice here and there. Indian scientists are probably doing more than scientists elsewhere to produce inexpensive and easy-to-use contraceptives that are free of side effects. They have achieved a measure of success. From a communications standpoint, the production of such devices could herald a revolution in the country. An antinatal vaccine for women has already been tested and is likely to be ready for use shortly. This one invention could have farreaching consequences, due to its practical value in terms of cutting across time, and its obvious advantages in terms of convenience. With the development of a vaccine we will not have to wait for a sufficient number of hospitals to come up in rural areas before we can deal adequately with the population problem.

Prophets of doom, who predict there is no hope for India, are somewhat out of touch with the Indian scene, and particularly the Indian countryside. Attitudes are hard to change, particularly when education is lacking. The effects of 200 years of colonial rule, which is primarily responsible for keeping us backward, have not been wiped out completely, or even appreciably, in the past 27 years. It is not surprising, not irrational, that impoverished families continue to believe that children are their security in old age and the providers of supplementary income. Infant mortality is still high in India, and this accounts for both human wastage and a high birthrate. The rising status of women, following the enactment of laws removing their disabilities, when coupled with increasing family welfare, economic betterment, and the availability of improved family planning aids and an efficient delivery system, are all necessary for population limitation.

Enlightened laws, giving women their rightful place, have been passed, even though they are not always effectively implemented. Better family planning methods, as I said, are being evolved, but poverty is a problem. The developed world can render real help not by giving doles but through more just terms of trade and assisting in raising both agricultural and industrial production while rendering technical training to youth in order to generate self-employment. If there were more to distribute and a more just and equitable distribution system, poverty could be tackled, and couples could depend more on themselves and less on their children. Stuck in the morass of poverty, people cannot be expected to act on their own without assistance. There is wisdom in the nursery rhyme that runs:

> There was an old woman who lived in a shoe.
> She had so many children she didn't know what to do.
> She would perhaps have had only one or two,
> If the old woman didn't live in a shoe.

By spreading awareness the mass media have successfully taken one step forward. They must now go on to tackle other prejudices, like "sons are better than daughters," which sometimes makes couples go on bearing children until an adequate number of sons are born. In short, the very foundations of old values have to be shaken. A climate for raising the age of marriage must be created and a severence of the idea that sexual activity must necessarily lead to reproduction must be brought about. Only a decade ago a family planning poster was almost taboo. Today there is a demand for population education, and even at school, voices are heard about making contraceptive advice and help available to teenagers, married or not. Posters giving details of abortion facilities in newspapers do not raise eyebrows.

Indians are open to new ideas. The mass media have much to do.

DISCUSSION

Krishan Bhatia: I must confess that when I saw the list of the other participants I was somewhat overawed. I am virtually the only person here who is neither a social scientist nor a distinguished professor or economist nor a government person of some standing. The way the heading of this particular panel was phrased, the neutral way in which it was put, did not improve my morale either. For a long while, I could not make up my mind what to talk about. When you talk about population change and the communications media, does it mean the impact of population growth on the media or the role that the media is playing in coping with population growth? I finally let Promilla Kalhan decide the matter for me. She interpreted it in the latter way, so I have done the same.

In order to discuss it within that framework I will make certain assumptions. The first obvious assumption, which was also fortunately made for me this morning, is that population change really means population increase. It is a polite way of saying that the population in India has been growing at quite a rapid rate and that this is a phenomenon that needs to be studied and discussed. Second, I assume that the rate of growth is a problem. I am in no position to say whether it is yet a catastrophic problem reaching disaster proportions. I do not know when that threshold will be reached. Maybe we are very close to it. Maybe it is still some years away. I do not know. But I assume that it is a reasonably serious problem of some magnitude, to which we must pay attention soon.

I also assume that whatever communication has to be done by the communications media is to be done within the framework of a democratic system. Professor Carstairs visualized the possibility of a police state or a military dictatorship. I was glad to hear that he also suggested that it won't function because of the basic factionalism of our society. I would argue that a police state is not likely to even come about, because of our factionalism. Even the army needs to have a certain measure of unity, and the army too must struggle with factionalism; our factionalism prevents the army, hopefully, from establishing a military dictatorship.

Also, I agree wholeheartedly that such a police state, should it come about, would be a totally inefficient one, but not mainly because we have our own brand of corruption. We do have our own distinctive brand of corruption. But it will not be efficient because military dictatorships have not been efficient anywhere in the world. They have not solved a problem or governed a country efficiently and effectively anywhere. Even if you could say that Pakistan was contaminated, or suffering, from the same kind of social corruption that we seem to have, we can go a bit further and see in the whole continent of Latin America in the past 30 or 40 years many examples of military states nonfunctioning, whether or not they have been corrupt. Therefore, I assume that any communication of ideas that has to be done has to be done within the framework of democratically conceived concepts and ideas, not military acts.

Presumably, if there is a problem, the media's role would be to bring on the gravity of that problem and if, at a later stage, there is a solution visible, to suggest that solution and bring about an acceptance of that solution. Within that framework, I will discuss the role of the Indian news media and the Indian communications media, which comprise largely All-India Radio and, to a somewhat lesser extent, the newspapers.

I agree completely with critics who stress the inadequacies of the Indian news media. We are supposed to be very aggressive in many fields. We are noted for a refreshing "cheeky" independence and freedom of comment. But if you look at the Indian press, particularly those leading newspapers that have the resources—financial as well as intellectual resources—we have been totally lacking in initiative. The Indian press is not an initiative-oriented press. It prides itself on a certain intellectual arrogance, but that is about all. Its awareness of social issues, its interest in social issues, its willingness to campaign for something—even negatively to do a certain amount of muckraking—I'm afraid have all been exceedingly limited.

Having said that, I would say that even if we had such initiative the other important aspect of the media's role or the media's capacity that should be kept in mind is that, basically, India's conception of what it is about is lacking. What the government is thinking, what social leaders are thinking, what the intellectuals are thinking, what is being said and done in the universities, what various people and organizations who influence and make influential decisions, these are reflected in the news media. I am not referring only to what goes on in the government. Unfortunately, the Indian newspapers do give undue space to what the government is thinking, but, all the same, the news media do reflect the society and its nongovernmental leaders. If there is no element of clear thinking, if there is no planning or approach to the population issue, much of that lack, much of that inadequacy will unavoidably be reflected in the media.

Part of our trouble, then, is the inability of India to generate a flow of ideas. The top leadership—and again I do not mean by that only Gandhi or a few ministers—has not as yet been able to make up its mind as to how serious the population problem is. In fact they are

still expressing resentment against any suggestion that this is a very
serious problem or that we are on the brink of a disaster. Partly
this is a reaction, I believe, to the Western attitude or the Western
insistence that it is a very serious problem.

Left to ourselves we might have agreed that it is a serious problem, and that we ought to do something about it. But frequent rubbing
in of the idea by use of the distressing language that one hears in reference to India's population problem creates a certain amount of resistance on the part of top Indian leaders. For example, when the
Bucharest conference was held, some of the newspaper items in the
Western press for some weeks before the conference gave one the
general impression—perhaps a bit oversimplified—that the world's
population and resources crisis was a function primarily of India and
Bangladesh. The gist of many stories was that if these two countries
could do something about population and stop copulating everything
would be all right.

That kind of approach has created a certain amount of resistance
to accepting or recognizing the problem of population in India. When
the top leadership and the government does not have a clear policy or
a clear sense of purpose on this issue, invariably the press becomes
a reflection of that. All-India Radio reflects that inadequacy even
more markedly because it is more of an expression or a vehicle of
government thinking than the ordinary press is.

About five or six years ago, slogans were coined about family
planning. Some of the billboards that were put up were designed for a
period six years ago. On my last visit to India I found in Bombay, in
Delhi, in some of the north Indian cities, that they were still very
much there. New ones had been put up, but they were the same slogans. They were duplicates of the others. They were the old slogans.
It seems to me that if the media decide to do something, the least that
they can do or should do immediately is to create a new generation of
slogans. The old generation, the first set of slogans, had a certain
impact, and Kalhan's paper mentions that. The effect was probably
not as much as it might have been, but the effect was there. Now I
find that most people who see these billboards or hear these slogans
have developed a certain amount of immunity to them.

On this question of family planning, there are other means of
communication even more effective than All-India Radio or the newspapers. I regret to find that they have not been used at all. It may
seem very strange to suggest in a gathering of experts that a public
meeting in India is still the most effective means of communication.
It has been estimated that if one gathered a collection of all of the
newspapers—English, Urdu, Hindi, and so forth—and allowed that
perhaps as many as four people read each copy, we still reach no
more than about 3 percent of the country's population, if that. But a

public meeting, and especially a political meeting, where social issues are also discussed, is still the most effective way to make certain concepts and suggestions known. The fact remains that for the bulk of our population, whether in the cities or in the rural areas, an occasional public meeting at which a local leader or a notable dignitary is speaking is still the principal diversion. Some of the meetings even now are attended by not tens of thousands of people but hundreds of thousands.

In the past these meetings have been used very effectively. To take a recent example, in 1971, when Gandhi was campaigning in the elections, she was fighting for her political life. She coined the slogan garibi hatao—"eradicate poverty." There could not be an emptier slogan than that. Not all of the press was cooperating with her in putting forward that slogan. Yet in a matter of a few weeks almost the entire country was aware of that slogan, and it had made an impact on a very large section of the populace. That was because of public meetings. I concede that garibi hatao is not analogous to telling the people that they should curtail the size of their families, but if there is a will on the part of the leadership we can still get across our ideas and get them accepted by people far more rapidly than the size of the country or the size of its population or the enormity of its illiteracy would suggest.

Words coming from a leader still have tremendous impact. As a people, we are described as highly individualistic. I would go one step further and say that we have a highly critical, almost destructive, cantankerous streak in our character. We are ready to demolish or question a leader at all times. But there is another part of our psyche. If a leader can establish his or her bona fides, can establish trust, then we are all too willing to accept his or her word, much more readily than we would accept the words of a newspaper or a radio commentator. I think this is one form of communication, or a medium of communication, that has not been exploited at all. We can exploit it only if people who are held in some esteem in the country are willing to talk about population as a social issue and have the tenacity to attend to it.

Religion is another field that can and should be used but has not been used at all for the communication of certain essential ideas. I was intrigued by this reference to a gentleman in Madras by Singer, a gentleman who quoted Manu in support of large families. I am not a practicing Hindu, and my knowledge of the scriptures is very limited, but I am quite sure that if you look hard enough in the scriptures you can find many justifications and much support for having smaller families. We can find a religious basis for curtailing population growth. This can be done quite easily I am sure. The religious leader, the priest, is still widely respected as a member of the community,

whether it be in south India or north India—perhaps in north India a
bit less and in other parts of the country more. We could use his influence to communicate and bring about a change in mass thinking.
This is something we ought to consider.

Phillips Talbot: I am reminded that in several Muslim communities
much of the acceptability of the Family Planning Programme depends
on what kind of fatwas have been issued by maulvis on the subject.
Both in Egypt and in Pakistan it has been important to get permissive
fatwas so that the official program could move ahead. Sometimes efforts to enlist the support of maulvis have worked and sometimes not.

Later on, I should like to question whether the press is too
modest in using a figure like 3 percent as its coverage of the country.
My recollection of a village experience some years ago is that one
copy of an Urdu newspaper would come into the village by mail once
a week. In the evening the local shopkeeper would read the various
items to the assembled males. This would often generate discussion
for an hour or more on what so and so had said or what the news developments were. What fascinated me was that because the shopkeeper naturally read out what he wanted to read out, what came
through from the newspaper to the villagers was precisely what interested the shopkeeper. An unpopular topic or one whose significance
escaped him might not get communicated at all.

That same village, like so many others, now has an official
village radio receiver. As the men sit around these evenings, therefore, they get what the government wants them to hear, and because
the news reports and comments are delivered orally, the nonliter-
ates get it direct. Then those who prepare the radio broadcasts determine what is to go into the ears of quite a lot of the villagers.

Yet the newspapers, so far as I know, still go into the village,
and with increased literacy more people may be reading them directly.
To that extent, even though the shopkeepers and others may still be
playing an important role, the villagers will be getting greater diversity of outside ideas than before. In this country, we too wrestle
with questions of press coverage of important topics, and sometimes
the press takes its own initiatives. I suppose a particular example
this year was the judgment of the editors of the New York Times
that the international food story was one of the worst covered stories
of our time. It was also one of the most difficult to get readership
for. Therefore, they developed a grand design of about 25 food
stories. By running the full sequence they began to create public
opinion on the food issue that became broader and deeper, I believe,
than the press had been able to achieve previously. Whether in the
circumstances of the Indian press such an approach would be feasible,
I do not know. We might try to get at the possibilities of this in our
discussion.

<u>Bryant Kearl</u>: I will take a slightly different line and deal with a few different things in this commentary than did Promilla Kalhan and Krishan Bhatia. This does not represent disagreement with them. I find myself very much in sympathy with them on most of the points they have made. What I'm trying to do is make this comment supplementary rather than repetitive.

I should also point out that, although I am talking about communications and about a particular problem that I think I see in it, this does not mean that I believe that this is the most important issue before India at this time. But I do think it is important enough to take the time at this meeting to discuss it.

I am struck by a curious contradiction as I've listened at this meeting to the points at which we have talked about communications. There have been a number of things said that it seems to me relate to communications. For example, someone made the point that what the villager has to say is important and that we are really not decoding what the villager has to say to us. "Not from me to thee should flow knowledge but from thee to me also." David Mandelbaum in his paper said that local cultural and social experience has to be understood and utilized in population policy programs. A couple of people have said that population growth patterns need to be viewed as a community concern; they need to reflect the relationships of the people within a community to other people there. Cassen points out that population will not come down until the community feels some responsibility for its numbers. I presume this means some local discussion of the issue, some local consensus about it. Carstairs said that there is a need for a sense of participation and control. I think he meant at the individual level, the family level, and I presume at the community level. I have a feeling that there is participation and control over choices and resources. Finally, of course, there has been some note that there are local and regional variations in resources and also in customs and values, and all of these have a bearing on policy.

Everything I have mentioned so far suggests the importance of two kinds of communications—upward communications to central policy-makers and internal communication within the locality—to discuss, review, and consider choices and to arrive at decisions. Then I look at the kinds of policies being pursued or suggested and find that whenever we talk explicitly about communications we talk about exactly the opposite. We always talk about communications from the top down. Virtually every public investment and every public policy choice that is made in the development of communications seems to be one that deals with the centralized or nationalized. It may deal with how to localize or decentralize that system, but it still deals with a system into which you can feed messages and convey them out on a sort of transmission belt.

I have a feeling that there is a dependence on traditional media at the local level—at the village level—while the newer mass media are plugged in at the national and regional levels. There seems to be something of a void in between. That is what I would like to discuss.

As I think about the reasons for this I look at the way national media systems develop. When they developed in the 19th century, they developed with a technology where there were very few economies of scale. The story in my part of the world 100 years ago was that anyone with a shirt tail full of type could go start a newspaper; that indeed is what happened. Type was hand-set. Hand presses were prominent even up to 100 years ago. Using hand or flat bed presses meant that when you got beyond 2,000 circulation or so you were in trouble. You simply could not get the newspaper out on time.

The 20th-century news media came along in a period of rotary presses. You cannot print 1,500 of anything now. You cannot afford to. You have to get up to the multiple thousands before almost anything becomes a paying proposition. In addition, the 19th century was an economic period when there were few national business and industrial concerns that generated income for the media, so the media drew their income from whatever community they happened to be located in. Some of it came through political subsidy, some of it through circulation, some of it from advertising, but the source of funding was local. The result was that the media system started out in this country as a highly dispersed system, in the form of individual independent self-sustaining enterprises scattered all over the country.

The media systems that started in the 20th century had these economies of scale, and this is as true for radio and television in this country as it is for the press. Television stations in America started out as local; the technology that tied them into a network came later. Radio stations started out as local—staffed in the community, programed in the community, listened to within the community—and the technology to make them more than local came later (10 years later in the case of radio).

The communications systems of the West and the systems of countries like India now appear to be converging. There are all sorts of forces in our system that are pushing toward centralization, and there are all sorts of forces in the Indian system that are pushing toward decentralization, but nevertheless I think the starting point has some significance.

What are some of the consequences of a system that starts out as a centralized system? Here are some, I would think. First of all, there will be tremendous emphasis on quality of performance, and especially technical performance. When a media system starts out as a local system, no one really cares about performance. There are weekly newspapers in this state—and there have been for 140 years

—whose writing style and whose sophistication is appalling. But they have survived. No one fights for performance. When you start out as a central system you say, "What we put on the air should be of high quality," and, as you go through this centralization-decentralization process you say, "Can we really set up a broadcasting studio in a particular area and staff it locally and still maintain our standards of quality?" Probably not. You also start out in a national system with some criteria in selection of materials as to the generality of the news. There is an understandable bias in favor of national issues of general interest. You start out with the premise that everything has to appeal to almost everyone.

In the case of my weekly paper here there are admittedly items that appeal to only a handful of people. This is part of the psychology of the person who starts with a decentralized system. Another thing— perhaps more important—is that the staffing of a system that starts out national and centralized will tend to be predominantly urban and predominantly middle class or upper middle class from the commercial and population centers. It will be a good deal harder for this kind of person—no matter how hard he tries—to hear the voice of the village than it will be for the other person who started out on a local medium and may have moved up (as did one person who started with a local newspaper in Mississippi and moved up to the editorship of the New York Times). I presume it was harder for him on the New York Times to forget what it was like on the main street of his village than for someone who had come through the other route to hear the voice of the village.

I don't by any means want to say that I am describing a typology of Indian communications, of which I do not know enough, but I do want to suggest that these are some of the consequences. I suggested the possibility that India may be moving to a point where there are national and regional media and traditional and local media and not much in between. This would not be a problem if these conditions were met. First, if there were few or no variations in local needs. Second, if there were no community or group action necessary. If community consensus or support were not important, if there were no need for continuing information on changing local conditions, if you did not want to hear the voice of the village, or if you were confident that there were other ways for the voice of the village to be heard, then there would be no problem.

But John Cool says that as population doubles many market towns are likely willy nilly to become urban places. I presume that what he means is that there is going to be a steady and quite remarkable growth of market towns and bazaars of 20,000 to 50,000 population. They are going to have local problems that are not susceptible to solution from Delhi but require responses from state and local gov-

ernments. They are going to have other problems that require that
local voices be heard in state capitals and in Delhi, and I suspect
that traditional communications media are not going to be adequate.
One thing that might be thought about is whether there are constructive
steps to improve the communications at this level as the size of the
population increases. A centralized national system serves some
functions, but it does not serve them all.

John Cool also points out that these market towns and bazaars
will become urban places without piped water, without closed sewers,
without zoning, without planning, without effective government. He
seems to be saying that these communities might be able to reduce
appreciably their problems if somebody would now think about what
could be done to develop the communications opportunities and system
there. I am reminded of a point that Milton Singer made about William James's definition of democracy. When people holler, the government does something. When people holler again, the government
does something else. The national system, it seems to me, operates
more on the philosophy that when the government hollers, people do
something, when the government hollers, again people do something
else. What is the mechanism by which the holler that people make
can be articulated, can be heard? This is the question I would like
to raise.

Milton Singer: Obviously the hollering goes from the bottom up and
also from the top down. I suppose that should be the first axiom of
any communications analysis. Perhaps a good deal more attention
has to be given to these different kinds and levels of communication.
What are the existing ways in which a point of mutual translation occurs? There is a disposition to assume that communications from
the center to the local units somehow must all be translated into a
uniform language or uniform slogans before they can be understood
and also for the reverse communication. The few observations that
exist on this seem to question that. There are ways in which a process of communication occurs that does not conform to that kind of
requirement.

I give an example from a village 40 miles from Madras that I
saw a little of in 1954. There was a very active village development
committee that had gotten a community center there. It had also
constructed a small library. They were very much interested in getting a new school built. They asked me to intervene with the local
district collector at that time to see what I could do to persuade him
and also to help get some new roads for the village. This was a rather active group. To use John Cool's typology, they were following
the optimistic scenario.

It turned out that the head of the village development committee was a local Brahman and quite traditional in all other respects. The other members of the village development committee were quite conservative. The president of this village development committee expressed unusual motivations and a philosophy of village development. He said that "Nehru had a guru, Gandhiji, who tells us to improve life in the villages, and Nehru is my guru and I am his disciple. We have decided to do what he has requested us to do." The use of this very traditional language about a chain of gurus and disciples was a local translation of national mandates by a local village development committee. At that very time we happened to hear then Prime Minister Nehru give a speech at Awadi near Madras; he did not hesitate to pull rank as a guru or as the follower of Gandhi. He told his audience what the government was planning and what they should do to cooperate, including the instruction to do more exercise and keep healthy, as he was doing.

This is one example, which could be multiplied many times, where a modernistic kind of five-year program formulated at the center gets translated by some villagers into a traditional cultural language and idiom. W. H. Morris-Jones, the British political scientist, has an interesting article dealing with this problem of the different kinds of cultural idioms that are involved in national-local communication.

John Mellor: I am stimulated to a very complicated question to the people who are on the communications side and who have some special knowledge in that area. I'd like to look at the question in the context of the economic development path along which India is proceeding. India is a country where a high proportion of the population is fairly concentrated, not in the sense of being in a few large urban centers but in the sense that the population density of what we would normally refer to as the rural areas is very high for a portion of the country that includes a high proportion of the people. I'm excluding those areas where the density of the population is much lower.

One also has a picture of a very rapid growth of both nonagricultural activities and what we tend to think of as the industrial sector, but again not concentrated in a very large metropolitan center or series of centers. For the rest of this century, then, one might expect—and here I draw very heavily on some of John Lewis' early work on market towns growing to rather substantial proportions—the growth of vast numbers of cities with concentrated populations to say 50,000 to 300,000 people, with the distance between those centers perhaps not being very large. Particularly if we are looking ahead to a population of say one billion people, that in a sense is the vision.

The question I raise, if one has that kind of a vision of population distribution and concentration, is this: Is it reasonable to accompany that vision with some vision of the kind of society that would be entailed in the process of reaching it? To come directly to communications, how would people communicate in that society? What would be the communications mechanisms?

I think the ideal vision from my point of view would be much different for India than it is for much of the United States, because of the population factor. To take the U.S. case, I have a definite impression of the communications network in this country as one in which we occasionally have some national policies pressing for a localization of communications. I take it that the cable TV people, for example, are being forced to mount local programs on their cables. This suggests some desire in this country to have local participation in communications and allow people in local areas to communicate one to another. It also suggests some support for this in the national government. I take it too that communications between local areas through the mass media have declined over the last few decades.

I would think that if one were taking the visionary view of India, one would raise questions of this type. What kind of communications do you want? To what extent do you want people in a localized area to be able to communicate to one another through the mass media? What kinds of implications does that have for the government's efforts to deal with radio or television or the newspapers? I have a lot of questions along these lines, and these may be way off the topic that we are supposed to be taking up. On the other hand, I think these do have relevance to the question of population growth as a positive matter, rather than to the negative aspects. It is especially relevant to the kind of concentrated population areas that may grow up. I see a relationship between the way a society is organized in population groupings and the nature of the communications processes and ideals that one may have.

Talbot: In the United States we have seen the break-up of the once dominant radio networks and a reemphasis on local radio. This is a phenomenon that some believe might possibly be followed in television in the coming years. This localization of our media, however far it may go, is a definite factor in our social communications and might, I think, be borne in mind as we consider possibilities in India. I would assume that on the holler-up side someone would raise the question of political communication.

John Cool: I have two observations to make, one referring to something that Krishan Bhatia had focused on, namely the degree to which even today in most of India we are dealing with a society in the oral tradition. Mukerjee made mention of the village meeting as a place where information is introduced, consensus is reached, and people are informed. I would like to highlight that as a reality that is borne out by the limited field studies that I have done.

I was once in a village in the Terai that was seven miles away from an outstanding agricultural experiment station that had been there 15 years. In looking at crop practices, cultivation, and so forth and how they had been affected by new technology, we had to conclude that the extension program had simply not spread even seven miles. In the process of doing that work we learned something about how new information got into that village. We found that some of the people who walked between villages—for example, the postmen—were important links to the outside world, not because of the printed matter that they carried and occasionally dropped off in the village—this was very limited—but because of the fact that they sat down and had tea and talked. When the road got into that village the bus driver began to take on the same functions. The ticket collector, who would get off the bus, and the <u>tasuir wallah,</u> who moved from village to village showing pictures and telling stories to the children, these were other communications links.

We know very little about these channels, and therefore we tend to disregard or underestimate or discount them. We certainly don't enrich the flow of information they have to disseminate. I would argue that this could be a fruitful field if we are to use communications as an effective policy instrument to handle the increased complexity of an India that is going to double in size. Recognizing that probably even with our best efforts literacy has been pushed up to only 30 percent—it is still less than 20 percent for women—if we hope to reach the rural illiterate people we ought to work to understand more about the media that they use.

In this respect I also want to mention that one of the "Second India" studies that has been completed is focused upon communications. In this, I was quite interested to see, the authors have devoted great attention to the postal system. The importance of the post office is something we don't think much about. Perhaps we should. They argue that there was an essentially antimodern bias in the very policy-makers who, in other contexts, were advocating modernization. When allocations are made to telephones and TV, these are regarded as elite instruments and at least in principal are frowned upon by political leaders as communications links with the masses. Telephones, telexes, anything that really facilitates the speeding up of communications internally, is somehow now recognized as a critical element of modernizing the means of reaching a whole range of people and speeding up the transfer of information. Communications is not, as yet, understood to be a critical dimension of the process of governance, development, and modernization.

Talbot: Both ends of the spectrum are important, I believe. In the Family Planning Programme, efforts have been made in villages to use local religious leaders and wandering minstrels to convey the message. At the other end of the spectrum is the preparation of television programing for the new satellite that is to be put into orbit. Between them—and with the traditional channels of press, radio, and personal networks—the scope of social communications could well be expanded, I should think. These might help bridge the great gap that has existed even between top leaders and the people. I remember that in some villages neighboring Mahatma Gandhi's ashram in Sevagram the people were sufficiently awed by the presence of the ashram in their neighborhood that they were revering it rather than getting the practical lessons out of what Gandhi was trying to do in terms of increasing education. It may well be that this kind of phenomenon remains, but the multiple channels of communicating the message may get through better.

Robert Cassen: When I was an Agency for International Development (AID) economist one of the things that used to turn up on my desk every now and then was the communications satellite and the program of TV for the villages, which was said to be likely to provide all manner of beneifts for family planning, agriculture, and so on. I used to write memoranda expressing some polite reservations to the effect that this was from the top down. I argued that the economics of it were rather dubious, that communications would be in the language of the establishment, that it would provide global, not local information, but primarily that what it would do would be to maintain employment of TV repair men, if any could be found. Then I would send my memorandum on and wait for the proposal to come round again, which it regularly did. I now discover that one of my colleagues has gone off to India to investigate the uses of this potential instrument of communications, and she informed me that things have been moving. They now have TV sets allegedly "ruggedized" to meet tropical conditions. I would like to know if anyone in this room can tell me what is happening to this program and what the villager thinks about it.

B. R. Deolalikar: Two things. One, Bhatia referred to newspaper circulation and its penetration to the village. At one stage, about four or five years back, we explored certain aspects of the communications media and in fact all organized communications media taken together—newspapers in all languages, radio, movies, and so forth. We found that about 13 to 14 percent of the population was exposed to all of these media put together. Even if you take all the major cities, and the exposure to all these media together, in the major cities, it doesn't come to more than 40 or 45 percent. So there remains a very

big question as to what expectations for the media can be considered
realistic.

Second, I have done some work on TV in one city. It is going
on, but at the present moment most of the work is organized under
the hardware systems. On the software side, there are some groups
working, so that when this satellite goes into orbit and gets working
the hope is that people in the backward regions in the country will be
exposed to satellite television. Some work is going on, partly through
All-India Radio, partly, in Ahmedabad, through the space research
program. On the hardware side, all sorts of developments have taken
place. The software people always think that they can deliver pack-
ages that never seem to come about.

In this context, however, I must say that the government of India has recently taken a very bold step. The whole communications
and advertising program in family planning is now being handed over
to a consortium of advertising agencies. The decision was made just
a few months back, and I guess 15 or 20 of the agencies will be involved in the circulation of all of the advertising programs.

Talbot: We will get some new slogans now.

Deolalikar: I hope so. At least this is one positive step. We now at
least have the participation of the creative advertisers.

Morris Carstairs: We've been asked to remind ourselves that the
theme of this meeting is, What will be the effect of the rising population on successive topics. Just now we are discussing the media.
We are really addressing ourselves, I suspect, to the question of
communications with those who really matter, that is to say with the
poor, among whom illiteracy is the highest and among whom contact
with the media is relatively low. I am reminded of a passage in David
Mandelbaum's paper that touched on the inappropriateness of certain
confrontations in the village, particularly in the Family Planning Programme. A lady doctor and her assistants were hardly able to con-
ceal their disdain for the villagers among whom they were compelled
to tarry for a while, doing this rather tiresome chore, and there was
a gulf of distance between them and the people to whom they were sup-
posedly purveying information and help.

I suppose one could say that this example represents the barrier
to successful communication; but it reminded me of the experience
that many of us have had, when living in a village, of the extraordinary
self-defensive outlook that the villager holds toward the outside world
in general when any well-dressed city man or woman comes there.
They are very polite—really exemplary in politeness and hospitality—
but what a splendid defense they have against believing anything that

person says! It's always put to the test of discussion in village
groups gathered around the sitting place or the panchayat area, after-
ward being mulled over again and again before they themselves give
it the stamp of their acceptance or, more often, their rejection.

I was just thinking, what is the avenue of communications here?
One can more easily see the ones that are <u>not</u> likely to penetrate their
guard. Certainly when I was living in a Rajasthan village, the only
person from the outside world to whom the villagers really listened
was a holy man, a <u>maharaj</u>, a guest of the village. He was there not
only to entertain but also really to be listened to. I also knew a dear
old itinerant Christian from not very far away who adopted the style
of a Hindu maharaj, and when he came to the village they entertained
him and he talked in verses, in couplets resembling Sanskrit <u>sloks</u>.
He had adapted the New Testament, or rather "gems from the New
Testament," to this form. The reaction of the villagers was, "There's
a good man, there's a worthy man!" He had no pretensions about
converting but was intent only on communicating a <u>satsang</u>, or spiritual teaching, and they were quite willing to accept anything good that
he had to impart. This was partly because he too was a villager. He
came from a village not very far away. His dress, his idiom, and
his accent were familiar to them.

If we are going to have effective communication on family planning let me say first of all that when the number of children increases
then the motivation will also increase. Even as long ago as 1950 I
remember a villager coming to me and saying: "Dr. Sahib, I've got
seven children already—what can I do to stop having children?" When
I finished explaining what he could do, he said, "Oh, I will never get
around to that"; and he was quite disappointed. That was 25 years
ago in an illiterate and very poor community. I am sure that as the
numbers increase the number of villagers with motivation will also
increase, and, while I still believe that the effective adoption of techniques won't come until they have hope and some confidence in the future, still the communication has to be made about how it is to be
done.

I don't exactly see ourselves enlisting holy men in this task,
but I do think we will have to enlist people of the village to share the
task of communication. I think this is entering increasingly into the
planning of the health services: The employment not only of doctors
and of paraprofessionals but also of assistant nurse-midwives is the
great slogan in health planning now. The assistant nurse-midwife is
a simple barely literate person who has a few skills; and as we know
in the Chinese pattern the "barefoot doctor" who is a member of the
village community is another such person. Among his or her few
skills are included contraceptive advice, and the means to put it into
practice.

Talbot: The differential between China and India in terms of success, of course, has not been that great.

John Lewis: I want to draw a very sharp and deep line between television and radio. At least back in the middle of the 1960s—and I haven't gotten over it yet—I developed a very great allergy toward the idea of television for communicating with villages, and later that got focused on the satellite. It has, I think, all sorts of problems. For one it does suggest a highly centralized form of communication, even if you are able to communicate in all the languages. It all emanates from one point. From an engineering point of view, even if the sets have been "ruggedized," it's a very small instrument. It's a very small screen, and the messages to be put through it are all on taped film. India already has a lot of experience running around with film projectors with very big pictures that really are much better for community communications.

On the other hand, it seems to me that radio—and we thought, particularly, transistor radios—have enormous potential. It may even go to something that Morris Carstairs suggested. There is a suspiciousness of the outsider coming in. A very little gadget that belongs to the villager himself, which he can turn off at will, is in some respects much less threatening and interesting.

Now there's a problem here in terms of equality because these things cost something. But they can cost relatively little. Unfortunately, the Indian transistor industry (I don't know about it recently) had developed in the 1960s just for the upper-class urban market and was producing rather fancy transistors in very small volume, therefore at high cost. If one used Japanese or Singapore norms—and I think Indian production now is quite capable of adapting to those—at that time we figured a transistor probably could be made and marketed for only 35 rupees, which is not an enormous amount. Of course it would be somewhat more now.

The whole idea of radio, however, would be to decentralize the source. It would be quite possible to establish a set of districtwide radio stations that would program in local languages. The capital costs on this would be quite small. Not only could the receivers all be made in India but, even 10 years ago virtually all of the sending equipment could also be made in India, as I say at relatively low cost.

There was a lot of discussion about this in the middle 1960s. The U.S. government was prepared to make a small loan, and then a very unfortunate thing happened. Some of us were on home leave. Somebody got the very bright idea that it would be nice to buckle together with this a more imaginative deployment of American Peace Corpsmen, so that they could go in and help with the proposed district radio programing. Some of us recognized this was a very sensitive

business—intruding upon a nation's communications network—and the
government of India reacted with predictable sensitivity. Perhaps
other things would have been sufficient also, but this was enough to
throw an ample amount of water on the whole proposition to cause it
to sink from sight.

It still seems to me that, quite without regard to outside help
(because it could be done almost completely indigenously), it still
represents a fairly sensible kind of communications strategy. I
have been hoping for almost 10 years now to hear some word of its
starting up again, but I haven't heard any.

David G. Mandelbaum: To follow up on that, I have noted that the
most popular radio talk programs among villagers are the agricultural
programs. They are listened to, and they are helpful, particularly
for the wealthier and better-educated farmers. We also have an example of an informal but very effective communications system in relation to the Family Planning Programme. There was a very rapid
spread of rumor about the deleterious effects of the IUD. In the
course of repeated tellings, the rumors became wonderfully fantastic.
They started with women who did have trouble with an IUD insertion.
When women married in other villages came to visit their natal villages, the news was carried from village to village to village. That
is one kind of communication network that has been very effective.

Another new development in communications that I mentioned in
my paper is quite significant. It has to do with the increase in population and with the complexity of running a modern agricultural enterprise. That is the increased patronage of the cafes. The cafe has
augmented the previous sources of news and gossip spread through
the hookah groups, which were largely groups of kin or allies. Now
a man can find a cafe in which he can meet all kinds of people and can
exchange information, especially about crops and land.

The importance of fairs and pilgrimages has been mentioned.
These now offer new means of communications. I attended a local
fair in the Nilgiris a few years ago where a large pavilion had been
put up by the Family Planning Programme. Many villagers were going around looking at depictions of a fetus in position and similar educational exhibits. At the exit the district health officer had stationed
himself to answer questions. I'm not sure what the effect of all this
was, but a lot of villagers did go through that pavilion.

Talbot: I suppose it's still true, isn't it, that the poor man's or the
poor woman's cafe is the village well?

Mandelbaum: Yes.

A. M. Shah: I would like to make two small points. One concerns
which part of the message conveyed by the mass media is accepted
by the people or rejected by them and with how much conviction. Second, although it is true that the agricultural programs are listened to
by the villagers, the most popular programs on the radio are the mu-
sic programs.

What I really want to address myself to is the important problem of communication involved in the personal interaction between
people. There has been a considerable increase in the movement of
people in recent years by railway, bus, rubber-tired bullock cart,
and bicycle. More people are now moving from one village to another
village and from village to town and back. There is an enormous increase in the movement of people around the country. More people
go on pilgrimages, and there are more pilgrimages of various sorts.
Now we find that people combine tourism with pilgrimage. They visit
dams and factories, radio and TV stations, the Parliament in Delhi,
and the assemblies in state capitals. They tour around the cities.

There is also communication by word of mouth. My own view
of the villager is that he is a very gossipy and nosy fellow. There is
so much conversation going on throughout the life of the villager from
morning to midnight. People sit for hours and go on discussing all
sorts of things. There are not only hookah groups; there are other
focal points as well. When a landlord is supervising the work of untouchables or laboring groups, he keeps talking to the people he is
supervising. Temples are another center. Women gossip at the well
and the tank. Great communication goes on at weddings. Weddings
are huge affairs. They collect people from a very large area, especially in north India, where you do not have cross-cousin and uncle-
niece marriages. There is hypergamy all over north India. Hypergamy means a man's sister and daughter are married in one set of
villages and his mother and wife come from another. Frequently
one's sister and daughter are married into towns and cities. This
means there are extended kinship networks that serve as communications foci. So much information is passed by word of mouth. A maternal uncle comes from the town to the village, and he brings lots
of information. Much talk goes on at weddings, including that of family planning. The same is true of other rites of passage and, of
course, of mortuary rituals. The most effective communication is
between kinsmen and among friends. The people with whom you have
the most intimate ties are also the most effective communicators.

Rakesh Mohan: It struck me that no one has mentioned the Bombay
films. Most of us usually like to look down on them as something vulgar, something of no use, except that they provide an amazing amount
of entertainment for a large number of people. It is true that a lot

of rural folk do not see these films, but it is also true that a lot of
them do. This is one aspect of communications that is often neglected.
Instead of merely making documentaries, which are heavy going for
most of us—and the villager has enough heavy going as it is—if he then
has to listen to serious dry programs preaching at him, this switches
him off. Making glossy, interesting, vulgar, colorful Bombay-type
films, fiction rather than documentary, would be quite a useful thing
to do.

But the main point that I want to make is the part of communications I know something about, which is agricultural extension. You
might take people from the village and train them, and then send
them back. One of the most interesting things to note is this constant
coming and going from village to town and back. Construction people,
construction workers, are people who move around the most because
they move from site to site. These people could be particularly
good targets for messages. Messages that are particularly good for
people get around anyway.

Robert White: I'd like to return the discussion for a minute to the subject it started out on, namely the more formal kinds of communications. It struck me that Bhatia was being a bit too modest in accepting the usual criticism of the Indian press. At least in a comparative
sense, if you look anywhere around in that part of the world, by and
large what I have read of Indian newspapers stand out in superb comparison; in fact, it compares favorably with newspapers almost anywhere. That's not to say that they cannot stand a lot of improvement.

The usual criticism understates the intrinsic importance of the
kind of press there is in India. There's a difference too that ought to
be noted between readership, percentages of people who read newspapers or hear the radio or see television, and what they get out of
that. I was thinking as Krishan Bhatia was talking about percentages,
of a survey that our polling department ran of young adults, people
under 20, relatively new voters. There were two questions asked.
The first question was, "Do you generally approve of the policies of
the Mayor of Minneapolis?" The answers were something like 60
percent "no," with the rest either "yes" or "no opinion." The second
question was, "Who, by the way, is the Mayor of Minneapolis?" To
my mind there was an astounding response—something like only 10
percent could identify him by name. The point is that there is a distinction between who the readership is and what they are getting out
of it.

A final comment on the difference between regional and national
communications. I was struck by the comment on the different kinds
of communications that take place in India and, of course, in different
places too. The dilemma in this country is that it is a country of re-

gional newspapers. The perpetual problem is, how does a newspaper
—or radio or a television station—do a competent job of informing its
audience about wider things, given its limitations of space, time,
and so on? There are lots of competing forces that work in this,
and I suspect we're talking about similar kinds of problems in India.
John Lewis' talk about use of radio at the village level is fine. This
should be encouraged. But it's not to discount the importance of doing that to suggest that you have problems of quality control there and
here.

Bryant Kearl: I would like to go back to the question that John Mellor
raised. We keep returning to the question, How do you get family
planning information out? If I understand it correctly, that is not the
theme of the meeting. The theme of the meeting is, What are the
changes that are likely to occur in India because of population changes
in the years to come, and what impact will they have on the media?
      One change that certainly seems likely to occur is that by the
end of this century, there will be about 20 new cities of multimillion
dimensions and probably 150 concentrated population areas of 100,000
population or more. Whether or not you quarrel with these figures,
these are communities for which there is no communications pattern
now because there isn't any community. As they develop I cannot
believe that All-India Radio, no matter how much it decentralizes,
can perform the function I am about to describe. On the other hand,
I can't believe that the traveling postman or markets or pilgrimages
or weddings or whatever else one finds traditionally can perform the
function either.
      That function is letting that community look at its resources and
look at what it faces and, within its own boundaries, within its own
jurisdiction, make the decisions that affect its own future. I'm saying that some things will have to develop in the communications pattern that are different, not copied from anywhere else necessarily,
and more imaginative than we've seen before. I like very much the
one that John Lewis has mentioned, of local transmitters locally controlled, with not even anyone from Delhi involved in the program,
much less anyone from the American Peace Corps. The pattern, if
it is to be effective, has to involve people in that community, putting
on that station whatever things the pressures in that community force
the station to carry. It's this kind of problem that I raise as an unan-
swered and maybe unanswerable question, but it's the one I think is
most important.

Krishan Bhatia: I am trying to think of what a city like Karnal—on the
road from Delhi to Amritsar—could develop by way of communications
at that point when it has a population of 100,000 or 200,000 rather

than 20,000 or 30,000. I visualize it would have a multilanguage press and a radio station operating out of a neighboring city. This would be the case unless there is a drastic change in government policy, which I don't foresee. Communication from the people to the government—the reverse of the top to the bottom—would have to be through the conventional newspapers under these conditions. I can only see for the next 10 years or so what changes will take place. Beyond that I cannot go.

Talbot: There is an honest futurist.

Kearl: I think you are quite right. There will have to be multilanguage newspapers. If you believe this to be a good thing, then you have to ask yourself, Are there policies that should be thought of now, and whether these are policies of newsprint development, postal services, or whatever. Policies adopted now could promote what might be a good development; or is this the sort of situation where you simply wait until economic forces bring what may? Some things can be hastened and some things can be delayed by policy choices. The speed with which local newspapers can develop in a community like that can be affected by policy choices.

Bhatia: I do not know what recent policy decisions consist of. I have not recently watched the government of India as closely or as carefully as I have watched the Ford administration in Washington. But I don't think there is any sort of realization in Delhi that a few years from now such and such a development might take place and we should now go about meeting it. Should we increase the production of newsprint? Should we denationalize some of the broadcast media? I don't think any serious thought has so far been given to such questions. Like most governments anywhere, the Indian government will be drawn into some kind of a policy decision by economic forces and compulsions.

Asok Mitra: A few years ago I was the office boy in the Ministry of Information and Broadcasting but was still working for the census. There are several media within the Ministry of Information and Broadcasting. One is TV; a second is All-India Radio. The third is advertising and publicity, which distributes posters, pamphlets, and so on. Then there is the publishing bureau, which disseminates news. The next is the Registrar of Newspapers, which estimates the demand of newsprint and determines the areas they cater to. The next is the Films Division, which puts out documentaries, screens commercial films, and also screens films for rural audiences. The other is the song and drama division, which is mainly concerned with traditional media.

It seems to me it would be a very interesting exercise to attempt projections for 1980. One would have to take into account the probable rates of growth of literacy, probable rates of growth of urbanization, probable rates of growth of numbers of women getting educated and getting jobs outside the home, and the probable rates of growth of organized labor and industrial establishments for whom better forms of communication could be organized, and also the necessity to concentrate on communication among tribes and backward peoples, particularly for the establishment of new radio stations. I think this is an area where some people in this room might be interested in working out the possibilities of this kind of projection. The two I have in mind especially are Anrudh Jain and Deolalikar. If they would take this up, I suppose the Asia Society might be sponsoring a very important area of research and a useful activity.

Wendy Dobson: I want to put three people on the spot. Professor Mandelbaum and Professor Shah and Rakesh Mohan in their interventions mentioned various media, although they were talking about family planning. I was curious—if we come back to this question of the consequences of population growth for social and economic change— what would happen in the instances that you have referred to from your own experience? What would happen to these particular kinds of media when population doubles? Do they just disappear? Do they become more effective as mass media or forms of mass communication? Or do they just stay the same?

Shah: They become more effective.

Mohan: I don't think it will have much effect.

Mandelbaum: More effective, and also, as Carstairs mentioned, one may get the emergence of millennial prophets.

Dobson: I was just curious, because what each of you are saying is that there is a relationship between certain modes of communication and population increase.

Talbot: Which is not at all what Bryant Kearl said.

Dobson: Yes.

Galanter: Kearl's comments on localization do, however, relate back to the tensions between decentralization and equity that were mentioned this morning. When you propose local control, it is another way of saying you are going to give the dominant groups in these local communities more power.

8

PLANNING AND THE PROVISION OF SERVICES IN CALCUTTA: A TEST CASE OF SOCIETAL RESPONSES TO POPULATION CHANGE
Asok Mitra

There is no wiser saying in the writings of John
Stuart Mill, the classic economist of the last generation, than his reminder that, if we would improve
the condition of the people, the improvement must
be on a scale that they can observe and realize, not
frittered away piecemeal as are so many municipal
improvements. In these cases the changes pass un-
noticed and are neglected. In the former case they
are appreciated and the people rise to the occasion.

Patrick Geddes
A Report on Town Planning
in Balarampur, 1917

In some ways, Calcutta is a very special and unique city: a primate city situated at the edge of an impoverished hinterland, sucking
in whatever the latter produces, much of which goes for export at
severely competitive prices. In other ways it stands as the archetype
of a primate city in the underdeveloped world. All primate cities in
the underdeveloped world are, at bottom, large reservoirs for rural
poor turned urban by migration, whose level of consumption and nutrition in the city is little higher than that of the poor in rural areas and
whose main field of employment is still in the unskilled poverty-induced tertiary sector. Because of the extreme degrees of poverty
and degradation so visible in Calcutta, it has become the uneasy con-
science of all primate cities in the underdeveloped world; one faltering
step, and they are there tomorrow where Calcutta is today. Despite
its vitality and tremendous activity, its Baudelairean beauty as a flower
of evil, its fierce assertion of life in the general odor of decay, its
peculiarly satisfying personality and cultural ambience, which grows

on the visitor as he stays on, Calcutta still serves as a somber warning for those undergoing processes of urbanization throughout the underdeveloped world.

By way of background for a more complete understanding of the extent to which this is so, it is important to mention briefly two outstanding facts, liable to be ignored even by those who know, that have gone into Calcutta's uniqueness. The first of these is that, until the beginning of World War II Calcutta was perhaps one of the most satisfying cities in the East, not excluding Singapore, Hong Kong, and Bombay. This writer would attribute the reason for it to the fact that Calcutta's industrial growth and diversification kept pace with its population growth, inasmuch as levels of unemployment in Calcutta prior to 1940 were low, being contained well within 7 percent of its adult male population. At this time too, Calcutta's efficient port and transport facilities matched the city's industrial activity, which in turn were well sustained by an abundance of industrial water and power. The city's stock of skilled human resources and entrepreneurship was the richest of its kind, not only among all cities in India but also among those in the entire East.

World War II converted Calcutta into a major forward military base and quickened its industrial enterprise, thereby attracting an unprecedentedly large volume of unskilled and semiskilled labor to man feverish and mushrooming industrial enterprises addressed to war supplies. Housing, water supply, sanitation, sewerage, and general municipal infrastructure, including metropolitan transportation and communication services, were strained beyond limits, and these very palpably failed to keep up with a burgeoning rate of population growth, caused by new rural-urban migration in the years 1941-43.

It was in the early 1940s, then, that civic amenities in Calcutta began to fall apart. The gap between population and industrial growth accelerated with the influx of refugees from East Pakistan after the Partition in August 1947. By 1951, when the census was taken, it became clear that about 1.5 million refugees from East Pakistan had settled in the Calcutta industrial region (roughly 150 square miles) in the space of four years, with Calcutta and Howrah cities alone accounting for over 900,000 of these international immigrants. This new population influx from East Pakistan, which continued into the decades of the 1960s and 1970s, culminated in the Bangladesh avalanche of 1971, and this in turn caught Calcutta's industrial pace totally unawares, widening the gap between the city's population and industrial growth rates and consolidating a new type of urban poor.

The new urban poor in Calcutta, the ranks of which are still being steadily reinforced by migrants pouring into the city from other states of India, have little alternative but to fill the cadres of the poverty-induced tertiary sector, by claiming services that are created by nothing other than the physical growth of population itself. Ever since 1950 industrial growth in the Calcutta metropolitan region has failed to keep up with population increases. In fact, except for a short spell in 1961-66, the gap between population growth and industrial growth has steadily and rapidly widened. Owing to the lack of a desirable rate of industrial growth, and the languishing of the port of Calcutta, the city's infrastructure has grievously and continuously suffered for lack of sustenance. The problem of Calcutta, then, is essentially the problem of population and industrial growth rates parting ways suddenly and sharply, in all too brief a space of time.

A second neglected fact about Calcutta, which adds fuel to the flames of the population problem, has to do with a series of wage tribunal awards made between 1947 and 1952. These awards destroyed whatever degree of solidarity between blue-collar and white-collar workers had previously obtained in the city. For the first time, the blue-collar workers, who traditionally hailed from a lower cultural and educational level, began to earn more than the white-collar worker, normally recruited from a higher cultural and educational level. This led to rather sad consequences in attitudes toward productivity and demands for municipal amenities and social benefits. The blue-collar worker, being in the main immigrant, had less stake in the city and, being more intent on sending savings home, was less intent on improving his surroundings. Bereft of the support of his blue-collar colleague, the low-income white-collar worker, who was non-migrant and more conscious of civic needs, was unable to prevail in his appeals for municipal improvements. As time passed, the white-collar worker also became less interested in parting with his earnings by way of rates that would benefit the blue-collar worker more than himself.

It has often been argued that the edge over other cities that Calcutta has lost in the last 25 years can be easily recovered once Calcuttans have made up their minds to do so. This sad fact is that it will prove very difficult for Calcutta to retrieve its primacy on the industrial map of India. A large number of industries moved away from Calcutta to other cities of India between 1958 and 1973. Most important among those to move away to new pastures were the entrepreneurial and head offices of important corporate and financial bodies. Equalization of prices of most important raw and processed materials, like coal and steel, during the past decade or two has robbed Calcutta of the locational advantage it had enjoyed up to the middle of this century. Since investment and entrepreneurial skill have now been dispersed all over India, it is simply wishful thinking to hope that they could be readily restored to Calcutta again. Then, too, the claims of other regions of India for balanced industrial growth will be difficult to ignore from now on, in spite of the obvious natural resource endow-

ments of West Bengal. All things considered, it will be unrealistic
to imagine that West Bengal and Calcutta will be able either to replace all of their obsolescent plants, import masses of new technology, and recover the kind of industrial primacy that Calcutta enjoyed
in the past or to manage the level of industrial investment that could
give Calcutta this kind of primacy in the foreseeable future.

Nevertheless, if the present period represents a deep economic
trough for Calcutta, it is also an appropriate moment to ask a number
of serious questions about it, like whether, why, how, and with what
kind of overview investment might logically be made there. What
have been the responses of Calcuttans and others to the nightmarish
events that have affected Calcutta in the last three decades? Assuming that this is not a human situation where one simply throws up one's
hands in despair, what can we learn from responses that have already
been made to some of the most massive problems in modern urban
life? In short, if we are going to deal with population variables of
the most severe kind, in one of the world's most seriously affected
urban areas, where do we go from here?

INVESTMENTS IN CALCUTTA

At the recent informal discussion, Shri S. K. Roy, director of
Planning for the Calcutta Metropolitan Development Authority (CMDA),
observed that the questions we are entitled to ask about Calcutta today
we would have been scarcely competent to ask had our level of expenditure been substantially lower than Rs. 110 crores ($137.5 mil-
lion) in the space of the last three years. It is this level of investment, at an average of Rs. 35 crores ($43.75 million) per year, that
lends validity to questions about Calcutta that are now legitimately
salient.

However, before we deal with these questions, it should be
pointed out that an investment of Rs. 110 crores in three years, in a
city that caters to about 8 million people, is not something to write
home about, particularly when it has been made after more than three
decades of gross neglect. Since 1940 Calcutta city has hardly seen
any maintenance investment, not to speak of renewal, and still less
of improvement or augmentation. It received no attention, even when
it functioned for more than five years as Allied headquarters for South
Asia during World War II, and no succor against the ravages of famine,
internecine strife, and sudden and grievous dissection of ethnic and
linguistic territory during the 1940s, the wounds of which have never
quite healed. With the partition of India in 1947, Calcutta suffered
from a complete loss of one of the richest hinterlands on earth, and
from the recurring traumatic experiences of massive migration, cli-

maxing in an unprecedented avalanche of 6.7 million migrants in the space of four months in 1971 (another 3 million immigrants came to other parts of India from Bangladesh in 1971). Calcutta then became a major theater of the Bangladesh war in late 1971, which in turn disrupted all semblances of normal existence, to be followed by a crippling void, characterized by human and physical exhaustion. In this atmosphere, the fairest appraisal of what has happened to Calcutta might well be the popular Bengali notion that throughout more than three and a half decades Calcutta was chewed dry, until people came to realize that it must be moistened a little, if only to get on with the chewing again. A sum of 110 or 120 crores of rupees—a total of Rs. 127.38 crores in the Fourth Five Year Plan (1969-74), inclusive of administration overheads, debt service charges, and stock of scarce materials—is very small compared to what has been continuously invested on Delhi since 1940 or even on Bombay since 1947. Indeed, it is perfectly valid to argue that perhaps nothing less than about a thousand crores ($1.25 billion) in the space of 10 years will be enough to render the Calcutta metropolitan region reasonably viable again.

Perhaps the best way to begin to analyze the investment needs of Calcutta, however, is by taking a quick look at some of the positive fruits of investments that have been made there during the past three years. Ever since planning began in India, private investment has not preceded, but has rather followed, closely, with a slight time lag, in the wake of public investment. This is the case in every sector of India's life one can think of, but it is particularly striking in industry, power, construction, trade, and communications. Private investment has also followed public investment territorially. In the Calcutta and Asansol-Durgapur regions, for example, private industrial investment responded handsomely to state investment between 1954 and 1962. In Asansol-Durgapur, private investment did not measure up with public investment, whereas it did measure up in Calcutta, primarily because government investment in Calcutta went mainly for infrastructural components like augmentation of power, servicing, and port facilities. To take the most striking example, as early as 1957, following a state government decision to build the Bandel Power Station in order to enhance power supplies for the Calcutta region, the Calcutta Electric Supply Corporation wanted to put in another 100 MW or so in Garden Reach for the same puspose, which in hindsight seems an excellent idea wasted. At any rate, new private industrial units in Taratolla, Budge Budge, Triveni, and Howrah (all in the Calcutta metropolitan region) were the private sector's response to the public sector's effort. In fact, even without the Garden Reach addition, the Taratolla-Budge Budge region, with its sophisticated capital and skill-intensive units mushrooming, held the promise of industrial growth for Calcutta in the late 1950s that Thana later fulfilled for Bombay.

In the last three years, the private sector has found a new way of responding to public investment in the Calcutta region or, rather, has revived a channel of investment that gave Calcutta a crop of new buildings and localities as long ago as 1927-39. Between 1945 and 1966, the Rent Control Act had a crippling affect on Calcutta's building trade. Real estate and the apartment construction industry then came into its own for a brief period in 1967-69, only to go dormant again during the new politically unstable period of the United Front coalition governments in 1969-70, when rents crashed and construction for renting or sale became unprofitable. The new money that was pumped into the CMDA in a big way in 1971-72 accelerated a movement that had appeared first as a sign in a small way in 1954-56 but as a definite trend in 1967: that of high-rise, high-density apartments, meant primarily for high-income groups. Curiously enough, in three different periods, the fashion for building was set by the public sector, later to be imitated by the private sector. In 1952-54 the state government first built Calcutta's tallest building, the New Secretariat. The Bengal Chamber of Commerce followed with its high-rise apartments in Alipore. The trend setter in 1967 was the central government and Air-India, and in 1971-72 the ice was again broken by the central government.

The earnestness of the government's intentions in various outlays for the CMDA and its own housing policy in 1971-72 has now led to a fresh spate of private capital in real estate, for which the groundwork had been prepared in 1967-69. This activity has in turn found an outlet for pent-up capital, which had stopped flowing in any quantity into industry around Calcutta after 1962-63. If one were to stand at the top of any high-rise building in the Theatre Road area of Calcutta today, one could count at least 50 silhouettes of high-rise, high-density apartments either completed or nearing completion. On closer inspection, one could also spot a few more looming up. At a conservative estimate, the cost of these new structures would amount to a little less than Rs. 75 crores ($93.75 million), not counting the black money that goes to the internal embellishment of these flats through the use of expensive marble fittings, and superfluous ornaments and decorations that appeal to the new rich.

The occupants of these high-rise flatted growths have contributed to the professional, entrepreneurial, managerial, scientific, and technical manpower resources of the city. Belonging to a status category with much higher consumption levels than the bulk of the city's population, they have also stimulated a perceptible amount of local industry, wholesale and retail trade, and a wide range of skilled and unskilled services. But it has also to be remembered that a considerable number of the residents of these new apartments are either immigrants into Calcutta or are dependent for their dwellings on recent immigrants into Calcutta, and in this sense they have added to its population and have made a significant addition to its municipal services requirements.

It can be argued that these growths have been almost a direct result of the CMDA investment program, with some credit being given to a return of confidence in the city's future after 1970. Along with this real estate spurt has occurred a resuscitation of all of the industries and trades concerned with building activity, which accounts for a certain briskness in medium and small industries in Calcutta and a certain stimulation of employment, not only of domiciles but also of immigrants. Large numbers of immigrant construction workers—the majority of them being unskilled but accustomed to heavy manual labor—and of workers connected particularly with road transport, transshipment, loading and unloading, have found their refuge in the city. This has stimulated Calcutta's transportation fleet—both public and private—with attendant side affects. Above all, it has stimulated a very large number of tertiary trading and service jobs, mainly to service the large population of immigrant construction and transport workers. These range from eating booths to personal services like barbering, and a vast array of pavement shops vending an astonishing range of perishable and durable consumer goods, all catering primarily to the pavement dweller and the low-income resident family. Indeed, the vast majority of the new immigrant population engaged in the real estate and construction industry in Calcutta resides in pavement dwellings, and the daily needs of this population are also satisfied, to a remarkable extent, on the self-same pavement. This happened not in Calcutta alone, but also in Kanpur, Delhi, and Bombay, although the extent to which this is the case may be greater in Calcutta than in other Indian cities.

CONCENTRATED DEVELOPMENT

In the case of both the earlier Calcutta Metropolitan Planning Organization (CMPO) and the later Calcutta Metropolitan Development Authority (CMDA), the principal professed goal has been the development of the Calcutta metropolitan region as a whole, of which Calcutta and Howrah are admittedly the core but, nevertheless, only a part. Yet, in terms of concentration of technical appraisal, development of data, and last but not least, investment, the Calcutta Corporation area has enjoyed almost a monopoly of funds and priority in project execution. Its immediate peripheral areas, like Howrah, Bally, Baranagar, Bhatpara, and Dum Dum, have received the bulk of what was left over. One reason for this was the simple fact that this core area offered the largest amount of manipulable data, thanks to the

TABLE 1

Total Expenditures in Fourth Plan Period, 1969–74, Calcutta Metropolitan Development Authority Area (CMDA)

Head of Expenditure	Total CMDA Area (Rs. in crores)	Expenditure on Area Outside Calcutta Corporation (but including Howrah and Dum Dum) (Rs. in crores)
1 Water supply	17.20	3.87
2 Sewerage and drainage	31.08	6.19
3 Garbage disposal	2.57	—
4 Environmental hygiene	0.46	—
5 Traffic and transportation	23.18	7.66
6 Traffic: other schemes	11.48	—
7 Special projects, like gas distribution, hospital facilities, primary schools, parks, and playgrounds	7.88	—[a]
8 Housing and new area development	8.77	0.04
9 Bustee improvement scheme	10.61	—[b]
Total	113.23	17.76

[a]Breakdown not available, perhaps about Rs. 1 crore.
[b]Expenditure on Baranagar, Kamahati, Rishira, Champdani, and fringes not obtained.

Source: Planning Commission of India.

work of the CMPO and the preliminary plan of the World Health Organization (WHO) on water supply and sewerage. In addition, there were a number of executing organizations ready at hand, who knew the immediate Calcutta area best and who also knew how to set about solving problems in it. Finally, Calcutta's needs and political and economic weight have always loomed so much above those of the peripheral areas that funds have automatically gravitated to Calcutta (with some fallout to Howrah), despite occasional protests from non-Calcuttans. Table 1, constructed from statements of the last CMDA Review Committee, provides a summary view of the geographical distribution of funds.

As can be seen from Table 1, only 17.76 crores of rupees ($22.2 million) was expended during the Fourth Five Year Plan period (1969-74) on areas outside of Calcutta, while 113.23 crores of rupees ($141.55 million) was expended in the entire CMDA area. This means that the immediate Calcutta area received more than 80 percent of total funds. Moreover, while almost 20 percent of total expenditure was professedly made in areas outside the Calcutta Corporation, perhaps most of it was in fact intended simply to buttress the infrastructure of the Calcutta Corporation area. A more searching analysis would be necessary to find out how much of it really went to augment the resources of municipalities outside of Calcutta Corporation and Howrah.

At any rate, it is clear that the bulk of government expenditure in the Calcutta area during the Fourth Five Year Plan has benefited not much more than 50 square miles of space, even though the Calcutta metropolitan region extends over an area of about 550 square miles. This inordinate concentration of investment on less than one-tenth of the total area, comparable in its enormity of disproportion to the income distribution curve of our country, has had the effect of accentuating almost all of the problems of Calcutta proper, instead of relieving them. In addition, of course, the problems associated with such investment have been concentrated in this one core area, rather than being distributed more equitably in the Calcutta metropolitan region as a whole.

There has been a noticeable increase in the human density of Calcutta proper ever since the CMDA began to spend large sums of money at the end of 1971. Part of the sense of overcrowding, of course, has been contributed by the dug-up roads, the stockpiling of construction material at prominent open spaces, and the working of large machinery. But it will hardly be disputed that contractors, skilled and unskilled construction workers, and even groups of beneficiaries being largely immigrant, the population of Calcutta has swelled at a more rapid rate since 1971 than was the case previously. The rumor of job availability attracts more people than can actually find jobs. This applies particularly to the accretions to the pavement population and the preternatural increase in the number and range of services that have mushroomed on them, threatening to choke even pedestrian circulation. Needless to say, this has meant great strain on the augmented filtered water supply, conservancy sewerage, and the regular sewerage services of the city.

The more development is concentrated in Calcutta proper, without a substantial fraction of it being directed to the surrounding region and, if one may venture to suggest, the more starved the district and subdivisional towns are, the more overwhelmed will Calcutta proper be with Bengali and non-Bengali immigrants. Ever since 1947 the district and subdivisional towns in West Bengal have been starved and neglected as they have never been in other states of India. They are now failing to stem the tide of immigrants to the Calcutta region for lack of the meanest amenities, and because of an excess of filth and congestion. The community development movement in the rural areas of Bengal dried up around 1960. Unless these countermagnets are revived through some strenuous self-help activity, with assistance pumped into them from the state government, the load on Calcutta will increase unbearably. The fact is that the CMDA's efforts in Calcutta since 1971 have accentuated the population pressure on the city very demonstrably, by threatening to choke up vehicular and pedestrian circulation not only on the smaller streets and lanes but along the main arteries as well. It is only in very small isolated neighborhoods, where the population is entirely homogeneous and the areas retain some semblance of privacy, that the lanes and narrow streets are still comparatively free.

Let us consider what is threatening to happen to Calcutta when certain major projects swing into action. Conceivably, there are going to be 40 to 50 more large, high-density, high-rise blocks, no ban being contemplated on them yet. In addition, three major projects will begin soon: the underground north-south mass transit system, the second Howrah Bridge, and the flyovers on Brabourne Road and the Sealdah area. These three projects will require not only the displacement of populations but also their reconcentration in less space, since none of the displaced populations are likely to be persuaded to leave Calcutta proper. On top of this, these projects will demand, at a conservative estimate, a minimum of 50,000 persons—contractors, technicians, administrative personnel, skilled and unskilled workers, transport fleets, with their servicing facilities—and a minimum of another 5,000 to 10,000 persons to provide services on Calcutta's pavements for this contingent. What is more, the majority of these people are likely to be short-term immigrants from other states of India, who will prefer to live on the pavement, on minimum investment or commitment for the duration of their employment, which means that they will enjoy whatever meager services Calcutta Corporation will have to offer, without being compelled to pay for any of them or without even any psychological or civic stake for keeping Calcutta clean and habitable. This is a matter that, as far as I gathered on my visit to Calcutta last month, had not yet been thought out. The thought of Calcutta adding more than 50,000 adults to its pavement population in the brief space of a year or so, with its open spaces still further contracting under pressure of construction, can be rather distressing, particularly when there are no positive plans in readiness for cushioning the impact.

CONSEQUENCES OF CONCENTRATION

If the process of redensification through high-rise construction for the affluent goes on apace, and if major improvements are made in the circulation system of the city by multiplying the inlets and outlets and improving the velocity and ease of transportation, there is bound to be a rapid thinning of Calcutta proper, resulting from a steady squeezing out of the lower and lower-middle income groups. Calcutta will grow into a city with fewer shades of social and economic classes and will consist mainly of the rich and upper-income groups, on the one hand, and the very low income service and working-class groups dwelling in the bustees on the other. For it is becoming increasingly clear that Calcutta's taxes and rates will have to keep on multiplying, with new imposts on many permanent and casual activities thrown in, to pay for the maintenance and renewal of freshly created assets. This alone will most likely bring about a dramatic reduction in the population of long-time residents.

Something like this happened for refugees in the decade of the 1950s. The census of 1951 was taken four years after Partition, and it counted 686,000 persons in Calcutta proper who were born in Pakistan, mainly in East Bengal (then East Pakistan, now Bangladesh). In 1961 this figure dwindled to 528,000. Similarly, Howrah District in 1951 counted 94,000 persons born in East Bengal, and only 80,000 in 1961. On the other hand the urban areas of 24-Parganas showed an increase of persons born in East Bengal, from 366,000 in 1951 to 490,000 in 1961, while rural 24-Parganas showed an increase from 255,000 in 1951 to 297,000 in 1961. Hooghly, adjoining Howrah, showed an increase from 72,000 in 1951 to 131,000 in 1961.

An interesting process started in the decade 1951-61, continued in the next decade, and probably continues to this date. There is plenty of evidence that the first rush of immigrants from East Bengal during 1947-52 concentrated for obvious reasons in Calcutta and Howrah cities proper, but large numbers of refugees felt compelled to

leave this core area for the peripheral and nonmunicipal areas, in
order to preserve some semblance of their former life-style. They
either squatted on or bought small plots of land all around Calcutta,
and built small cottages or substandard brick buildings for themselves,
using either tile or tin for roofs. This kind of growth in the urban
and rural areas around Calcutta, Howrah city, and the towns of
Hooghly and Nadia districts is there for all to see. It is particularly
impressive from a low-flying plane. Within their small plots, acquired by purchase or trespass, the families retain a semblance of
privacy, make their own arrangements for water supply, sewerages,
and sewage, and, in addition, grow considerable quantities of vegetables and small fish, which feed the markets and pavement shops.
Of all the cities of India, Calcutta retains its pride of place for vegetables and small fish, thanks mainly to the enterprise of people who
were too poor to go on living in Calcutta. These people have managed
to live estimable lives in their own way, educating their children in
professions and skills, engaging in self-respecting livelihoods, and in
numerous other ways discharging social responsibilities. Their way
of life, though much constricted by lack of resources, is perhaps in
many ways worth more socially than the kind of humanly wasteful
lives that many people, who may have displaced them, live in affluent
flatted growths in Calcutta proper. The country has to choose the type
of life it prefers for the majority of its citizens, instead of leaving it
entirely to random choice.

     Around 1969-70, two experts invited by the Ford Foundation to
work for the CMPO on the prospects of low-cost housing in the Calcutta
metropolitan area produced a report that goes by their names. This
is the Kingsley-Kristof report, which, unfortunately, failed to receive
the attention it deserved, either in Calcutta or from the central government. Kingsley and Kristof arrived at the conclusion that, land
values and building costs being what they were, there was no hope for
families in the income bracket of about Rs. 300 per month ever to acquire a residence of about 260 square feet for themselves in Calcutta
city. However, Kingsley and Kristof concluded that the semiurban and
rural spaces in the Calcutta metropolitan region might still provide
propitious circumstances for purchasing such residences, provided
costs were reduced by operations of scale and with standardized materials and specifications.

     If these remarks applied to conditions in Calcutta, they would
apply equally to corresponding income groups with corresponding levels of consumption in other big cities of India, and this brings us to
certain fundamental considerations as to the kind of urbanization that
deserves to be articulated and assisted in India. In the present context, I shall attempt to provide such consideration by focusing on ways
that articulation can be stimulated in the Calcutta metropolitan region.

INTEGRATION AND THE WESTERN MODEL

It is now common knowledge that the degree of industrialization and white-collar services that one associates with urbanization in the Western world does not exist in the majority of the developing countries in Latin America, Africa, and Asia. It certainly does not exist even in the most citylike city of India, Bombay. In most urban areas of the Western world, the level of consumption of the lowest-income deciles of the population is decidedly above that of the corresponding groups of their rural populations, whereas Dandekar and Rath have demonstrated, and their contention remains by and large undisputed, that the level of nutrition of the lowest-income deciles of India's urban population is often below that of similar groups among her rural populations. This yields the conclusion that a substantial proportion of India's so-called urban population has very little to do with the kind of blue- and white-collar jobs one associates with urban areas of the West, but mainly subsists on (1) very low-paid menial jobs, which often fetch incomes as low as those of landless agricultural laborers in depressed areas, or (2) extremely low-level domestic service, trading, and other pursuits, which in the West used to be known as "breaking the book"—for example, selling cigarettes or biris by the stick and not by the pack, or selling other articles of very low-income consumption—in short, what Bhabatosh Datta once called the poverty-induced tertiary sector, or services that are generated merely by the growth in numbers of poor population and not by economic investment.

For a long time to come, or at least in the foreseeable future, industrial investment in India is unlikely to reach the level where it could support all but the lowest-income decile or two of India's population in the appropriate blue- and white-collar jobs that one associates with an industrialized country. Places like the Calcutta or the Bombay metropolitan regions will be lucky if the second or third lowest-income deciles of their population are enabled to have a consumption level that will give them reasonable nutrition and shelter against exposure. In other words, India's urban population should have reasonably arrived if, in the foreseeable future, all but its lowest-income decile or so is enabled to have a minimum consumption of Rs. 350 to Rs. 400 per month at 1968-69 prices. Even with population control, such an income would have to sustain at least a family of five, provided such a family is not made to pay fully for all the civic services and amenities that a city like Calcutta is supposed to maintain. These brutal facts, taken alone, will put to severe test India's ability to go ahead with adequate levels of investment for her industrialization program, which is far from adequate at the present time.

In such a situation, even if India went full steam ahead with her program for reducing income disparities and drastically reducing the individual ceilings on urban property, the level of investment that is being currently undertaken by the CMDA for Calcutta or the Bombay Metropolitan Authority for the twin city project of Bombay or the Delhi Development Authority for Delhi is far above what the vast bulk of their resident populations can bear, pay back, or maintain with reasonable ease in the future. In short, the developments under way under the auspices of the CMDA are pricing themselves out of the competence of the Calcuttan either to maintain, augment, or replace them with his own resources. At this rate, all of the big cities in India will have to be on perpetual charity or subsidy. The improvements on hand are on scales much larger than the traffic can bear, for the present economic structure of Calcutta's population and the system of municipal rates and taxes cannot ever raise more than a small fraction of the money required to pay for them. If Calcutta is to sustain the improvements it has embarked upon, it will shortly have to squeeze out a substantial proportion of its domiciled population and still fall flat on its face some day.

On the other hand, if the Calcutta metropolitan region can devise a system by which it can house and service the bulk of its domiciliary population at an average consumption level of Rs. 350 per month at 1968-69 prices for a family of five, it will have achieved conditions much more worthwhile, though less spectacular and less demonstrably modern than the on-going projects in Calcutta. What must be found is a means by which the Calcutta metropolitan region can be rendered much more livable for far larger numbers of people, and more endowed with human dignity, than the present projects promise.

When the CMDA originally was set up, the idea was to place all of the following areas in nine clusters, under equitable development programs:

1. Calcutta, South Buburban, Garden Reach
2. Baranagar, Kamarhati, Dum Dum, South Dum Dum
3. Panihati, Khardah, Titagarh
4. Barrackpore, North Barrackpore, Garulia, Bhatpara
5. Howrah, Bally
6. Uttarpara-Kotung, Konanagar, Rishra
7. Serampore, Baidyabati, Champdani, Bhadrawan
8. Kanchrapara, Naihati, Halisahar, Kalyani
9. Chandannagar, Hooghly-Chinsurah, Bansberia

Moreover, within the CMDA, the proposal was made and accepted that all local self-governing units, which include towns other than Calcutta in the Calcutta metropolitan region, be placed under one central authority. The original idea was to obliterate separate statutes and individual municipal identities by placing all of them under one authority, thus making it possible to provide an equitable spatial development plan to ensure comparable levels of amenities throughout the region. As events have shown, these expectations were belied. In fact they were bound to be belied, if only because of the inordinate political weight that Calcutta pulls by virtue of its wealth and importance. As things worked out, Calcutta's influence preordained the lion's share of available resources for the core, regardless of any plans to the contrary. In spite of the arrangements for sharing Calcutta's octroi resources, for example, the other units have not received anything at all like the attention and resources they deserve according to their area and population, although they encompass in their urban structures large and valuable industrial complexes that are the pride and chief wealth of West Bengal in terms of capital and human skills.

So long as the idea of integration dominates the discussion, so long as the present apparatus of an inefficient information system for the non-Calcutta areas of the metropolitan region holds sway, so long as apathy and neglect obtain, and so long as the decision-making body is composed in the main of representatives who live in Calcutta and have their major political and economic stakes in this core, the non-Calcutta areas of the metropolitan region will continue to suffer from grievous neglect and fail to discharge that adequate complementary role of extended suburbia that is essential to the operation of the metropolitan region as a homogeneous going concern.

ALTERNATIVE MODELS OF DEVELOPMENT

It seems important, therefore, to talk practical politics and think of dividing the region into several clusters of municipal-rural continuums around Calcutta, each with its own unique homogeneous entity of demographic, social, economic, human settlement, transportation, and servicing features. The better course would seem to be the evolution of a three-level structure whereby (1) at the lowest level a municipality would be in charge not only of its own area but also of the contiguous rural interstices, which, by virtue of their transportation, servicing, and human settlement patterns, would conveniently and legitimately fall within its ambit; (2) at the intermediate level the single municipality and its rural appendages, with a number of similarly constituted and geographically contiguous municipal-cum-rural areas, would make up a large cluster of five or six such bodies, each with its own confederate body of representatives from each constituent unit; within each cluster, the confederate body of representatives would take decisions of common and interwoven action; (3) the

metropolitan region itself would become the apex body of these clusters, each of which would enjoy considerable autonomy in decision-
making, planning, and executing and in personnel programs and funds.

The formula of sharing of grants and loans among the clusters
and individual units ought to be on the basis of weights, which will
take into account: (1) the degree of backwardness in respect of standard norms for (a) each municipality and (b) each cluster; (2) the burden of population in (a) each municipality and (b) each cluster; and (3)
the geographical area of (a) each municipality and (b) each cluster.
Some machinery in the nature of a federal award body would have to
sit at stated intervals to adjudicate and fix the shares and proportions
of each constituent. Otherwise there seems to be little prospect of
each constitutent of the region receiving its due share of attention
and resources. The three levels of tiers should be matched with
three levels of planning and executing bodies, each connected to well-
lubricated channels of properly functioning vertical and horizontal
information systems. Unless certain measures of decentralization
and autonomy of decision and execution are consciously and deliberately built into the structure of the Calcutta metropolitan region, the
present lopsided concentration of resources on Calcutta will continue
to hasten the denudation and deprivation of the rest of the region.

Neglect of the non-Calcutta portions of the Calcutta metropolitan
region has also resulted from the multiplicity of implementing agencies, the overwhelming majority of which are entirely Calcutta-based,
with their expert knowledge mainly confined to conditions in Calcutta,
and their ideas of scales of working and technology mainly suited to
Calcutta's conditions. Moreover, these bodies have lately hitched
their wagons to the star of the urban arrangements and aspirations of
Western and, of late, American supercities, and, what is worse, they
wish to forget about compromises on the scale of amenities that the
people in the other municipalities of the metropolitan region can more
realistically observe and realize. Of the 24 agencies operating in the
CMDA, not more than four or five have sensible ideas of what will
actually work in non-Calcutta conditions, as is indicated by a look at
the agencies and their distribution according to areas of knowledge
and interest.

Although on paper there are as many as nine or more estimable
organizations that claim expert knowledge of non-Calcutta conditions
(Table 2), none of these, as we have seen before, have yet been fur-
nished with a surfeit of funds, nor do they find it possible to ask fundamental questions, or to experiment on possible policy alternatives.
For example, why should the norm be 40 gallons of protected and filtered water per person in Calcutta, when there is hardly a gallon of
water per person available in Bansberia or three of it in Uttarpara?
Why should it be necessary to go in for underground sewerage and

sewage instead of individual or group underground septic tank latrines
or decentralized small-scale sewage purification plants? Why should
garbage disposal in the municipal-nonmunicipal continuums not be
worked out in terms of small-scale compost grounds, the composts
of which would assist in truck gardening within the region, which in
turn is so vital for keeping up nutrition levels? Why should we not
build internal networks of narrow roads of lower specification within
each municipality or cluster, which would be suitable both for intra-
cluster pedestrian safety and the low density of passenger car and
freight transport, and supplement these with arterial passages through
clusters, or ring roads around clusters, using better specifications
for mass transit and rapid intercluster circulation? It seems to be
in the very nature of the structure of the organizations themselves,
as well as their interrelationships, their vested interests, and the
authority they have wrested for themselves over the years, that new
nonconformist, or inconvenient questions are hardly allowed to break
into any serious discussion of future plans. And, as everyone knows,
when people who know all the answers sit around a conference table,
new ideas fly out of the window.

Having invested about 130 crores in the space of three years,
over and above currently budgeted outlays—and again, of course, I
would repeat that 130 crores is not a figure to boast about, particularly when viewed in the light of the age-long neglect that Calcutta
has suffered relative to other Indian cities like Delhi and Bombay—
it may be time to pause and reflect whether the scale of investment
and distribution of new assets that is presently being contemplated is
going to benefit the Calcutta metropolitan region in the way that was
originally envisioned. For one thing, even if we can scrape together
the money by way of grants and loans—international and national—for
the improvement of Calcutta, can we prevent grievous fresh influxes
of populations into the city? Without doing so, increased migration
into Calcutta will speedily bring to nought whatever investments have
been made. Are present investment plans the way to distribute
equitably the population in the metropolitan region, or to guide populations away from the core? For one thing, again, it is becoming increasingly plain that for at least those Indian cities that have a population of a million or more, there is no way out but to introduce a permit system for screening fresh immigration, so that immigrants will
either have to pay an entrance fee or a terminal tax, or submit to some
other such device to fill identifed new jobs in the city. Such a device
would help to raise funds sorely needed for improvement, maintenance,
and renewal and would also help to keep down both the level of unemployment and the numbers in the poverty-induced tertiary sector of
very low levels of employment, which have a way of consuming more
than they produce or invest. Such a device also seems inescapable, if

TABLE 2

Agencies Operating for CMDA with Specialist Knowledge of Calcutta
Proper and Knowledge of Working in Non-Calcutta Areas

Specialist Knowledge of Calcutta Proper	Knowledge of Working in Non-Calcutta Areas
1 Calcutta Corporation	1 Howrah Municipality
2 Calcutta Improvement Trust	2 Howrah Improvement Trust
3 Calcutta Metropolitan Planning Organization	3 Other municipalities
4 Irrigation and Waterways Directorate	4 Public Health Engineering
5 Housing Directorate	5 Health Directorate and Hospital Facilities
6 Public Works Department	6 Public Works (Construction) Board
7 Public Works (Roads) Directorate	7 Zilla Parishad
8 Calcutta Port Commissioner	8 CPHERI
9 Calcutta Tramways Co. Ltd.	9 Forest Directorate
10 Calcutta State Transport Corporation	
11 Oriental Gas Co.	
12 Calcutta Metropolitan Water and Sewerage Authority	
13 CMDA and others	
14 Central Public Works Directorate	
15 Bustee Improvement Agencies (a) CMPO (b) Central P.W. Directorate (c) Calcutta Corporation (d) Howrah Improvement Trust (e) CMDA	

Source: Compiled by the author.

only to rationalize and keep down growing interstate tensions and
scrambles for jobs as between the "sons of the soil" and alleged intruders. It is no use pretending that migrant-nonmigrant tensions, particularly in large cities, are a passing phase. They will increase, and it
seems imperative to build in rational, well-designed safeguards, well
ahead of time, to contain them.

While it is obviously essential that Calcutta and Howrah cities complete some of the schemes that are already under way, it also seems important in the greater metropolitan region to opt for standards and norms that the people will be capable of observing and realizing, instead of thrusting on them standards and norms of development that are too precious and irrelevant, being more suited to highly developed economies. Instead of spending patently on consumption areas, the greater needs in the Calcutta area today are to develop low-value lands and to build up solid new blocks of electricity generation and industrial water supply. If Calcutta could have an increment of 200 megawatts (MW) of electricity and a fresh supply of industrial water, it would be psychologically and economically in much better shape than it is with its newly acquired attributes of conspicuous consumption.

It is quite plain that India will not be able, at least in the next two or three plans, to afford the level of industrial investments that will transform the populations of major cities into blue- and white-collar earners of the Western breed at the latter's income level. It should be enough for India's purposes of socioeconomic development, modernization, and cultural change if a level of economic activity is generated that gives each metropolitan region family an income level of about Rs. 400 at 1968-69 prices and a level of consumption of about Rs. 325-350 for a family of five. Such a family would be an estimable asset builder to the region, even if it could not afford a house in Calcutta proper. It is important to provide for such families within the Calcutta region, but such provision would also be in the national interest.

CONCLUSIONS

The great bulk of the population, even in major cities of India, lives in the environment of urban villages, where the level of their economic pursuits is below those required for Western urban living. At the height of their gracious days earlier in the century, cities like Calcutta, Allahabad, Lucknow, or Madras were no more than conglomerations of urban villages. People can be quite happy in urban villages, built around a modern city core, provided certain amenities are assured in terms of settlement lots. First comes housing and shelter, particularly for the very low-income groups, which the CMDA has neglected not only in the non-Calcutta parts of the region but even, sadly enough, in Calcutta and Howrah proper. Here, as we have discussed in respect to the East Bengal refugees, houses need not be of brick, steel, and concrete but rather of brick or semidurable material, with mud or lime mortar and tiled roofing. In any case, India will have to forget about steel and cement for low- and middle-income housing, for steel and cement will be scarce, prohibitively expensive, and sorely needed for more urgent national purposes. Second, economies of scale work up to a certain point, but it is becoming increasingly plain that a central water supply, as well as sewage, sewerage, and drainage systems for the entire Calcutta metropolitan region, such as has been planned for Calcutta, are things the resource traffic will not bear. They will have to be broken up into smaller mini-systems, designed to bring about self-sufficiency for defined geographical spaces of say 10 to 15 square miles each, conceived, planned, and executed on scales that local resources can maintain and replace. All of these, but particularly water and drainage mini-systems, can be connected by light grids to contiguous mini-systems for emergencies like breakdowns for short periods. Thus, large central water-purification plants will have to give way to small decentralized plants, catering to defined units of populations while receiving supplies of water from large-bore deep tubewells or from nearby rivers, or even from large protected surface tanks. Similarly, sewage, sewerage, drainage, and garbage disposal systems will have to be decentralized and broken up into smaller mini-systems and located in the shape of a network within clusters, each of which can be conveniently maintained by either a municipality or the cluster itself. Portions of these systems could then be conveniently renewed, without the necessity of renovating the entire network. Finally, garbage disposal and nightsoil treatment must certainly be undertaken in such a way as to produce compost, in order to assist the raising of vegetables and crops for city consumption.

But the most important element in such cluster growths that will contribute to the integration of a metropolitan region is a well-designed network of light and heavy traffic roads and railways, arterial and circular, which will ensure fast transit from cluster to cluster and to the core, and yet provide reasonable facilities within each cluster. This is of the essence if we are to assist actively in such things as a dispersal of population and an adequate interaction between rural and urban habitations. If such measures can be initited, they are likely to stimulate, with a ripple effect, wider and still wider rings of pleasant semi-urban territory around the metropolis.

Maintenance of services will also need reexamination, as I indicated in 1970-71, at the beginning of the new CMDA Bustee Improvement Scheme. During a discussion of the unused and unemployed educated manpower of young men and women in the bustees, I pleaded in 1970-71 that each bustee should be divided conveniently into blocks of population of about 600 to 1,000, or at most up to 2,000, and the amenities provided in each should be put under charge of educated unemployed young men and women of the block, appointed to work in four-hour shifts on stated days. The duties of this corps of young people would be (1) to undertake house-to-house visits, making sure that taps, water points, sewage, drainage, street and drain pavings, and conservancy services are working properly; (2) to see to it that young children are regularly attending school, that their uniforms and meals are all right, that they have received the right inoculations, and so forth; and (3) to check on pregnant and lactating mothers, newborn infants, and children in general, in order to ascertain the extent to which they are receiving adequate care from community health centers.

For each two blocks of 4,000-bustee population, there should be a schoolhouse-cum-clinic-cum-nonformal adult education center, which would similarly be looked after by semitrained young men and women drawn from the community, who would run such things as primary or middle school education up to standard VI, rural health clinics and child and mother health care and nutrition centers, and nonformal adult education centers to be conducted in four-hour shifts, all in the same community building (which should have a playground attached to it). The community itself could be responsible for these services. Payments to young men and women need be made only on a part-time basis, at rates not exceeding Rs. 150 to Rs. 200 per month for four-hour shifts per working day. Nodal services at levels higher than these would have to be provided by either the municipality or the cluster authority.

Some system of this kind seems imperative, both to generate stakes in the community and to stimulate community participation in preserving and renewing what has been invested. Otherwise, as in the improved bustees in Calcutta, an improvement accomplished becomes nobody's business to maintain and nobody feels called upon to regard it as his own. A sense of involvement through remunerated recruitment from among local young men and women seems essential for propagating a much-needed sense of community involvement, which in turn seems a precondition of the new urban movement. That this is no utopian wish is borne out by the fact that the most successful and eagerly sought schemes of the CMDA have been offers of school-houses, health centers, and short connecting roads on a matching contribution basis to small communities in the outer suburbs of Calcutta.

At the moment, however, the most important thing seems to be to think anew about the type of metropolitan urban renewal process that will really suit our economic and social condition. This applies equally, or perhaps even more, to the district and subdivisional towns of West Bengal, the utter neglect of which for three decades has not only added to the problems of the Calcutta metropolitan region but has grievously hurt the state's agricultural development. Undoubtedly there is a great deal of thinking, planning, studying, and experimenting to be done.

But it is clear that attempts to transplant wholesale the apparatus of renewal of large cities in developed countries will hardly work. The most important thing is to own up to the fact that they are a trifle too precious, and a bit too irrelevant, to our process of development. What has now become imperative is an attempt to upgrade our semi-urban conditions by providing such attributes as will endow them with self-sufficient urban services on a reduced or modified scale, all the while adopting technologies that will put each citizen on the path of modernization, but in a manner more appropriate to his socioeconomic status. Above all, services must be such that the citizen will be enabled to sustain and, when necessary, renew them. Linkages can be obtained by welding urban villages together with a skillfully devised system of internal roads and lanes and intercommunicating fast traffic highways, as well as railroads, all connected to the metropolitan core.

In order to begin to translate such ideas into practice, it would first be necessary, of course, to work out a viable three-tier system by virtue of which planning and executing responsibilities can be decentralized and fiscal arrangements laid down within overall centrally articulated goals and targets.

It is unnecessary to rush headlong to repeat the mistakes of pollution, congestion, and displacement of resident populations so often made in expensive city renewal projects. It is much more important to preserve an existing metropolitan population, and to help it in its growth, all the while striving to keep levels of pollution and congestion as low as possible. Above all it is important to go in for those improvements that will work, and those that the resident population, in the words of John Stuart Mill, can "observe and realise," that is, maintain and renew with no great difficulty. A vast network of well-knit contented urban villages, with low levels of pollution, but with greater degrees of decentralized community participation, may well be India's answer to sweltering high-rise, high-density, high-pollution, circulation-choked cities, such as Calcutta is speedily degenerating into. India's metropolitan growth can yet proceed on a path that will fulfill its own needs. It can also provide useful clues for dealing with urban growth in poor-income countries.

DISCUSSION

<u>Robert Cassen</u>: What I have to say revolves around what I would call the marriage of two themes that are found in the literature today. One of these is concerned with economic development, the theme of distri-

bution with growth, which talks about the failure of development during the past 20 years to do much about the condition of the poor; the other is perhaps the main theme in the population literature, that it is only by providing some decent form of life for the mass of people that you have a chance of containing population growth in the long run. These two themes, it seems to me, relate to almost everything we have been discussing, and very much to what Mitra has been saying in his paper about Calcutta. I think he was excessively modest about the paper. Anyone who would dare to talk about Calcutta's problems in the presence of Asok Mitra would be very daring indeed. Therefore, I want to talk about other problems that relate to what he has said.

There are really two faults of planners that one can perceive on our topic. One is planning as you think people are going to behave or as you would like them to behave and not as they actually do behave. I think the planners of this conference experienced that a little. The other is the use of false standards in creating plans and estimating requirements. It is really this latter one that seems to me the key to what Asok Mitra has said; and this is true, I think, of urban plans in developing countries. I think it's true of Calcutta.

The typical thing is for an economist to estimate requirements by developing some standard of provision in health, in education, in housing, in urban development. He works out the cost of this provision for the growing numbers of people, and he decides that a huge volune of resources is needed. This volume of resources is not available, and therefore we just do part of the plans, and the part of it that we do is nearly always the part that benefits the privileged members of society and not the rest. That is why so many cities in the world and in the developing countries have highways right through the middle of the city, to help people with cars get to their elegant offices from their elegant homes despite the fact that these roads hinder the mass of the people, who have transport problems in getting to work.

The same is true in a large range of planning services. I have seen estimates of "housing need" in India where even the estimators have themselves despaired; they say that you can call "housing need" 1 million dwellings, 10 million dwellings, or 40 million dwellings, depending on where you draw the line and what you think are intolerable standards in which people are already living; whatever they do with these numbers, they can't come up with the necessary sums for the provision of housing. The funds do not exist and will not exist for several decades.

Yet there is something that one can do instead of going through these exercises. This is a different approach, which consists of the marriage of the two themes that I was talking about. If one looks at the situation in India, it isn't happening yet, although all the pressures are present to make it happen. For example, what the government has tried to do is to spread rural health with a network of Primary Health Centres, staffed by doctors and other personnel. But the system does not cover the needs of the poor. There is a way of doing something different, and the Fifth Plan proposed this. It proposed a scheme of development of paramedicals, who would be far less extensively trained but who would be able to bring primary medical care to the mass of the people. This was unfortunately shot down, mainly by the Indian medical profession.

This is terribly important because all the talk now is of integrating family planning with health. But there is no health system with which to integrate family planning, and unless this development of paramedicals becomes a reality you cannot hope to achieve a family planning program that reaches poor people. I think you can see many similarities in the process of planning, whether you look at health or whether you look at some of these other things.

However you look at the two-way process—planning for growing numbers, and how the way you plan will affect the growth of those numbers—you come to exactly the same conclusion, that the key to everything is the provision of employment. If you try to add up the cost of providing services, you come up always with these impossible numbers. But you have some hope that if you give people jobs with incomes, they will be able to find services for themselves. Hence, the move in urban development toward the "site and service" approach.

You don't build housing for people anymore. You give them a water tap and electricity and other services and hope that if you produce jobs for these people they will provide some sort of rudimentary shelter for themselves. There is some prospect, in this way, to give people housing—by no means comfortable but at least a relatively sanitary way of life—and this represents an alternative approach to the false standards and false estimations, in the absence of resources, to implement a program.

But without employment we are not going to solve anything, just as the food problem is not solved by growing more food, because unless people have income with which to buy it the gap between the existence of food and the abilities of those who need food to purchase it is never crossed. This is just as true and just as relevant in rural areas: If you have funds, they should be used to provide employment and income for the mass of the people, and you only have to do certain very basic things by way of services.

Talking of false standards, Asok Mitra has mentioned one of those here today. There is a standard of 40 gallons of drinking water. This is a false standard. It would be very nice, but it is not necessary. Studies have shown that the provision of a very small amount of very clean drinking water has a tremendous effect on health. For the rest of human water needs, you can have much less well-controlled water, but for drinking needs you require a very small amount per person of very good water; that is possible to provide. If you follow the WHO standards for water provision, you cannot provide that. The WHO standard is also usually in terms of piped water supply to houses, which it is not possible to provide for more than a tiny fraction of the people. What is needed is a stand-pipe with access for everybody, even for poor people.

Well, one could go on and on, but the message is always the same, that you shouldn't set a false standard and then find that you cannot afford it. You think of what you can pay for, what people can benefit from, and then you struggle to do that. I think the possibilities of going in that direction are favorable, and I think Asok Mitra has shown the way in which that works out for the intelligent planner in Calcutta. I think the first Calcutta plan document had some very good ideas about how to go in that direction. The difficulties in pursuing that policy are partly caused by economic factors but partly also by fundamental political problems.

I would like to make one additional point about density. A lot of the conversation we have had has been speaking about density as if the growth of population is inevitably going to provide living conditions for groups of people in proximity, to an extent that one has never before seen. What in fact we are likely to see is a growing proportion of the community living in conditions of the highest density currently experienced. Not that people are going to get closer and closer together to the point where they are six feet apart. There are just going to be more people living at the highest existing densities.

Central Calcutta has actually been losing population in the last 20 years, no doubt due to what Ashish Bose talked about when he said that migration is often discussed in terms of "push-pull" factors, and, as he noted, in Indian cities you have a "push-back" factor. The "push-back" factor seems to be operating in Calcutta. The density of central Calcutta is declining.

What is going to happen in India is that the large conglomerations will spread so that the densities will reach a peak beyond which they will not pass. What we will have eventually is a situation where people will not look on cities as places where it's worth migrating to, and then you will get the growth of other urban centers. So this picture of John Calhoun's mice in the mouse cage is terribly deceiving. Calamitous densities are not necessarily going to occur. We have probably already witnessed the maximum density in which people are likely to live and they have been there for hundreds of years. "The streets of Delhi, though broad and not greatly encumbered with wheeled conveyances, are permanently thronged with the inhabitants whenever the abatement of the heat permits. If one looks inside the houses which seem piled one upon the other they are teeming with in-

numerable families. Of every ten who pass me by on the street
eight or nine are ill clad." This, or something like it, was written
in 1666 by Francois Bernier. I do think we have to be careful with
this talk of density.

One interesting corollary of Asok Mitra's paper that has to be
drawn out and is of great interest to everything we are discussing is
the question of controlling rural-urban migration. He points to this
as a possible necessity for India's future, and I think this may well
be so. It is certainly a very interesting theme to think about because
if you really do succeed in providing employment and improved living
conditions in the city of Calcutta then you just intensify the problem.
It then once more becomes an attractive center, so anything you do
to solve the problem reintroduces the problem.

It may well be that the control of rural-urban migration is a
key to part of the problem. One of the difficulties, of course, is that
it is not very easy to control migration. Even in China, they have
tried to control migration and have had only partial success. But I
think it is going to become a growing subject of interest in terms of
what I said the other day about the importance of communities taking
responsibility for their own numbers. It does make a great difference
to have a village that will think about coping with its own growing numbers, if it is actually made much more difficult for members of the
village society to go outside to earn their income. They will then
have to concentrate their minds on the village.

I would like to close with a remark about Calcutta that I found
in a book by Geoffrey Moorehouse. He said that when one watches the
Howrah bridge during rush hour it is like seeing a gigantic colony of
refugees struggling to escape their impending doom; only the refugees
are so bewildered that they are fleeing in both directions at once. I
have a feeling that economic planners are somehow in the same situation, fleeing in all directions at once. What I have tried to suggest is
that this is not necessary, that if one does combine these two themes
in the stream of intellectual work on development at the moment, with
employment as the key to the problem of development, and also the
problem of population growth, we will find a way ahead.

B. R. Deolalikar: Cassen has preempted almost everything I was going to say. I will, therefore, just raise a few of the points that came
up after reading Mitra's paper. I cannot relate them directly to Calcutta, which is a city I do not know very well. Calcutta is a unique
city in many respects. Mitra has described the range of problems
that affect the nature and the quality of services in that city. If you
look to other states and other cities in India, the problems are similar, if not quite so extreme.

Mitra referred to the fact that over a period of time, investments in urban development and services for some of India's major cities have been quite large and that cities have suffered significantly. In the two states that I know, Gujarat and Maharashtra, the growth of cities of a second order—cities with a population of less than 100,000—have suffered significantly. As a matter of fact, a kind of decay is occurring in these cities. Governmental schemes of town planning, of investment in the city, have really come to a halt.

When you look at the whole situation in this light, one can begin to get a sense of the problems of these urban conglomerates like Calcutta, Bombay, Ahmedabad, and a few other cities around the country. Can we really look at the problems of these huge urban conglomerates in isolation from the rest of the countryside and hinterland? One naturally raises the question. Though we have begun to look at these problems, in a piecemeal way, should we really look in the future at a growth policy? Do we have a growth policy that will take cognizance of the range of problems right from the village to the problems of the huge city?

I also want to emphasize a few points that Mitra has brought out very clearly. If the city is going to be viable, the participation of individual members of the city will contribute to its development. Mitra estimates that if you can bring it to a level where there is marginal participation, then you have to bring people to a level of income of around 400 rupees.

Mitra: . . . consumption, not income.

Deolalikar: I'm sorry, consumption of around 400 rupees per capita. Well this is true, and unless this is brought about, little can be done. At present maybe 40 or 50 percent of the population is below these levels. The result is that a callous attitude develops: The city management, the municipal corporations develop a callousness toward people who are not participating.

I was involved at one stage in a study of seven cities in Gujarat with 100,000 population or more. At no stage in the growth of these cities does one really see any involvement on the part of the city to really look after poor people and attend to their needs. After all, what would one expect the concern of the city to be vis-a-vis people who do not in any way contribute to the city or to the coffers by way of taxation or by participation in any other process?

Another distressing factor is that in some cities—I cannot speak for all—participation in wage employment among women, which has always been marginal, is declining. During the last 20 or 25 years, women have almost been shoved out of wage employment sectors in the textile industry in Ahmedabad. As a result, stresses and strains on the family earner—the male family earner—have been increasing.

One series of questions by way of conclusion. Asok Mitra uses urban villages as a model. But can we really adapt ourselves to a low level of technology? Can we change our building codes, our housing codes? Urbanization rates in India are not high. A few cities are growing, but the urbanization process is still very slow. The quality of life in our cities has something to do with both the physical environment and the nature and quality of the services provided. Data for these kinds of things do not exist. Hard data particularly are lacking. One therefore goes into this with a lot of guesses.

The occupancy rate of housing in urban areas is growing, but significantly we have noted in one of our studies that the occupancy rate in the villages is also growing over a period of time. There is also degradation of housing. Family size is increasing, and this causes acute housing problems in the villages as well as the cities. The question of educational spread is coming at us, and it's a question not only of how to have more teachers. It's also a question of how to have more buildings.

A more significant problem is that related to the entire area of health and health delivery services, affecting the treatment of diseases and illnesses, sanitation, and public health. The question of a reasonable amount of safe drinking water arises not only in the cities but more significantly in the rural areas. Hardly any work has been done on it. There has been hardly any work on developing a simple technology for these matters. Talking about water as a base for urban viability, in four cities in Gujarat in the region of Saurashtra over the past four years, the problem became so severe that the government had to think in terms of shifting the urban population out of Rajkot and Jamnagar. Such crisis situations are developing in other places.

The question of management of services is an equally important question. I have a feeling that, after an initial surge of interest in this question in the 1950s and early 1960s, the quality of management is slowly being eroded away, both in rural services management and in urban management. The preoccupation in the last few years has been to <u>contain</u> problems arising out of shortages rather than <u>deal</u> with them.

<u>John Mellor</u>: I must say I found Professor Mitra's paper fascinating. I have had some little knowledge of the situation in Calcutta, and I know it is a very difficult situation. I think what we get out of the paper is not only a perspective about what the problems are in Calcutta but also something that relates very much to the topic of this conference.

I notice in our discussion, however, a tendency to slip away from the theme of population and its social and cultural consequences. I suppose one of the reasons for this is that, since India's population will be growing so rapidly and so inevitably over the next few decades, this opens up a series of possibilities that would not otherwise be there. I suppose some of us might wish there were not quite so many possibilities, because any one of them might well create enormous problems. If one has a very static structure, it is quite difficult to change the way in which people are organized. In the past there has been considerable drift almost everywhere—among both high-income and low-income countries—as to the form in which we organize a growing population.

One of the things we might turn our attention to is whether we have any views about the best way in which to organize growing population centers. I would like to hear some statements of the options here. Perhaps Professor Shah could respond on this score and get us into the social and cultural factors involved and the implications of different-sized organizations with respect to the services question. It seems to me we should bring in something from that side on this general topic.

There has been a great deal of talk of smaller urban concentrations, perhaps some of it resulting from John Lewis' book of the early 1960s. These small urban concentrations have often been seen as an option to the large massive cities of South Asia. I would like to make one comment on that. I think that in most countries, the market town kind of approach has not been very noticeable in its success, and I would like to suggest that there is a very simple reason for that. It does not make sense to have smaller urban centers growing in a situation where you have to bring raw materials to that center from the previously existing urban centers and then move the produce produced back to the urban center. In other words, if the existing source of income is in the older established urban center, this makes it very difficult from an economic point of view to develop smaller urban centers.

A very important potential role of the agricultural sector in this milieu is to experience rapid growth in incomes through the processes of technological change in agriculture. Those incomes then provide a very powerful market base for those market towns, not just in selling inputs to rural people with their higher incomes (which will be a relatively small proportion of the way in which rural people spend their new higher incomes) but to sell consumer goods to them as well. It is the consumer goods industry that provides much larger economic possibilities for smaller and medium-scale firms in smaller urban concentrations. Inputs like fertilizer have to be produced in massive plants in order to get your costs down, because of technical factors. When one talks about consumer goods one has a wider range of options.

What I am suggesting is that, so far as the economics are concerned, despite not very great success in the past, there are options
for much smaller urban concentrations. I am not sure quite what I
mean by much smaller. I have a suspicion that much smaller does
not mean 5,000 and thereabout, but it probably means 50,000 to
300,000 people. The point is that there are more options where you
have vigorous and rapidly growing rural incomes and a growing massive demand for consumer goods. I make that comment particularly
to throw out the option question for discussion. As population grows
one has to bear constantly in mind this question: How will the population be concentrated?

Mitra: The main problem in the case of Calcutta is how to convert a
city that has been historically impoverishing the countryside, fatten-
ing itself at the latter's expense. At the end of a colonial regime a
country is left the poorer in the quality of its manpower and in the
quality of both its agricultural and industrial products. It is rather
exhausted and even devastated. Of course, by the time a protest
grows up it is also accompanied by a considerable new enrichment
process. But the dominant role is one of impoverishment.

Several of my graduate students at Nehru University are working on the problem of the outreach of the former colonial city. One
is working on the tea plantations of Assam. The problem she is working on is how to assess the position of the tea estates in Assam during
the colonial regime. Assam tea estates were almost entirely British-
owned until 1947. On the other hand, the Bengal Dooars, the Bengal
tea plantations, were a product of Indian entrepreneurs. What unequal effects did these two have on the growth of the hinterland, on
the city, and the early establishments, the road and transport network, the infrastructure, and so on, in Assam as compared with
those in the Bengal Dooars?

Fortunately, the British Parliament has always suffered from a
sense of guilt and so a great deal of parliamentary data exists on this
field of exploitation, as the word goes. Even after 1942, in the parliamentary debates, British members of Parliament produced data to
show how the country was being impoverished because Assam tea
plantations insisted upon importing even the utensils for laborers
from England, not to speak of pruning knives and so on. There is
evidence that even toilet articles and clothing for indentured labor in
the tea plantations were imported from England rather than bought from
the Indian market. And there were ghettos of indentured labor in the
Assam tea plantations!

I have another student who is working on jute. He is looking into
the jute industry and the circumstances under which jute cultivation
was controlled by British interests in Calcutta or Dundee or Aberdeen;

and the way impoverishment grew in jute cultivation in Bengal and Bihar. Another student is expecting to work on the history of the indigo plantations that impoverished Bihar and Orissa, and still another on the iron and coal industry and the British concessions in the Bengal-Bihar coal fields. Interesting comparisons are possible between the tea industry in Assam of the Calcutta hinterland, and the Madras hinterland of the Nilgiris, or the Kerala tea and coffee plantations where labor was not indentured and there was some kind of give-and-take between the foreign investor and the rural economy.

Foreign rule led to a lot of impoverishment of the countryside. As a result, it upset the balance of relationships between the primate city and the hinterland, and this did not help the hinterland to grow. What we have in Calcutta today, then, is an overhang of history that has come about during the last 150 years, until about 1947. I am of course simplifying a great deal of historical material, and I am sure that in the process of oversimplification I am leaving out a good many relevant factors. But the fact is that Calcutta built up a great deal of technical, managerial, and entrepreneurial experience on which Amiya Bagchi of Calcutta has written one of the most authoritative and exhaustive accounts. I believe some of you have read Bagchi's books on the subject.

When any machinery went wrong, say, in a tea plantation, however small it might be, technicians and mechanics would be fetched from Calcutta to do the repairs. Nothing grew up locally in Assam by way of repairing and servicing facilities. The classic tussle came after the establishment of the Tata Iron and Steel Industries in Jamshedpur. Throughout history the tussle between the Indian bourgoisie and the Indian government resulted in a situation where Indian products would be resisted, even for repair and services, in British concerns. Most British houses in Calcutta insisted on importing all of their material directly from England.

But every movement has its countermovement. I have written on this in some detail in the Bengal census report of 1951. This was first remarked upon in 1828 by a perceptive Englishman in the Bengal Gazette. He observed the birth of a Bengali middle class between 1818 and 1828. This was the first modern middle class in the whole of India. The Maharashtrian and the Gujarati middle classes came a little later. This middle class had an interest in getting hold of iron ore and coal concessions. It also wanted to enter into partnerships with the managing agency houses in Calcutta. It is this infrastructure that assisted the hunger for agricultural and social institutions and created a climate of positivism. The result of this was that Calcutta, toward the end of the 19th century, acquired a great concentration of talent—and this was native Indian talent—not only within the city but also through denudation of the countryside.

Denudation of intellect followed denudation of material wealth
from the countryside: A greater denudation than draining of material
wealth, because after all the middle classes have always been great
protagonists of agricultural development in all countries and it was
this middle class in Bengal that was enticed into the Calcutta offices
for other enterprises. The first casualty over this long period was
Bengal agriculture and the demands for irrigation that came only in
the 1930s, after the great depression. This continuous concentration
went in two ways, to produce eventually what one could call the Anglophiles and Anglophobes.

The Anglophiles were the landed gentry and middle classes that
went into partnership with the British with a great deal to gain. Part
of this gain of course percolated into various public institutions in
city and country. On the other side were the Anglophobes, who saw
the impoverishment caused by imperial rule: This led to resentment,
which in turn led to the terrorist movements in Bengal. This, what
one might call a love-hate relationship, continues even today in the
sense that the average Calcuttan or Bengali is always on kind of
"treaty terms" with the rest of India. He often sees himself as an adversary. This adversary role has continued from one historic period
into another, even though the adversaries have changed.

Arising from this adversary role, there have been various kinds
of prescriptions for the upliftment of Calcutta. What I have tried to
say is that even the World Bank scheme for the Calcutta Metropolitan
Development Authority is based on an imperfect appreciation of how
to proceed in the matter of transforming the role of a primate city
from an impoverishing agent to an enriching nexus. A great many
plans for improvement of primate cities in most colonial countries degenerate for lack of appreciation of this need, to cosmetics. Here
you have a captive population in a primate city, where conditions are
often unspeakable. Some alleviation has to be done and services have
to be provided, and these services naturally come from the European
or the U.S. model because these are the only models that people generally think of.

But it is really questionable whether that model applies to the
situation in India. The situation of the country now, as I have indicated in the book on Population in India's Development, 1947-2000, is
still the situation of a peasant country, of a peasant community where
industrialization is still an overlay. It has to be recognized that industrial and ancillary activities in India are still secondary phenomena, the main activity still centering on a peasant community.

As in most peasant societies, there is no way but to proceed
part of the way through the process of primitive accumulation of capital. Everybody gets tired of giving alms, and charity has its limits.
Even with the best of international aid, there has to be a tremendous

amount of self-help activity and a fresh balance between formation of wealth in rural areas and its investment in the urban centers. To pull oneself up by one's bootstraps gives one a sense of fulfillment and a certain contentment and also an appreciation of the art of the practicable.

There is still another aspect that will perhaps surprise you, and that is that the rate of population growth in many West Bengal towns has been less than the rate of growth of the national increase for the state as a whole. This perhaps is a situation that is difficult for a demographer to conceive or appreciate. The question really is one of providing and maintaining social services in the cities and towns of West Bengal that would nourish a more viable relationship between urban and rural growth. The World Bank project reminds one of a line in a Tagore poem, which says that a jeweled necklace is an embarrassment: It cannot be worn because it hurts; it cannot be torn because that too hurts.

On the one hand, the level of investment that has gone into Calcutta since 1947 is nothing compared to what it needs or nothing compared to what Delhi has invested on itself. On a very rough calculation, since 1947 Delhi has invested on itself something like about 15 billion rupees, of which 82 percent has been government subsidy and the rest by way of taxes. Against this figure, Calcutta has received only about 1.30 to 1.35 billion rupees in the last three years. But, that apart, my more fundamental point is that I doubt that Delhi is the kind of prototype that can be followed in India if one is to establish a viable relationship between a city and its hinterland.

I believe one will have to think of another kind of metropolitan or urban growth that will be far more modest, based on self-help, in which the entire metropolitan area is conceived in terms of constituent units, with each unit having its own modest way of providing municipal services. Yet, through a network of communication-transportation units, this expanding cluster would cater to the needs of both the city and the wider metropolitan hinterland.

A M. Shah: I will confine myself to a few comments on local responses to development. I am glad that Mitra has focused his attention on self-help and that he has derived inspiration from Patrick Geddes, who was one of the founders of sociology in India.

It seems to me important to identify the local attempts at self-help in different parts of the country. For example, there are certain districts in Gujarat, Maharashtra, Mysore, Haryana, and Punjab that are going extremely well. What are the causes of these bright spots? At least one of the causes is the emergence of local leaders, such as the corporators in large cities, the chairmen of the zilla and taluka panchayats in the rural areas, and even the leaders

in villages and small towns. I have come across a number of perceptive and resourceful local leaders in central Gujarat. They may not
think in the same manner as do academics, but they think about the
problem; they are quite aware of the problems.

We need to know more about the question of local leaders, how
they arise and how they perceive problems, and especially how they
go about solving problems. At least in the district that I know well,
in almost every village, there are leaders who are genuinely trying
to solve the problems of their community. In the village that I have
studied at length you find water taps, not because of attempts made
by the government but as a result of a local effort to improve. Villagers have come together and have tried to build a community building without any grant whatsoever from the government. In this manner there are a number of attempts made in different parts of the
country every day to improve one's local condition. It is possible,
I suppose, that you do not find this in Bengal. But then it is necessary
to find the reasons for this.

The second point I would like to make is that, unfortunately, we
do not have enough political scientists at this conference. After the
academics have done all of their exercises and even after the local
leaders have done all of their exercises, a great deal depends on the
politicians these days. For example, Deolalikar was mentioning the
problem of water in Gujarat. The Gujaratis are crying for water,
but nobody is sanctioning the Narmada project. It has been hanging
fire for many years. It is because of the politics of the country. We
cannot really think of the provision of services and distribution of
resources without bringing politics in, and this in turn ties up with
local leadership. Local leaders are not just social service or social
administration people. They are also hard-headed politicians. So
unless we bring in politics, it will be very difficult to analyze this
problem of the distribution of resources and provision of services.
Even within the village, if the people want to have something, they
have to mobilize the politicians at various levels outside the village.
I would say then that one of the reasons why you find bright spots in
various parts of the country is because of resourceful local leadership.

Milton Singer: About 20 years ago, in 1954, I was invited to a conference on urbanization at Chicago that was organized by Bert Hoselitz.
There were economists, geographers, anthropologists, and sociologists there from whom we learned the importance of making distinctions between the patterns of population and urban growth in the United
States and Western Europe and the urban patterns of growth in the rest
of the world. There was not much in the way of comparative urban
studies at that time. Twenty years later, a very masterly analysis,

such as Asok Mitra has done on Calcutta, gives the kind of answers
that we had hoped for 20 years ago.

Many people in this field recognize the importance of comparative studies and of relating them to basic social theory, to the experience and problems of planners, and the like. We take this more or
less for granted. So I was somewhat surprised last night when, in
the informal meeting at the motel, John Mellor gave his impression
from the discussions at the conference here this week that anthropologists and sociologists had not struggled with these problems in the
way that economists have been struggling with them. Although I did
not lie awake struggling with these problems.

Mellor: That is the difference. We lie awake struggling with them.

Singer: On other occasions I have stayed up.

Partly in defense of the sociological and anthropological contributions, I do want to point out that in his recent introductory book
The Human Consequences of Urbanization, Brian Berry, a colleague
of mine at Chicago who is in urban geography, has put together a
very useful round-up of the anthropological, sociological, geographical, and economic studies of these problems in Africa, Latin America,
Asia, Europe, and the United States. This book tends to confirm what
Asok Mitra, Rakhesh Mohan, and others have been saying.

I was nevertheless impressed in reading Asok Mitra's paper by
the striking similarities with the most recent problems of American
cities. Asok Mitra is probably right in concluding that a vast network
of well-knit, contented urban villages with low levels of pollution but
with greater degrees of decentralized community participation may
well be India's answer to sweltering high-rise, high-density, high-
pollution, choked cities such as Calcutta is speedily degenerating into.
Let me assure you that many of us living in places like Chicago or
New York or Detroit are coming to share similar ideals. Across the
country I have the impression that this is a direction in which many
people would like to go, to such an extent that small towns and smaller
cities are beginning to try and pass ordinances to keep newcomers out,
or to have systems of permits.

Along with this trend, the preservation and restoration movement is increasingly coming into direct conflict with a more modernizing type of urban renewal that wants to demolish old buildings and
build high-rises, shopping centers, and parking lots. In many areas
of the country, this is increasingly important as a problem at the
same time that provision of housing for the poor and disadvantaged is
running into great difficulty because, as the population flies from the
central city to the suburbs or beyond, the factories, offices, and
stores move with them, so the residents of the central city are left

without jobs and services. Granted, of course, all of the historical
and cultural differences between Calcutta and American cities, I
think, at least in one respect, the tendencies and problems described
by Asok Mitra are present in the European and American city and
are worldwide. Brian Berry describes some of these similarities
as well as some of the differences. The sociologist, the anthropologist, as well as the urban geographer, are certainly very much concerned with the problem.

Mitra: I have little to add to what I have already said, but since you
have asked me and since I am a compulsive talker I will say one or
two more things. I realize that what I advocate for Calcutta may not
catch on readily, but what can one do? One cannot just sit down and
contemplate doom forever. One lives in hope and keeps on trying.
If one area of thought exhausts itself one must go to another while
one is alive. It is enough for the time being if my paper interests or
disturbs people, and I am glad that when I produced the first draft
of this paper in a Calcutta seminar, although it wasn't really discussed at length, both S. K. Roy and Sivarama Krishna were suitably
disturbed by it.
        I should like to conclude with two literary references. First,
the opening passage from one of the first chapters of E. M. Forster's
novel Howard's End, where the author says: "We are not concerned
with the very poor. They are unthinkable, and only to be approached
by the statistician or the poet." Since I am a statistician of sorts I
cannot but be concerned with the very poor.
        The second reference is to a cautionary verse by Hilaire Belloc,
where he speaks of Jack and his pony Tom. Now Jack was so fond of
his pony Tom that he would ply it with all kinds of delicacies that
were not good for horses—like bread and chocolate and apple-rings—
the most of which do not agree with poly-ponies such as he. And all
in such quantity as ruined the pony's digestion wholly. As a result
Tom swelled and swelled and swelled until the pony died, and as it
died kicked Jack severely in the side. Hilaire Belloc then proceeded
to draw the moral that kindness to animals should be attuned to their
brutality. Indeed, the situation that we have in many cities is a brutal
rather than a human situation.
        I think I shall stop at that, believing that my references some-
how tie in with what we were discussing. Unfortunately I am a statistician of sorts and I cannot be wholly unconcerned.
        You have been good enough to ask me for a summary on the sub-
ject we discussed the other night after dinner. If I may enter straight
into the subject, you already have disturbing evidence of recession in
the United States. Thousands of automobile workers are being laid
off in a country that consumes about a third of the world's resources.

Here we have a combination of recession and inflation, in a situation where shop shelves are overflowing with goods.

In other parts of the world we have a different kind of inflation, arising from few consumer goods on the shelves and essential articles, including food, in short supply. In this context, the whole question of international aid is fraught with serious implications. How the different segments of the world will adjust themselves, particularly the richer vis-a-vis the poorer and vice-versa, is the real problem. At this very moment the World Food Conference is going on in Rome. From what you see in the papers, nothing really worthwhile seems to have been arrived at in that city.

Most of you know Jean Mayer, to whom I could listen for hours on the subject of nutrition. He was in Delhi last month and very kindly called. He told me that he had a column in Newsweek and other U.S. journals with a total readership of 30 million. He said that he was starting his column on how much food could be offered if the American people did not eat that much meat, particularly when excess meat-eating was leading to so many sad consequences in the state of health of the country. He added that beef or other animal flesh is a very inefficient means of converting straight grain into food because, while one head of cattle consumes 3,200-3,400 pounds of grain per year, a human being could be maintained at the optimum nutritional level with only 350 pounds. I ventured to tell him that while such a thing was good as an occasional reminder, a person who was bent on having his dinner on steak in the evening was unlikely to be deterred by this counsel.

In this connection, I reminded him of what I found at wayside restaurants in the city of Kyoto in 1972. These restaurants were filled early in the evening with what looked like lower-middle-class housewives from traditionally conservative families—they all wore traditional kimonos and had shopping bags on their arms—evidently returning home after a late afternoon of shopping. Most of them were avidly putting away beefsteak, first because that is the fashion with the upper classes in Japan today, and second because they had not acquired the art of cooking steak in their traditional kitchens. To preach to them about the evil effects of starting off on steak at their stages of life would be madness. Besides, we would have to think of other things, set in a much wider horizon, if we were interested in taking a public stand on the shape of things to come.

Let us for a moment think of the second industrial revolution in the West between 1947 and 1974. From 1947 onward, following the great inventions and the great leaps in technology during and immediately following World War II, you have a situation in which the second industrial revolution in the West has achieved immeasurably more than did the first industrial revolution of 1775 to 1850. Standards of

living, wages, the range of consumption of goods, housing, transportation, amenities, and social welfare services have improved in the
West to points that could never have been imagined, say, in 1938.

This spectacular, almost magical improvement in the level of
living in Europe and the North American continent has been achieved
in the last 25 years through the use of raw materials and other mineral resources from the underdeveloped countries, obtained at prices
that are far more exploitative than those found in the colonial period
1775-1850, when these countries were directly ruled by the Western
metropolitan countries. In return, the underdeveloped countries
have received very little by way of plant, machinery, or technical
know-how, and wherever these have been received, they too had to be
obtained at exorbitant prices.

You will remember the statement by the Iranian Minister of
Economic Affairs at the World Bank-IMF Group meeting last month,
when he said that, if there was inflation of 14.5 percent in 1974 in the
Western world, then petroleum and oil would account for only 1.5
percent of it. The rest of the inflation was contributed by the transfer of goods and services from the less developed countries to the developed countries, at rates that were far more exploitative than in
any comparable historical period in the past.

If the Western world is troubled over pollution today, it has
now the means very successfully to fight it. Let me give an example.
As a student in England in the late 1930s, I could never see the London sky. It was always full of smog. In November 1971, I was returning from a seminar at MIT Cambridge and stopped in London for
the night. Standing at Aldwych, I was astonished to find every speck
of light burning bright down the Strand beyond Trafalgar Square. The
stars in the sky were bright and big, like tennis balls. This had been
possible, I was told, not only in London but in Birmingham, Manchester, Leeds, and Liverpool. On the other hand, the underdeveloped
countries have very little comparable means. Even the Delhi sky,
which used to be so bright and pure throughout the year as late as
1960, is now invariably murky.

There is so much concern about malnutrition of vulnerable
groups today. But it is curious that total food aid has been steadily
diminishing several times over, in inverse proportion to the talk generated on the subject of nutrition. In the 1950s and the first half of
the 1960s, the total of nutrition aid in terms of food from the developed
countries to the underdeveloped world would perhaps be a sum of
about 20 million tons or more. Today it is difficult to get a pledge of
even 200,000 tons of grain, and direct aid on nutrition for the vulnerable groups, which is small compared to the talk about it, is substantially taken back again by experts or consultants appointed to super-
vise nutrition programs, or by special foods sold to support these
programs.

Most less developed countries (LDCs) have their problems of balance of payments and problems of balancing food and agricultural production with the production of cash crops. Lately, all the world over, on account of rapid population increase, there has been much insistence on the production of food, but let us look at the implications. Let us talk of India. If we are going to have a reduction of income disparities from a concentration of 0.33 to 0.25 in the Lorenz curve in a space of 10 years, then against a rate of population growth of 2.2 percent compound, you would have to have a growth rate of food grains of a little over 4 percent per annum compound and expansion of employment opportunities of over 7.5 percent per annum and an expansion of production of cash crops at around 5.5 percent per annum. The performance of none of the LDCs is anywhere near these figures.

On the other hand, in recent years, not only in India but in other countries, there have been large diversions from land under cash crops to land under food crops because of the heavy demand for food. In India, there is evidence that land has been diverted from cotton, groundnuts, and jute to food crops. A worse case is Bangladesh, where large diversions have taken place from jute to paddy, and yet, as you know, jute is almost the only export earner in that country. I am afraid, in thinking about the population problem and the need for growing more food, even very thoughtful people are developing a blind spot in their eyes in the matter of the need to grow more cash crops in less developed countries. It is that area that, in most countries, holds the prospects of reducing income disparities.

If, then, we are thinking of global plans and not regarding ourselves as instruments of advancing our own country's narrow and short-term commercial interests, thinking men and women will have to put their heads together in at least three areas.

First is the area of research and development and the propagation of the fruits of research and development. It is quite obvious that a great deal of research has to be concentrated for growing crops on dry and arid areas, and particularly how to make cultivation profitable in dry and arid areas by growing cash crops more than food crops. A great deal of research is going on in the world; ICRISAT at Hyderabad is an example. But extension of the fruits of research costs great amounts of money, management, and coordination. This is where the international community can help.

The second would be a more rational attitude toward fertilizers. When I was visiting the United States in April, there was reference in the Washington Post that the United States was thinking of external and internal political considerations in organizing the international and internal sale of fertilizer. It is common knowledge that it costs much less to export fertilizer to a country than it does to export food,

and it costs much less to a country to manufacture its own fertilizer
than to import food. It is also a fact that LDCs today have to buy a
ton of U.S. fertilizer at more than twice the internal rate of the United
States.

It is also a fact that in an LDC today the rate of return by way
of crops for one pound of fertilizer is much higher than in the developed countries of North America or Western Europe. So, on balance,
the world as a whole will gain a lot more if you could locate fertilizer
factories with bilateral or multilateral help in strategic parts of the
world, nearest to large areas engaged in growing food and cash crops.
Let us, for example, reflect for a moment how immensely the fertilizer position will improve if only the more glaring instances of wastage of flare gas could be harnessed for conversion into fertilizer,
say in Saudi Arabia, the Persian Gulf, Nigeria, Venezuela, or Indonesia. There is much secretiveness even on the export of fertilizer
technology to the less developed countries.

The third area, of course, would be the area of integrated rural
development through the expansion of irrigation and harnessing of
power resources, particularly hydroelectric power. Here too, instead of going in for large power stations, it would be worthwhile to
think of appropriate technology that would install power stations and
connect them in an appropriate network. The Swiss power stations,
for example, before World War II, used to be rather small units but
well distributed over each canton. Such small power stations also
serve the purposes of community participation of the kind that we have
been discussing. This area of irrigation and power development is
one that ought certainly to engage the attention of the international
community.

Similarly, in the matter of local development, including urban
development, the sooner the international community gets interested
in a range of possibilities rather than sticking to the models of highly
developed countries, the more we can think in terms of down-to-earth
programs. So far as the World Food Conference at Rome is concerned,
one would not mind if they did not settle the matter of short-term food
aid, but one would certainly mind if they did not tackle the problems
of agricultural research and development, long-term schemes of expanding fertilizer production over the world, and schemes for improving irrigation and power generation.

John Lewis: I agree overwhelmingly with what Asok Mitra has said.
I think I would put a little different emphasis on naming the kinds of
things that the rest of the world needs to do. He said that he sees aid
somehow drying up, and he indicated pretty cryptically the need for
much more responsiveness on the trade side, including the pricing of
raw materials and so on.

On the one hand, I would sound a note that he did not happen to in this particular set of remarks, and that is that we may expect to see some attempt to do the OPEC kind of thing in other commodities. There will be some attempt (which I personally as an observer applaud) to mobilize the poor power of the world and use the market—if you will, market power—to alter the world's sharing of resources.

But I am bearish as an observer as to how far the poor countries will get away with this. I think there are a number of things that make oil quite a special case. Also, I have to point out that the distribution of potential benefits from such tactics among the developing countries is very, very uneven. The economic rents that are there to be exploited are not uniformly distributed. I would guess that, particularly among those who do not have a lot of them, the most prominent is India. If one could get a really good iron ore cartel going, that would be helpful, but that does not look terribly promising. So I don't see "poor power" doing the job.

The job is basically one of coping with these really extraordinary disparities among countries of income and economic welfare per capita that, as Asok Mitra says, have come into being only quite recently. There is no historical precedent for the scale of these disparities, and, it seems to me, there is no social ethic operative anywhere that offers any continuing justification for it.

I am rather bearish about the adjustability of advanced country trade policies for some time, although I do think that things need to be pushed hard in that direction. Therefore, I was going to argue, more than Asok now has made it necessary for me to do, about the need for net transfers. When he talks about doing big things in irrigation and in fertilizer production, he is in fact talking about some kind of net transfers, and about concessional transfers at that. I would simply emphasize that need. As unpopular as aid seems to be, the continuing case for net transfers is to me inescapable.

Rather obviously, from a political point of view, both the donors and the recipients will want these transfers to take a form that is not called aid. The business will have to have quite a new look. I think it has to be more routinized and almost surely much more multilateralized, and it has to come much less in the manner of largesse or of charity or philanthropy than as a matter of right to the poor, through mechanisms that are analogous to international progressive taxation.

There are some such mechanisms already in view, such as the so-called Special Drawing Rights (SDR) link; seabed royalties (if we manage to keep the commons common and not all divided up among the coastal nations); much more sophisticated kinds of debt adjustments; and possibly in due course something that literally amounts to transnational taxation.

Now that all sounds like pie in the sky. But let me add quickly why, as a forecaster, I would at least quite seriously entertain such possibilities. I won't say I would firmly predict them, but I would say that in the long run we are likely to move in this direction, partly because of the pressure of "poor power" but partly also because of what I once called, in something I wrote, subversion in high places.

What I mean by the last is the following. One of the common throat-clearing exercises that many social scientists go through just now as they approach such subjects is to say—of course, we all recognize that nationalism is rising all over. I think it is rising and is still very strong, particularly in the new nations, maybe in Japan, certainly in China. I wouldn't speak about the Eastern European countries with any confidence. I am rather sure that nationalism as a secular matter is declining in the West, and this is simply because I believe very much in the powerful influence of elites in forming opinion over time. The elites in the West have increasingly seen that the problems that are really overwhelming the world, the ones that John Cool has talked about so eloquently, are essentially transnational problems. They simply don't submit very well to coping by the nation-states we have ourselves organized into. At any rate, they cannot be coped with in any way that's rational from the point of view of the planetary self-interest, by policies that are in any narrow parochial way simply responsive to national self-interest.

As a matter of fact, I think our bureaucracy in this country and Western Europe—our press, the academic community (for what that's worth), even our business community, some of our interest groups otherwise—already are honeycombed with subversives. These are people who tend to think in planetary self-interest terms, at least part of the time. I think it will be the guilty consciences of the affluent that will constitute part of the mechanism for pulling policy in the directions that it needs to go. I think it is very easy for a person to see this if he or she happens to work in a place that tries to cope with young people who have declared for activist careers in public affairs. They are not starry-eyed idealistic folk at all. They do not see themselves as humanitarians. They are simply very impatient with the parochialism and antiquity of purely national-interest views.

I sensed this very much this past summer in meeting with a bunch of young Europeans working in the development field, most of them bureaucrats. One of the most radical happened to be a captain in the West German Air Force. The people in the aid agency in Bonn were somewhat more conventional, but still very much globalists. On the basis of that experience and the one here, I think there is a very strong chance that we are being subverted, some of us being subverters.

P. M. Beliappa
Jawaharlal Nehru University
New Delhi, India

Krishan Bhatia
Foreign Correspondent
The Hindustan Times
Washington, D.C.

G. Morris Carstairs
Vice-Chancellor
University of York
United Kingdom

Robert H. Cassen
Fellow
Institute of Development
  Studies
University of Sussex
United Kingdom

John C. Cool
Deputy Representative
The Ford Foundation
New Delhi, India
and
Center for Population Studies
Harvard University
Cambridge, Massachusetts

B. R. Deolalikar
Consultant
Operations Research Group
Ahmedabad, India

Wendy K. Dobson
Special Assistant to the
  President
International Development
  Research Centre
Ottawa, Canada

Joan M. Dunlop
Associate of John D. Rocke-
  feller 3rd
Rockefeller Plaza
New York, New York

Kempton Dunn
Assistant Director
Department of Meetings and
  Studies
The Asia Society
New York, New York

Joseph W. Elder
Professor of Sociology and
  Indian Studies
University of Wisconsin—
  Madison
Madison, Wisconsin

Marcus F. Franda
Associate Professor of Politi-
  cal Science
Colgate University
and
Staff Associate
American Universities Field
  Staff
New Delhi, India

Marc Galanter
Professor of Law
State University of New York
  at Buffalo
Buffalo, New York

Adrienne Germain
Program Officer
Population Office
The Ford Foundation
New York, New York

David E. Horlacher
Chairman
Department of Economics
Susquehanna University
Chairman
Population Panel
Southeast Asia Development
   Advisory Group/SEADAG
The Asia Society
New York, New York

Anrudh K. Jain
Assistant Director
Biomedical Division
The Population Council
New York, New York

Bryant Kearl
Chairman
Department of Agricultural
   Journalism
University of Wisconsin—
   Madison
Madison, Wisconsin

John P. Lewis
Professor of Economics
Woodrow Wilson School of
   Public and International
   Affairs
Princeton University
Princeton, New Jersey

David G. Mandelbaum
Professor of Anthropology
University of California at
   Berkeley
Berkeley, California

Rama Mehta
Author
New Delhi, India

John W. Mellor
Professor of Agricultural
   Economics
Cornell University
Ithaca, New York

Asok Mitra
Secretary to the President
   of India
New Delhi, India

Rakesh Mohan
Fellow
Research Program in
   Economic Development
Princeton University
Princeton, New Jersey

Bhupendra Nath Mukerjee
Visiting Member
Faculty of Law
Banaras Hindu University
Varanasi, India

John Newmann
Economist
Office of Asia and the Pacific
The Ford Foundation
New York, New York

A. M. Shah
Head
Department of Sociology
University of Delhi
Delhi, India

Milton B. Singer
Professor of Anthropology
University of Chicago
Chicago, Illinois

Phillips Talbot
President
The Asia Society
New York, New York

Irene Tinker
Director
Office of International Science
American Association for the
   Advancement of Science
Washington, D.C.

Beba D. Varadachar
Senior Research Fellow
Center for Advanced Study in
  Sociology
University of Delhi
Delhi, India

Lawrence A. Veit
Research Fellow
Council on Foreign Relations
New York, New York

Abraham M. Weisblat
Director
Research and Training Net-
  work
The Agricultural Development
  Council
New York, New York
Chairman
The India Council
The Asia Society

Rapporteur

Vonetta J. Franda
Hamilton, New York

Observer

Robert White
Editor
Minneapolis Tribune
Minneapolis, Minnesota

The Johnson Foundation Staff

Leslie Paffrath
President

Henry Halsted
Vice-President—Program

Rita Goodman
Vice-President—Area Programs

Kay Mauer
Conference Coordinator

MARCUS F. FRANDA is Staff Associate of the American Universities Field Staff in New Delhi and Associate Professor of Political Science at Colgate University. He holds the Ph.D. degree in Political Science from the University of Chicago. From 1968 to 1970 he was Director of the American Institute of Indian Studies in Calcutta and New Delhi. He is author of Radical Politics in West Bengal, Political Development and Political Decay in Bengal, and West Bengal and the Federalizing Process in India, and co-editor of Radical Politics in South Asia.

JOHN C. COOL is Ford Foundation Representative in Pakistan. From 1974 to 1975 he was Visiting Scholar in the Center for Population Studies at Harvard University. Recipient of the Ph.D. degree from the London School of Economics and Political Science, he has served as Deputy Director of the United States Agency for International Development Mission in Nepal and as Assistant Director of the Mission in India. From 1970 to 1974 he was Deputy Representative of the Ford Foundation in India.

MARC GALANTER is Professor of Law at the State University of New York at Buffalo. He holds a law degree and an M.A. degree in Philosophy from the University of Chicago. He has served as Fulbright Scholar on the Faculty of Law at the University of Delhi and as Faculty Fellow of the American Institute of Indian Studies. Currently he is editor of Law and Society Review and a member of the Board of Directors of the Association for Asian Studies.

PROMILLA KALHAN is Special Correspondent for the Hindustan Times in New Delhi. She holds an M.A. degree from Punjab University and completed a postgraduate course in Social Science and Personnel Management at the London School of Economics and Political Science. She is the author of Kamala Nehru: An Intimate Biography.

DAVID G. MANDELBAUM is Professor of Anthropology at the University of California at Berkeley and former Chairman of the Department of Anthropology and the Center of South Asia Studies. He has been Visiting Fulbright Professor at Cambridge University and Senior Fellow in the American Institute of Indian Studies. He holds the Ph.D. degree from Yale University and has written Society in India and Human Fertility in India.

RAMA MEHTA holds the M.A. degree from Delhi University and was a Fellow of Harvard University's Radcliffe Institute. She was one of the first women to be admitted to the Indian Foreign Service. Her books include The Western Educated Indian Woman, Inside the Haveli, India: Now and Through Time, and the forthcoming The Hindu Divorced Woman.

ASOK MITRA is Professor at Jawaharlal Nehru University, New Delhi. He has served as Secretary to the President of India and as Secretary to the Government of India's Ministries of Information and Broadcasting, Tourism and Civil Aviation, and the Planning Commission. Educated at Presidency College in Calcutta and Oxford University, he holds the D.Sc. (hon. causa) degree from the Academy of Sciences in Moscow.

LAWRENCE A VEIT is Deputy Manager and International Economist in Brown Brothers Harriman and Company in New York. From 1969 to 1972 he served as Treasury Representative for India and Nepal in the American Embassy in New Delhi, and from 1972 to 1975 he was a Research Fellow in the Council on Foreign Relations in New York. He holds degrees from Yale University and the New School for Social Research and is author of a forthcoming book on India's development.

ECONOMIC GROWTH IN DEVELOPING COUNTRIES—MATERIAL AND
HUMAN RESOURCES: Proceedings of the Seventh Rehovot Conference
edited by Yohanan Ramati

EDUCATION, MANPOWER, AND DEVELOPMENT IN SOUTH AND
SOUTHEAST ASIA
Muhammad Shamsul Huq

FOOD, POPULATION, AND EMPLOYMENT: The Impact of the Green
Revolution
edited by Thomas T. Poleman and
Donald K. Freebairn

THE MICRO-ECONOMICS OF DEMOGRAPHIC CHANGE: Family
Planning and Economic Wellbeing
Frank J. Jewett and
Theodore K. Ruprecht

PATTERNS OF POVERTY IN THE THIRD WORLD
Charles Elliott

PLANNED CHANGE IN A TRADITIONAL SOCIETY: Psychological
Problems of Modernization in Ethiopia
David C. Korten with
Frances F. Korten

THE UNITED STATES AND THE DEVELOPING WORLD: AGENDA
FOR ACTION, 1974
edited by James W. Howe and the
Staff of the Overseas Development
Council

WORLD POPULATION CRISIS: The United States Response
Phyllis Tilson Piotrow